The Psychology of Blindness

Donald D. Kirtley

The Psychology

of Blindness

nh **Nelson-Hall**
Chicago

Library of Congress Cataloging in Publication Data

Kirtley, Donald D.
    The psychology of blindness.

    Bibliography: p.
    1. Blind—Psychology. I. Title. [DNLM: 1. Adaptation, Psychological. 2. Blindness. HV1598
K61p]
HV1598.K5   155.9'16   74-17155
ISBN 0-88229-178-5

Copyright© 1975 by Donald D. Kirtley

For information address
Nelson-Hall Publishers, 325 W. Jackson, Chicago,
Ill. 60606

Manufactured in the United States of America

To
My wife Joyce
And
My daughters Melanie and Vanessa

Contents

Preface

Being blind does not in itself make one an authority on the psychology of blindness, so on that ground I make no special claims for the present book. I have been blind for a little over twenty years and in that time have known about as many sightless as sighted persons who were ignorant or misinformed on the subject. However, it is true that my own personal experience of blindness, together with the reactions of other people to it, provided the chief motivation for my interest in this field, as well as for my undertaking of the present project.

At this point, it would be appropriate to offer a few words of clarification regarding the title of the book: *The Psychology of Blindness.* It is not intended to imply that there is any unique psychology of the blind—that is, a psychology essentially different from that of the seeing or, for that matter, any other particular class of human beings. No new or special psychological principles are required to explain the behavior of the blind or attitudes toward blindness; certain established principles of general psychology are fully adequate to this task. Indeed, the blind are different from the sighted, but, as the reader will learn, this difference is not characterized by any particular pattern of personal or social development, character traits, or motives that are distinct from those found in the visually normal. The difference of the blind lies solely in their experience of visual deficit and certain behavioral limitations inherent in that deficit. It will be seen, however, that such limitations are much less extensive than is generally thought, for blindness is not nearly so severe a handicap as most people believe it to be. While blindness does constitute an internalized stress condition, it, like most stresses, can be mastered, given certain psychological prerequisites in the individual (viz., adequate ego strength, intelligence, motivation, and physical and mental health), plus a favorable social environment—or at least one that is not too negatively inclined toward the individual. Blindness is by no means synonymous with personal misery and defeat: the sightless can be, and very frequently are, just as happy and productive as their seeing peers. Years ago such a statement would have been received with considerable doubt, if not outright disbelief; yet today, among professional workers for the blind, it would be regarded merely as a truism. Consequently, in this book the term "psychology of blindness" simply refers to the various topics on which phychological theory and research have been focused within the broader fields of practical work for the blind and the scientific study of visual disability.

With respect to attitudes toward blindness and the impact of the handicap on the behavior of the individual, those who work with the blind are at times inclined to take strong opposing views. Often such positions are more a matter of tendentious rhetoric or philosophical speculation than of sound scientific hypothesis or empirical fact. A wide variety of theoretical concepts have been employed in the attempt to understand the relation of blindness to behavior, and just as diverse an array of research techniques have been used to collect the data on which such concepts are based. It is not my purpose to assume any particular stance, theoretical or methodological, to defend at the exclusion of other competing approaches. No one theory, no one research method is sufficient to do justice to all the psychological facts at hand. Moreover, it is my conviction that a number of seemingly incompatible approaches in this field are ultimately reconcilable with one another. Thus, the character of the book is essentially eclectic and integrative; however, the reader will notice some special emphases—e.g., my application of Freudian and Jungian theories of personality to the subject of attitudes toward blindness and my advocacy of quantitative dream research as a valuable tool for the understanding of personality. The use of Freudian and Jungian concepts is justified insofar as symbolic factors play a critical role in the formation of attitudes toward blindness, and of all available psychological theories, those of Freud and Jung are the only ones that deal comprehensively with the psychology of symbolism. Also, up to the present time, the relevance of Jungian theory to the psychology of blindness has apparently been totally ignored. As to my stress upon quantitative dream research, suffice it to say that there currently exists an impressive body of scientific evidence supporting the validity and utility of this approach. Indeed, dreams, if objectively analyzed, probably constitute our best single test of personality. Still, such emphases do not entail a denial of the importance of other commonly applied approaches (e.g., attitude research based on the questionnaire method, social learning theory, or phenomenology). Certainly, I have tried to be impartial, and I believe that I have been reasonably successful in achieving this goal. In any case, the reader will be able to judge such matters for himself.

This volume serves two chief purposes: first, it is a critical introduction to the major areas of theory and research on the psychology of blindness; second, it presents recent, hitherto unpublished research on the dream life of the blind, conducted by the author and associates, and on attitudes toward blindness, independently carried out by the author. The book should, therefore, be of use to veteran researchers and applied workers in the field of blindness, as well as students and behavioral scientists new to it. Although the present work is written primarily for the professional audience (i.e., the psychologist, psychiatrist, sociologist, rehabilitation counselor, social worker, and special educator), the layman who is seriously interested in the problem of blindness will also find it informative, as should certain readers mainly interested in depth psychology (and only secondarily concerned with blindness), for much of the material discussed within these pages is relevant to both Freudian and Jungian theories of personality. This volume could fruitfully be employed as a text or source book in courses on rehabilitation counseling, insofar as the latter deal with the visually handicapped. It would also be of value as a supplementary text in courses on personality or abnormal psychology, to the extent that the instructor wishes to consider the psychology of physical disability, especially blindness.

In the past, the reader in search of a concise but comprehensive treatment of this subject has had no single source to which to turn, as the available scientific literature is scattered through a wide variety of professional journals, research bulletins, unpublished master's theses and doctoral dissertations, papers delivered at professional conventions, and the like. The few existing books that objectively deal with psychological questions have tended to focus on some relatively narrow aspect of the total subject matter—e.g., the adjustment of the visually handicapped, space and object perception in the congenitally and adventitiously blind, the dreams of the blind, or cultural reactions to blindness. The present text encompasses such areas (and others of central psychological significance) within the framework of two broad topics presented as Parts I and II of the book.

Part I: Attitudes toward Blindness, Chapters 1 through 4, asks the basic question: What do most people think about the physical condition of blindness, as such, and concrete persons possessing this characteristic?

Chapter 1 is historical in nature and describes the social-psychological environment and economic position of the average blind person from ancient times to the present. It is concerned with the role of historical forces as conditions antecedent to contemporary social reactions to the blind.

Chapters 2, 3, and 4 are more specifically psychological in nature and attempt to uncover the psychological roots of popular prejudices and misconceptions regarding blindness. Chapter 2 discusses the symbolism of the eye (i.e., of both normal vision and blindness) from the standpoints of psychoanalytic theory and observations in clinical psychopathology—viz., symbolic meanings imputed to the eye by patients suffering from psychogenic visual disorders or actual organic visual impairment. However, the chief portion of this chapter explores the nature of eye symbolism in the English language from the perspectives of both common linguistic usage and etymological origins. Included here are the results of the author's content analysis of all references to the word "blind" and cognate terms in *Bartlett's Familiar Quotations* and *Webster's Third New International Dictionary.*

Chapter 3 assesses attitudes toward blindness as these are expressed through depictions of blind characters in mythology, legend, folklore, music, the graphic arts, and literature. All major past research on this subject is reviewed at length, and the author's own findings in a related study of contemporary literature, fable, myth, and fairy tales are presented. Previous and current results are integrated, and all recurring blindness-related motifs are enumerated and discussed with respect to their possible psychological sources—including cultural conditioning, the authoritarian personality syndrome, and castration (or generalized sexual) anxiety. In addition, the final and most important section of the chapter examines the applicability of Jung's hypothesis of the collective unconscious.

Chapter 4, on the other hand, is a critical survey of contemporary social attitude research carried out by means of traditional social science methods—i.e., primarily the questionnaire and interview methods and, occasionally, controlled experimentation. Attitudinal findings in regard to blindness are not only considered in their own right but are also compared with the results of parallel studies on attitudes toward the physically handicapped in general.

Part II: Blindness and Personality, the last four chapters of the book, asks the fundamental question: What are blind people really like?

Chapter 5 deals mainly with the intelligence and creative capacity of the sightless. It presents representative cases of historically noteworthy blind people (for the most part, individuals outstanding for their contributions to government, the arts, sciences, or humanities) and indicates the psychological and environmental factors affecting their success.

Chapter 6 summarizes and evaluates the findings of a representative body of contemporary empirical investigations concerned with the personality development, social adjustment, and general psychological functioning of the visually handicapped. Discussed here are: the consequences of blindness for cognition, perception of the environment, and mobility; psychological aspects of congenital or early childhood blindness in contrast to blindness of later onset and of partial versus total blindness; characteristic emotional effects of sudden traumatic blinding subsequent to the early childhood years; personality attributes of well-adjusted as opposed to poorly adjusted blind persons; and considerations of importance for the psychotherapist, rehabilitation counselor, social caseworker, and special educator engaged in work with the newly blind, the aged blind, the multiply-handicapped blind, the blind child, and the family of the blind person. Also, the results of personality research on the visually handicapped are compared with those from analogous investigations of the physically disabled at large.

Chapters 7 and 8 deal with the dream life of the blind and are primarily concerned with the relation of dreams to personality. Chapter 7 contains a nearly exhaustive review of all scientific publications on the nature of dreaming in the visually handicapped. The sensory and thematic characteristics of the dreams of the visually impaired (viz., the congenitally and the adventitiously blind, together with the partially-sighted) are described and compared with typical contents in the dreams of the seeing, the deaf-blind, and other disabled groups. The investigations in question are methodologically evaluated in terms of their strengths and weaknesses relative to one another and in the light of recent research just completed by the author in collaboration with Calvin S. Hall and Katherine Cannistraci. Chapter 8 describes the results of a pioneering content analysis study, employing the quantitative scoring system devised by Calvin S. Hall and Robert L. Van de Castle in 1966—by far the most comprehensive approach of its type yet developed for the analysis of recorded dream reports. This investigation, conducted by the author and Hall, apparently represents the first attempt to apply quantitative content analysis to the dreams of a blind person. It focused on 307 written dream reports contributed by an adventitiously blind man—certainly the largest dream series from a blind person ever to have been scientifically studied. The purpose of this study was to explore the relation of dream life to waking behavior, as well as the relation of blindness to dream content and personality. A second and later content analysis investigation by the author and Katherine Cannistraci, dealing with the dream diaries of a group of partially sighted and totally blind subjects, is discussed in Chapter 7. This study was largely concerned with the nature of dream content in the blind, as contrasted with the sighted; in the totally blind versus the partially sighted; and in individuals blind from birth or early childhood as against those blinded during later childhood, adolescence, or adulthood. Each of these two studies clearly demonstrates the scientific superiority of content analysis over other methods heretofore used in studying the dream life of the visually handicapped, and, in addition, offers much important substantive information regarding the ways in which blindness does (and does not) affect individual personality and behavior.

Thus, aside from providing a needed overview of research and theory on the psychology of blindness, the present book is unique in contributing much original material on the subject (particularly in Chapters 2, 3, 7, and 8).

Donald D. Kirtley, Ph.D.

Acknowledgments

I take this opportunity to thank each of the following persons for his important contribution to the present book.

Most of all, Dr. Calvin S. Hall (with whom Chapter 8 is jointly authored): for his extensive advice regarding the organization of the original manuscript; for his constant moral support throughout the period of its writing; and for his critical reading of the final manuscript.

Judith Wolfson, librarian of the American Foundation for the Blind: for invaluable assistance in providing needed bibliographies, books, monographs, articles, and unpublished papers on the psychology of blindness.

Vernon Nordby: for indispensable assistance in the content analysis of the dream data of the Kirtley and Hall study, described in Chapter 8.

My wife Joyce: for reading and tape-recording material on the dreams of the blind.

Dr. Ernst Moerk: for his assistance in translating German sources and for his critical reading of a large portion of the manuscript.

Mrs. Claudia Moerk: for her help in the translation of French materials.

Dr. Thomas Breen: for his aid in locating and providing necessary reading materials on the biology of dreaming.

Mrs. Gwenn Wright: for typing major portions of the final draft and for proofreading the manuscript.

Kenneth T. Sabo: for his help in correcting errors in the original and final drafts.

PART I

Attitudes toward Blindness

I

The Place of the Blind in History

According to Lowenfeld (1964), the social and economic history of the Western blind may be divided into three distinct stages: (1) the primitive period; (2) the era of the asylums; and (3) the age of social integration. The initial stage occupied all of prehistory and pervaded the ancient period, when the blind were generally regarded as an economic liability, unworthy even of the fundamental right to live. During antiquity, they were treated with the utmost scorn, and begging became their traditional form of livelihood. The second phase began with the rise of Christianity in Rome and ended in the late eighteenth century with Valentin Hauy's founding of the first school for the blind in Paris in 1784. During this long middle period, the right to life was recognized, but education and independence were not encouraged. The sightless were still considered helpless, capable of a decent existence only through the benevolence of others, preferably as wards of the Church. The final stage commenced with the French Enlightenment and the advent of systematic education for the blind. Once equipped with the skills requisite to self-support, the sightless started becoming integrated into normal society, as full-fledged members; but this process of assimilation has been slow and piecemeal and remains even today only partial. Owing to a ubiquitous pattern of discrimination, particularly in the economic sector, the blind have yet to achieve their rightful place in society.

Antiquity

Throughout the ancient period, physically defective infants were commonly exposed, but according to French (1932), a distinguished historian of the blind, this practice was probably somewhat restricted in the case of the sightless since visual disability may not be recognizable at birth. Among primitive peoples, blinded children and adults, as well as infants born sightless, were frequently put to death. In old Prussia, for example, sons customarily killed their aged and infirm parents, while fathers, as a matter of honor, destroyed by sword, burning, or drowning all blind or otherwise defective children, including those with a mere squinting of the eyes. In addition, masters utilized elaborate means of torture to execute their sightless or lame servants.

In Rome, there were a few blind musicians, poets, lawyers, and scholars—e.g., Cicero was tutored in philosophy and geometry by the blind Diodotus, who won the lasting esteem of his famous pupil—but the vast multitude of the sightless lived in extreme degradation and penury. Blind boys were trained for begging or were sold as galley slaves, and blind girls were forced into prostitution. There was no official state aid of the unfortunate; nor was humanitarianism fostered by religion or philosophy. Stoicism recommended kindness to the poor and disabled, but scarcely any of its adherents took the idea seriously. Although the emperors and some wealthy citizens occasionally distributed food, clothing, and sometimes money to the masses, this largess was offered merely to promote the donor's popularity with the people or to demonstrate his power and social importance. The blind were loathed, and most were homeless, wandering beggars whose only possessions were dog or staff, knapsack, and the rags on their backs. Many were owned by ruthless slave masters, who derived a profitable income from this begging and were wont to beat their captives mercilessly when pickings were small.

On the other hand, the Roman army, in time, began administering aid to its blinded veterans, and the emperor Hadrian praised the welfare approach of the Egyptians, for a large number of their sightless were gainfully employed and independent. Nonetheless, neither the army nor Hadrian exerted any appreciable influence over the general condition of the blind in Rome.

In Israel, four major classes of infirmity were recognized: blindness, deafness, dumbness, and lameness. Of these, blindness was viewed as the most debilitating. The sightless were seen as "living dead," alien creatures whose mere touch might communicate blindness or disease. Public care of the visually handicapped was lacking, although religion advocated private charity, and some laws were established for their protection. Beggary was their typical occupation, yet numerous individuals were able to find more satisfactory means of support—e.g., grinding grain with the hand mill. By contrast, those sightless who belonged to the higher strata of society were less severely stigmatized. They were allowed education, and many became scholars and private tutors and were regarded as "living libraries," on account of their immense store of memorized knowledge.

In Greece, the status of the blind was somewhat more favorable. They were sometimes venerated as seers or prophets. The unsophisticated masses were inclined to attribute supernatural powers to the intelligent or gifted blind, but the bulk of sightless persons were not similarly revered. Blindness was traditionally considered as divine punishment for sin, and the extraordinary abilities of some blind were a compensatory gift of the gods. Euripides believed suicide to be preferable to blindness, and three centuries B.C. the aged Eratosthenes, eminent astronomer and geographer, starved himself to death rather than accept approaching blindness. The Greeks, like every other ancient people, regarded blindness as the worst of all possible afflictions, the effects of which could only be devastating unless countered by some special beneficence from "On High." Still, the plight of the blind was less severe in Greece than in most other ancient civilizations. For example, Athens issued its needy citizens a subsistence pension. Though small, it was at least not interpreted as charity but as a right of citizenship. Also, self-sufficient blind scholars, poets and musicians were more numerous in Greece than in Rome.

In the early West and Middle East, Egypt showed the most constructive attitude toward the visually handicapped. According to Ross (1951), another historian of the sightless, the priests of Karnak developed a fairly systematic program of welfare for the poor and disabled and, among the latter, fostered a degree of learning and economic independence. The physically impaired were perennial guests at the ceremonial feasts along the Nile, where sightless poets, musicians, jugglers, buffoons, and shepherds were plentiful. On the other hand, no blind artists or scholars of enduring distinction appeared in old Egypt.

Contrary to the usual Western belief, the ideal of individual, human worth first emerged in the Orient, not in the Middle East. In both China and India, useful occupations for the blind were found relatively soon.

In ancient China, blind scholars, soothsayers, storytellers, and musicians were not uncommon. Shihmien, who tutored Confucius in music, was a blind man; and Shihk'uang, also sightless, comforted Confucius through music and thereby artistically embodied the master's teachings. It was thought that his beautiful performances were, likewise, enchanting to the spirit world. During the Han dynasty, the blind soothsaying movement was launched by Luk'ai, who held high public office and, notwithstanding his sightlessness, wielded considerable influence over his contemporaries. Through him, schools were established to train the visually disabled in the art of fortune telling. The Han era also gave birth to a lengthy succession of blind storytellers who traveled about the country relating their romantic tales to the accompaniment of crude musical instruments. Via this oral tradition, the stories of old China were communicated from one generation to the next. For a time, there were also schools for this occupation.

Music, however, was the preferred vocation of the Chinese blind, and many joined bands that played or sang at teashops, private dwellings, and festivals. The more talented supported themselves by teaching music, and a handful achieved prominence; whereas the majority were itinerant beggars, identifiable by the traditional gong and stick, whose music and occasional clowning were devices for entreating the generosity of the public.

In India, Buddhism taught compassion for all the unfortunate. During the third century B.C., the pious Asoka the Great constructed hospitals at public expense and encouraged tolerance toward both the impoverished and the physically deviant. Moreover, some of the blind gained a respectable niche in society as transmitters of oral tradition, both secular and religious but especially the latter. Nevertheless, sightless mendicants were still to be found everywhere in India.

The Middle Period

The Christian communities of the first century A.D. assisted the needy blind, and rich Christians accepted them as guests in their homes. The

Church fathers were sincerely concerned for the well being of the sightless and dispensed as much aid as was practically possible. As the Church grew into a complex, monolithic bureaucracy, the blind became recipients of its general care for the poor and obtained food and shelter under the administration of individual bishops. With the eventual decline of church power and wealth, parish priests continued to give alms, which were derived from private offerings and religious fees. By the close of the Medieval period, the Church, as such, had ceased to be the primary benefactor of the poor. Centuries earlier, this role had largely accrued to Church-sponsored asylums.

The Congregation and House of the Three Hundred (or Quinze-Vingts) was the most famous of these institutions. It was founded in Paris in 1254 by King Louis IX, and according to legend, was built for blinded Crusaders. Later, blind women were also admitted. Each brother and sister joined with all personal belongings, which, at death, became the property of the asylum. They were obliged to keep the statutes and secrets of the House, observe certain religious rituals, and execute all allocated chores. In addition, they wore the House uniform—a long blue gown with a lily on the breast. The brothers and sisters could marry among themselves and retain their children for a prescribed period. To supervise the affairs of the institution, a master and an attending priest were appointed by the king. The master, moreover, was allotted a business manager and five sworn assistants to expedite his guidance. Originally, all major decision-making power was in the hands of the Congregation, but, in time, such control was usurped by the sighted administrators. The king granted the Quinze-Vingts exemption from taxation and the right of asylum. Clement IV and subsequent popes eulogized the organization and bestowed upon its church highly liberal indulgence privileges. As a consequence, the church of the Quinze-Vingts was able to attain great distinction. However, under Louis XVI this commodious asylum was abruptly sold, and the blind brotherhood was stripped of its possessions and thrust into inferior quarters. During the French Revolution, the new anti-Royalist government made partial amends for this infringement of rights, and the Quinze-Vingts once more began to function; but never again was it to have the prestige and wealth of former days.

In its heyday this institution was emulated all over Europe, an event analogous to the development of trade and merchant guilds during the same period. Furthermore, the populations of these asylums were not exclusively sightless, as some accepted individuals with other physical handicaps. In Italy, Germany, and Spain, the blind brotherhoods were notably successful.

One of the most outstanding of these was the blind Brotherhood of Palermo, which devoted itself almost entirely to music and its teaching. The asylum's thirty members were all instrumentalists, singers, composers, or rhymesters, who also published their works and sang for audiences outside the institution. They were under oath to eschew performances in brothels, as well as the singing or recitation of obscenities in public places. Additionally, they were compelled to carry out a variety of religious exercises and to submit their creations to the censorship of a Jesuit chaplain. Despite such restrictions, the Brotherhood won widespread acclaim and was quite justifiably proud of its tradition.

Throughout the Middle Ages, care of the destitute was typically accomplished through the Church in partnership with the state. However, toward the end of this period, such functions were increasingly assumed by single communities. The Reformation greatly reduced the Church's capacity to help the blind, while the ensuing local charities were grossly inadequate to the need then extant. Furthermore, even when the Church-supported asylums were flourishing, the great bulk of the sightless did not live within them. Most, like their fellows of old, were homeless beggars. For many, admission to charitable institutions was strictly forbidden, since blindness had come as a punishment for crime, often of a sexual nature. On the other hand, the Church itself had never possessed sufficient means to maintain all its blind and, therefore, had customarily allowed these unprotected persons to beg at holy sites. Indeed, in order to augment income, the asylums, likewise, encouraged begging among their inmates, and even the respected Quinze-Vingts procured a portion of its funds in this manner. Eventually, the impotence of the Church, coupled with the absence of systematic state aid, produced a vast wave of aggressive mendicancy throughout Europe.

The wayfaring victims of this social dislocation frequently traveled in large, noisy crowds, which sometimes attracted lepers, not to mention impostors. Unlike their more stationary, less impoverished predecessors, this new breed of blind outcasts roamed widely and begged with the utmost tenacity. To get about, most used dog, staff, or boy-guide. The public regarded them as unspeakable pests. The more fortunate members of this hated group were minstrels, who, in proportion to their talent, were able to mitigate somewhat the extreme wretchedness of their lot.

Until the modern era, the vocations of music and poetical recitation continued as the blind's typical means of achieving economic security. In Egypt and China, records of such occupations among the sightless date back as early as 1500 B.C., while in ancient Greece, the blind bard (with his boy-guide), reciting heroic verse to the melodies of the lyre, was a fairly common sight in town and village. The legendary Homer was just such a wanderer. Similarly, among the ancient Celts, sightless bards glorified the gods and heroes of their people and vilified foreign enemies. Out of this tradition arose the legend of Ossian (c. 300 A.D.), who lost his vision after a long and distinguished military career. Ossian, as the story has it, was a prolific poet, one of the highest rank—a traveling bard who sang his verse to the tune of the harp.

During the eleventh century, Hervaeus of Brittany, long since dead, was canonized and soon became the patron saint of Europe's blind bards. According to tradition, he had been born blind, of a pious mother and a musical father, and was himself a bard. He is often pictured in his native land, going from village to village with a white dog, where the local children would flock about him and, from his songs, learn the love of God, their fellow man, and their daily work. Supernatural powers were imputed to St. Hervaeus, such as abilities to communicate with the dead and to tame wild beasts by the beauty of his singing. It is known that he founded a monastery in Brittany, where he taught the neighborhood children, and that he died in the middle of the sixth century. His relics were kept at the Cathedral of Nantes until the French Revolution, when they were lost.

With the invention of the printing press and the propagation of printed materials, the sightless bards tended to be more and more supplanted by formally trained, thoroughly professional musicians. Thus, this once worthy vocation quickly came to be associated with common beggary. Such blind minstrels were found all over Europe but were particularly abundant in Italy, Spain, Germany, and England. They played and recited in castles, city streets, village squares, and at all sorts of celebrations—private, Church, and public. They often printed ballads, or told ribald stories. Many were known for their drinking and general roguery.

In some countries, sightless minstrels were able to garner, either through governmental or their own united actions, at least a small measure of security. In Spain, their begging rights were protected by law until the revolution of 1868, prior to which only the blind had been permitted to sing or recite in public places. On the other hand, in China and Russia, the sightless formed their own congresses and drafted rules to govern their begging activities, so as to insure optimal monetary opportunities for all their kind.

Still, mendicancy was not the universal fate of blind musicians, since some of them belonged to the new and more popular class of highly skilled professionals previously mentioned. During the late Middle Ages, there arose in Italy, France, and Spain (within the courts and universities) a small but eminently successful number of blind performers, as well as musical scholars. This group, of course, consisted wholly of men who had experienced probably the best type of musical education, both academic and technical, then available.

In the West, the Renaissance stimulated great intellectual and material progress, yet for the average blind person, it meant only more humiliation and want. Nonetheless, this epoch gave birth to at least one important flash of insight concerning the fundamental problem of the visually disabled, viz., their frustrated potential and need for optimal economic autonomy. The idea was first expressed in 1526, when Juan Luis Vives, the renowned Spanish humanist, argued that the blind were too often idle, despite the fact that they were quite capable of contributing to their maintenance through the performance of meaningful labor. Although Vives apparently failed to recognize the possibility of full self-support for the sightless in general, his view was still enlightened and even radical for its time. It was not until the eighteenth-century French Age of Reason that economic independence for the blind through socially valued work began to become a reality.

In early Islamic countries, the state of the blind was somewhat more satisfactory than in Europe. During the eleventh century, they were offered instruction at Cairo's University of Al-Azhar. Their education extended over a twelve-year period and was accomplished through memorization. Some of the sightless became teachers or preached in the mosques, while many others sang or recited the Koran in public and holy places. Egypt was one of the first countries to produce self-supporting blind scholars.

However, of all the early approaches to the blind, the most constructive was that of the Japanese. During the eighth century, Ganjin-Wajo, a sightless Buddhist sage, established a kaidan at Nara, and hundreds of Japanese, including the empress, became members of the order. Such recognition, in effect, made Buddhism a state religion. Its emphasis on humanitarianism was to benefit all the underprivileged.

After Prince Hitoyasu, son of the fifty-fourth emperor, became blind in 858, he and his father grew interested in the practical problems of the sightless. Following Hitoyasu's death, a group of blind men were appointed to investigate the condition of the Japanese blind. They created an academy and explored a variety of occupations that might be successfully carried out by the sightless, e.g., music, literature, religion, and massage. The academy officials were held in high esteem and possessed the power of feudal lords. This innovation led to a succession of degree-awarding academies and was probably the first institution for the systematic education of the blind, though this honor is generally credited to the previously mentioned Paris school on account· of its more comprehensive program.

By the close of the ninth century, the Todo and the Moso formed the two main classes of the Japanese blind. The former were laymen operating through the feudal academies, while the latter were Buddhist monks. The majority of the sightless belonged to guilds and were protected and controlled by law. In time, music, acupuncture, shampooing, and massage came to be the leading vocations of the blind. In the early seventeenth century, the sightless acquired a virtual monopoly over acupuncture and massage. Training in such skills covered a period of four to seven years. As Western influence grew, the practice of acupuncture declined to insignificance, but massage continued to be popular. Contemporary Japan, in its work for the blind, remains one of the most progressive countries in the world.

The Modern Period

The first glimmerings of scientific interest in the blind began in eighteenth-century France with the work of Diderot, who studied not only the gifted but also the ordinary blind. On the other hand, the objectivity of his investigations was seriously marred by a pronounced tendency toward overgeneralization—e.g., he concluded that the blind are characterized by a marked propensity for sadism, a damning view of the sightless thoroughly discredited by later research. Among the individuals studied by Diderot were Nicholas Saunderson, the distinguished Cambridge mathematician, and Melanie de Salignac, a French girl of average intelligence who had been taught to read with cardboard cutout letters and who comprehended the basic principles of algebra, geometry, and astronomy.

Voltaire was similarly interested in the capacities of the sightless, largely because of his relationship with the socially prominent Mademoiselle Du'Deffand, a blind woman who conducted what was then one of Paris's best known salons. Voltaire admired her keen mental powers and energetic temperament, which suggested to him that the general social level of the blind could be raised through education. At the time, however, opportunities for both applied and academic learning were entirely lacking for the great bulk of the sightless.

Valentin Hauy, a French philanthropist, crested this swelling tide of rationalism when he founded the first major school for the blind in 1784 in Paris. Its ambitious curriculum was practical, as well as broad in scope, and focused upon music, crafts, and academic subjects. The chief goal of the institution was to prepare the sightless to function independently in culturally useful occupations.

The success of Hauy's school soon inspired imitation. Johann Wilhelm Klein, in early nineteenth-century Germany, and Samuel G. Howe, a few decades later in America, were both prime movers in the founding of progressive schools for the blind. In late nineteenth-century England, another pioneering educator, Sir Francis J. Campbell (who was himself blind), helped establish an outstanding institution that was soon turning out successful blind organists, teachers, and piano tuners. Like Hauy, these later educators stressed training and readiness for vocational self-sufficiency. Today, of course, special schools for the blind exist in countries all over the world.

A graduate of the young Hauy school, Louis Braille (1809-1852), was destined to become the single most important figure in the history of work for the blind. Shortly before his fourth birthday, Braille accidentally blinded himself in one eye while playing with an awl, and the sight of the remaining eye was soon lost as well, owing to a sympathetic ophthalmia. He entered the Paris institute in 1819, and ten years later, while a member of its faculty, he began to develop his revolutionary system of reading and writing. The original discovery had been made by Charles Barbier, a veteran of the Napoleonic wars, whose initial purpose was the devising of a cipher language for the military. He christened his system "Nightwriting," as it was to be employed at night for the exchange of secret intelligence in war zones. In 1820, he attempted to interest the Hauy school in his invention, but the administration considered it unworkable. Braille alone recognized the immense value of Barbier's technique, and his contribution consisted in refining it for practical use. By 1834, the now famous Braille system had been perfected. However, Braille's great work was not to be acknowledged until after his death. In 1854 (when Braille had been dead for two years), the Paris institute at last adopted his method. By the end of the century, the Braille system had become the universally accepted means of written communication for the blind. Previous approaches had focused upon embossed, Roman lettering. The critical insight of both Barbier and Braille was that the fingers discriminate point stimuli more readily than the line properties of ordinary letters.

In America, early in the present century, a number of liberal educators fought to improve the social, economic, and educational status of the sightless. Two of the most effective of these rebels were Newell Perry and Robert Irwin (1955), both also blind. They were perhaps most important for their battle to win admission for the blind to public schools, including colleges and universities. Many visually handicapped youths attend such institutions today, largely as a result of the reforming zeal and political adeptness of Perry and Irwin.

In the British Commonwealth and the United States, organized work for the blind was predominantly an outgrowth of the two World Wars. In London, during World War I, Sir Cyril Arthur Pearson, a sightless newspaper magnate and philanthropist, founded St. Dunstan's, a pioneering rehabilitation center for the British war-blind. This institution's primary emphasis was upon vocational adjustment. Its notable achievements quickly led to the establishment of similar organizations in Canada, Australia, New Zealand, and South Africa. In the United States, rehabilitation services for the blind were negligible until the close of World War II, when, under the direction of the federal government, such programs were greatly expanded (Bauman, 1954, 1969).

Although their general cultural position has advanced significantly during the last two centuries, the blind are not yet fully accepted members of modern society. Even in the United States, with its comparatively enlightened approach to the blind, inequality is still the rule rather than the exception. For example, everyone familiar with the practical problems of the sightless knows that discriminatory employment practices in our country are still widespread—in fact, almost universal. In this connection, the situation of the blind is analogous to that of black people and other stigmatized minority groups.

On the positive side, however, contemporary social injustice toward the visually disabled is not going unchallenged. In 1940, the blind Jacobus ten Broek (1956, 1957)—a distinguished Constitutional historian, orator, and social welfare authority of the University of California—founded the politically militant National Federation of the Blind (NFB), an organization to promote the social and economic equality of sightless persons through public education and legislative action. Since its inception, the NFB has grown considerably in financial resources and political influence and today constitutes a potent force against anti-blind discrimination. To date, the work of the NFB has led to the passage of much sorely needed state and federal legislation for advancing the civil rights of sightless citizens, particularly in the areas of hiring practice, admission to educational institutions, and utilization of public facilities and conveyances, including housing.

The American Council of the Blind is another recent, influential, social action group, while the American Foundation for the Blind (AFB), founded early in the present century, is the country's chief nonpolitical organization for the blind. The AFB is primarily an informational service, providing educational communications regarding blindness to the general public, as well as support for research on blindness, including projects concerned with the development of improved mobility, reading, and recreational aids.

Conclusions

Down through history, social reactions to the visually handicapped have been preponderantly negative. During the ancient and Medieval periods, the average blind man was a beggar. Even today, the blind, as a group, occupy a marginal position in society. When employed, they are likely to perform menial types of labor at less than the minimum wage, viz., within the so-called "sheltered workshops," such as Goodwill Industries or the Lighthouse for the Blind. Of the jobless, many are supported, in whole or in part, by meager government aid and, to a much lesser extent, by humiliating, private charity. Some would contend that visual deficit per se, and not adverse social conditions, is the crucial determinant of the inferior status of the sightless as a class. In Chapters 5 and 6 of Part II, this fundamental question will be considered at length.

References

Chapter 1/The Place of the Blind in History

Bauman, M. 1954. *Adjustment to blindness.* Commonwealth of Pennsylvania: Pennsylvania State Council for the Blind.

Bauman, M. 1969. Dimensions of blindness. In M. Goldberg and J. Swinton, eds. *Blindness research: the expanding frontiers.* University Park, Pa.: Pennsylvania State University Press.

French, R. 1932. *From Homer to Helen Keller: A social and educational study of the blind.* New York: American Foundation for the Blind.

Irwin, R. 1955. *As I saw it.* New York: American Foundation for the Blind.

Lowenfeld, B. 1964. The social impact of blindness upon the individual. *New Outlook for the Blind* 58: 273-277.

Ross, I. 1951. *Journey into light.* New York: Appleton-Century-Crofts.

ten Broek, J. 1956. Within the grace of God. Presidential address to 16th annual convention of National Federation of the Blind, San Francisco.

ten Broek, J. 1957. The right of the blind to organize. Presidential address to 17th annual convention of National Federation of the Blind, New Orleans.

2

The Symbolism of the Eyes and Their Dysfunction

Objectively considered, the eyes are, pure and simple, the organs of sight. However, for man, the visual apparatus has always entailed more than mere physical seeing. The eyes and their functional condition also possess symbolic meaning. All languages, including our own, are replete with such extraphysiological referents. These additional significations indicate the operation of certain typical fantasies in connection with the presence or absence of vision. Words pertaining to the eyes—e.g., "sight," "vision," and "blind"—are often used metaphorically, and it is through such figurative usage that we are able to identify and understand the nature of the purely imaginary components in the meaning of the eyes. In the everyday utilization of language, such intrapsychic conceptions are usually unconscious, which indeed is the case with symbolic meanings generally. While it is not clear to what extent or in what manner fantasy is related to conscious attitudes or overt behavior, there nonetheless exists ample evidence, both clinical and experimental, to show that these realms of activity are by no means discrete. One's fantasies, whether conscious or unconscious, do, to some degree and through a variety of channels, affect one's attitudes and actions. It is my conviction that fantasies about the eyes, as expressed in the common language, constitute a critical factor in determining emotional reactions to blindness, both among the blind and the sighted. This exploration of the irrational bases of linguistic practice will, it

17

is hoped, shed some light on the immense problem of social discrimination faced by sightless persons.

The Normal Eye

Within the framework of psychoanalytic theory, Thass-Thienemann (1968) investigated the etymological roots of two perennial eye symbols: the eye as window and the sun as eye.

Let us first examine the window symbol. A popular figure of speech in English refers to the eye as "the window of the soul." This equation, as Thass-Thienemann demonstrated, has a long history and is not unique to our language. For example, the Greek *phota* signifies both eyes and window, while the Latin *lumina*—plural of *lumin* (light of the eye)—also denotes window. Similarly, the English *window* originated from the Old English term *wind-auga*, viz., "walleye." The walleyes of our primitive forebears were the eye-shaped windows that they cut in the timbers of their crude block dwellings.

In the view of this psychoanalyst, "the human body and its functions are the primary frame of reference in naming objects of the perceived world," though "this body language is unconscious in the modern speaker."

From this perspective, window shades assume the intrapsychic significance of eyelids. The window-eye that is covered by a pulled-down shade is, in effect, blind. Moreover, our language supports this interpretation through terms such as "Venetian blinds." Thass-Thienemann related the use of window shades to feelings of modesty, guilt, and aggression expressed in the "downcast look." At bottom, the embarrassed decency of the downcast eyes often constitutes a reaction formation against an aggressive impulse to look. The downcast look and the closed blinds are not intended merely as a safeguard against a guilty conscience or inspection by outsiders. More basically, they may aim to achieve the tactical advantage of spying on others from a protected position. One wishes to see without being seen, which is, as the investigator pointed out, a fundamental characteristic of animal aggression. Numerous symbolic references in the Bible bolster such an interpretation. For example, the Old Testament Hebrew term *arubhah* means "lurking" as well as window. In addition, Thass-Thienemann examined the Biblical "evil eye" and found that it designates various expressive movements of the eyes and not the sadistic omnipotence imputed to the evil eye of folklore. Peering through nearly closed lids is associated with stinginess (e.g., Prov. 28:22), whereas a sidelong glance, looking from one eye with the other shut, or the winking of one or both eyes represents aggressive dissimulation (e.g., Prov. 6: 13-14).

On the other hand, the downcast eyes do not invariably involve the foregoing type of reaction formation, for at times the look expresses genuine shame or guilt. According to Thass-Thienemann, one is thus seeking to elude his conscience by rendering himself invisible to it. Such behavior is observed frequently in children. For instance, a four-year-old girl was wont to shut her eyes whenever her parents apprehended her in some act of mischief. This behavior was a device for escaping punishment. Since she became invisible to herself, the child imagined that she was likewise screened from parental scrutiny. Consequently, when a person conceals himself from external light (e.g., behind Venetian blinds), he may be acting out a conscience-provoked fantasy, viz., he wishes to hide from his own punitive conscience, which is projected onto outer light so as to facilitate the self-deception.

Thass-Thienemann's discussion of the sun-eye symbol is relevant here. The sun god was the most widely worshiped deity among primitive peoples. In the religion of ancient Egypt, the sun possessed the power of vision and was artistically represented in the form of an eye, while among the early Greeks, the sun became the vigilant god Helios. Furthermore, the Old Testament alludes to the "sight of the sun." Likewise, in the words of an old German proverb: "The sun sees everything." And the Irish term *suil* refers to the eye and sun alike. All of these symbolic usages, in Thass-Thienemann's view, link the sun with an all-powerful, all-knowing superego, i.e., the omnipotent father-authority of early childhood. In fleeing from sunlight, one is attempting to extricate oneself from the inevitable judgment of the all-seeing father, or, more precisely, from the guilt-producing power of one's own superego, the childhood introjection of the parental superego.

The above analysis, though not concerned with visual disability, does, nevertheless, suggest some interesting hypotheses regarding the motivation of certain attitudes toward blindness. One such attitude associates blindness with immorality. In popular fantasy, sightless persons are frequently represented as evildoers, their visual deprivation constituting a well-deserved punishment for sin. This stereotype is perhaps related to the window symbol and the aggressive signification of window blinds. Because the "windows" of the sightless individual are "blinded," he could be a dangerous character and, therefore, one worthy of suspicion. In this connection, mythology and folklore ascribe occult powers to the blind, including prophetic vision. The more sophisticated, contemporary interpretations of visual handicap are by no means immune to such superstitions, for extraordinary abilities, both sensory and mental, are often thought to go hand in hand with blindness. A person endowed with magical abilities would, of course, possess a greater than normal potential for evil. Another prevalent fantasy identifies blindness with inscrutability, i.e., the condition is perceived as an impenetrable barrier that separates the sightless individual from the outside world, as if it were a screen, wall, or invisible force field precluding observation of the individual and, hence, knowledge of him as a person. If such fantasies are admixed with those pertaining to the window and its blinds, demonic overtones would, perforce, accrue to visual deficit. The blind person may be seen as evil simply because his handicap is interpreted as a castigation for iniquity or because it affords him camouflage, together with a threatening "second sight," or both kinds of fantasy may be important. Another possibility is that sightlessness is imagined as cutting one off from the influence of his conscience. The blind person is not only hidden from the light of the "seeing sun," but he is also blind to the inner "searchlight" of conscience; therefore, he must be regarded as immoral. Such a fantasy would be suggested by the image of the sightless as mentally incompetent, a stereotype even more widespread than its opposite, viz., that which assigns special cognitive powers, merely by reason of visual disability.

The infantile fantasy that equates not looking with self-invisibility is perhaps related to the ubiquitous image of the blind as helpless, as well as to the anxiety engendered by it. The infant's helplessness and fear of parental abandonment, the greatest fear of early childhood, are quite real. Invisibility may suggest freedom from punishment, but it also implies a renunciation of the parental protection necessary for survival; for if the child is invisible, he cannot be found—he is, in effect, lost to his parents. In this manner, the idea of invisibility comes to be associated with separation anxiety. When the child closes his eyes, he is temporarily blind, and he identifies this condition with his imaginary invisibility. Interestingly enough, "invisibility, darkness, obscurity," and "indiscernibility" are all archaic meanings of the term "blindness." Thus, via invisibility, blindness becomes linked with the child's fear of abandonment, being interpreted as a state of utter helplessness. In adults, separation anxiety is particularly evident in severe forms of anxiety neurosis, which are characterized by panic states, a sense of impending doom, and overwhelming feelings of incompetence, inferiority, dependency, and confusion. Furthermore, an appreciable residue of this infantile fear typically persists into normal adulthood, by which time strong psychic defenses have been levied against its potentially disruptive influence. In both the sightless and the seeing, blindness anxiety and the identification of blindness with hopeless inability appear, to a considerable extent, to stem from a reactivation of this previously unconscious separation anxiety.

The Impaired Eye

Schauer (1951) analyzed the symbolism of the eyes in fairy tales, mythology, folklore, religion, and proverbial sayings, as well as in the fantasies of both normal and neurotic individuals. His discussion suggests seven common, if not universal, themes: (1) the eye as devouring mouth; (2) he eye as an omnipotent, destructive organ; (3) seeing as identification with the thing seen; (4) seeing as a forbidden or forbidding activity; (5) blindness as punishment for sin; (6) blindness as conveying rare moral virtue; and (7) the blind as immature or childlike.

In certain fairy tales seeing is likened to eating, as objects are said to be devoured with the eyes. The eyes are employed as though they were entirely in the service of the mouth. In the everyday use of visual metaphor, persons, food, movies, books, and other external things and events are said to be consumed or incorporated through the eyes. For example, one may "feast his eyes" on a beautiful landscape or "take in" a movie. Such fantasies endow seeing with great destructive power. By implication, the person who cannot see is deprived of such power. This is one intrapsychic source of the belief that the blind are impotent.

The idea of magical power is also integral to the folk belief in the evil eye, which, at a single glance, can render its victim helpless and vulnerable to danger. Here the eye is used as a sadistic weapon, and looking confers absolute power over the object looked at. By visual fixation of the object, the looker compels it to behave as he wishes. The popular misconception of hypnotism, which imputes occult powers to the hypnotist, arises directly from this ancient fantasy, which is itself a further ingredient contributing to the attitude that the blind are helpless.

Since looking may often serve evil purposes, blindness naturally acquires the status of a punishment. In imaginative literature, this form of castigation occurs regardless of whether the sin is committed knowingly or unknowingly. The little hunchbacked tailor, Peeping Tom, is struck blind while watching Lady Godiva through drawn window shades. On the other hand, Oedipus blinds himself for his unintended sin of incest. Thus, the sightless person becomes immoral simply by reason of his sightlessness. At the moment of blinding, he is transformed into a wretched sinner. Nor may he, in his defense, cite a prior life of obvious virtue, for this can only mean that his sin was formerly hidden.

Contrariwise, fiction and folklore perhaps just as often portray the sightless individual as unusually good and innocent, even saintly. This interpretation emanates in large part from our Judeo-Christian tradition, which stresses spiritual growth through suffering. Among the uneducated masses, this teaching has long since come to mean that misery automatically leads to virtue. However, another possibly important factor behind the "saintly image" of the blind is the moralistic significance of vision in the unconscious. Since the blind person cannot look, he cannot commit the sins of looking, i.e., he cannot look at the genitals nor at the sexual behavior of himself or others, nor, indeed, at anything forbidden. At least in the visual sphere, he has no choice but to be virtuous.

Schauer found that such moralistic, infantile interpretations of sight were associated with visual disturbances in his neurotic patients. Some typical fantasies of hysterically blind patients ran as follows: "I can't see because it isn't right for me to see," and "I can't see because it's dangerous for me to see." These patients feared the emergence of socially unacceptable impulses of sex or aggression that might be gratified through looking. Certain common fantasies of voyeuristic patients focused upon a fascination with the forbidden, a need to identify with the sexual capacity and behavior of another and a wish to excite others sexually through looking at them. Inability to look was an occasional symptom among obsessive-compulsive neurotics. Though wishing to look, such patients were compulsively forced to avert their gaze and rely upon senses other than vision. The symptom was related to pressing sexual impulses of an infantile nature, viz., of exhibitionism, scopophilia, and the like. As the ashamed child averts his gaze in the magical hope that, by not looking, he will not be looked at, so the adult obsessive-compulsive avoids looking in order to escape his "immoral" impulses. Such visual fantasies are by no means restricted to neurotics. They are also found among normal individuals, though usually in a less intense form. The fantasies of neurotics merely provide a more dramatic illustration of the relationship between sight and immorality in the unconscious.

Seeing a thing may also imply an identification with it. We say we identify with interesting plays, movies, and novels, meaning that we become so engrossed in the imaginary characters and action that we temporarily forget our own unique self-identity and, as it were, become one with the ongoing drama. Psychologically, we become a part of that which we watch on the stage or screen, or see imaginally when we read.

Among scopophilic men, as previously indicated, a frequent fantasy centers on the need to identify with the presumed sexual prowess of some other man. For example, a male patient of one of my colleagues could not experience orgasm with his wife during normal coitus. Full sexual gratification came only when he observed another man copulating with her. During such episodes, he would masturbate to the visual scene while imaginatively likening himself to his wife's lover. In fact, he assisted her in procuring lovers, a plan that he had initiated with her consent and full cooperation. His feelings of sexual inferiority could be suppressed and replaced by a sense of potency only when he identified himself with the sexual performance of strange men whom he perceived to be ideally virile.

In folklore, to look at an object often means to acquire its properties, to be forced to imitate it, or to force it to grow like oneself. Fantasies of this variety constitute an inherent component of the evil-eye superstition. In horror stories, those who see the evil eye frequently become evil themselves. For instance, looking into the hypnotic gaze of Count Dracula ultimately engrafts an identification with him, for the blood-drained victim is himself transformed into a vampire. According to Schauer, sighted persons sometimes eschew empathizing with the blind out of the unconscious fear that to do so could render them similarly blind. In this connection, parents are wont to teach their children not to stare at physically disabled individuals. Consciously, this is done out of politeness; but at the level of the irrational unconscious, the critical motive may be fear of an ensuing identification with the person stared at. During antiquity, particularly in Israel (as has already been mentioned), to touch or to look upon a blind person was considered dangerous, since blindness was believed to be contagious. Many seeing individuals have told me that they avoid looking at blind people because the mere sight of them brings depression. Such persons characteristically conceive of sightlessness as the most unhappy of all human afflictions, as a handicap that obviates every possibility of self-fulfillment, not to mention the simpler, more casual pleasures of normal animal existence. To them, blindness is a miasma whose pollution may reach beyond the bounds of the affected person's body, insofar as the gloom of blindness directly assails the sighted onlooker. Though not consciously anxious over the other's blindness as such, these seeing persons nonetheless fear an invasion by the depression that they have projected into the sightless individual. Here, then, the identification pertains to affect and not the physical condition of blindness.

Finally, Schauer referred to the fact that the blind are often regarded as immature or childlike. Accordingly, they are apt to be overindulged, overprotected, patronized, or simply tolerated in the sense of the "good child" who is to be "seen but not heard." Schauer also ascribed this attitude to unconscious infantile evaluations of vision, since the actual limitations of sightlessness are insufficient to warrant so exaggerated a view of the sightless person's dependency. In addition, Schauer went on to point out that the inconsiderate, impetuous curiosity characteristic of children and mental retardates is frequently assigned to the blind.

The latter attitude appears most strikingly in respect to the tactile behavior of blind people. Many of the seeing believe that the sightless possess a voracious, insatiable appetite for feeling objects in the environment, including the bodies (especially the faces) of other persons. This inordinate need for touching is, furthermore, represented as being awkward and somehow unwholesome. I have found that blind persons themselves, mainly newly blinded adolescents, commonly share in this distorted attitude toward tactile exploration, with the result that they utilze this modality as little as possible and thereby exclude themselves from much useful and even needed information about the environment. The misconception, to a marked degree, derives from our culture's taboo against touch in general, for the moral proscription of genital touching has been extended to cover nonsexual tactile sensations as well. Consequently, the sightless individual, who requires more than normal touch contact, may come to be fantasized as sexually impulsive. In their play (when there is no immediate threat of adult interference), children, of course, indulge freely in erotic touching. The sighted adult's familiarity with such behavior is one important factor that leads him to associate the blind adult with the child.

According to Schauer, the preceding symbolic meanings of the eyes, vision, and blindness (which are almost always unconscious in any given individual) constitute potent forces in shaping social attitudes toward the blind. Their essentially negative character accounts, at least in part, for the virulent, age-old prejudices against the visually handicapped. In the seeing, as well as the unseeing, such fantasies give rise to anxiety, shame, guilt, disgust, and hostility wherever blindness is involved. They impel the sighted to reject the sightless, and the latter to reject themselves and each other. Among the seeing, they foster a compulsive need to help or avoid helping blind persons, while among the blind, they often issue in neurotic overdependence or an equally pathological counter-dependency reaction.

That our visual fantasies are frequently contradictory (e.g., the blind person is both saint and sinner, genius and idiot, etc.) should not be surprising, for as Freud long ago demonstrated, the unconscious takes little heed of logic or objective reality. Indeed, the psychobiological id, which comprises the deepest strata of this psychic realm, knows no rules or facts other than the images of its own tumultuous wishes and impulses, viz., its hallucinations, autistic ideas, and fantasies. Logic and realistic thinking are the province of the predominantly conscious ego. In the unconscious (as our dream life readily reveals), opposites not only coexist but also combine to influence the same conscious activities. Moreover, on Freud's principle of overdetermination, any given thought or act is, as a rule, caused by a number of related motives rather than by some single, isolated wish. Thus, certain diverse fantasies may all bear crucially upon identical attitudes and behavior.

In a further psychoanalytically-oriented investigation, Chevigny and Braverman (1950; summarized by Braverman in 1951) focused upon the negative stereotype of the sightless and amassed considerable qualitative evidence in support of the hypothesis that such attitudes result from the castration anxiety of the seeing. According to these investigators, it is important to recognize that the negative stereotype arises from the attitudes of the sighted toward the blind rather than from the latter's own self-evaluations, for innumerable blind people regard themselves as essentially normal and happy. If sightless persons, by and large, find that vision is not absolutely necessary to a meaningful life, why do so many of the sighted hold an opposite view?

Chevigny and Braverman traced the roots of this unjustifiable pessimism to the important role of sight in early personality development, agreeing with Freud, who considered looking a partial instinct in the unfolding of the sexual apparatus. The child soon discovers that he can procure erotic pleasure simply by the act of looking. In the healthy personality, this quasi-instinct (or drive) eventually abdicates its major pregenital prerogatives and accepts a subsidiary function in the sexual economy of the genital adult—with visual observation, as well as most other forms of sensory stimuli, becoming an instigator to sexual arousal rather than a vehicle of ultimate gratification, which in the mature adult is obtainable only through genital intercourse. If parental discipline foils the child's need for erotic looking, a visual fixation tends to emerge—i.e., looking acquires an inordinate sexual value, an enduring trend that will later manifest itself in adulthood as an influential trait of personality. If restrictions are extremely harsh, subsequent erotic satisfaction may revolve exclusively about the looking impulse, viz., scopophilia. The authors emphasized the point that vision is the chief sense associated with sexual deviations. Even tactile and olfactory perversions, the incidence of which is by contrast minor, usually involve a significant degree of visual imagery. Furthermore, since parents in our culture typically frustrate sexual looking (including the wish to be looked at), scopophilic or exhibitionistic tendencies exist in most of us. In support of this conclusion, Chevigny and Braverman pointed to the multifarious displacements of scopophilia and exhibitionism that, indeed, abound in our society, e.g., pornography, erotic movies, floor shows, beauty contests, nudist colonies, and the like. Today, such displacements are even more apparent, owing to the recent advent of topless-bottomless bars, nude therapy and theater, and the flood of motion pictures containing sexual as well as sadistic content that is far more explicit than that in the films of a generation ago.

On the hypothesis of these investigators, the blind man triggers castration anxiety in the seeing man, in proportion as the latter experiences the looking impulse as a critical component in his sexual organization. Moreover, in our society, where vision possesses intense sexual significance, mere sights or thoughts of blindness precipitate a certain measure of castration anxiety in the average man, while the full blown scopophiliac should interpret blindness as actual destruction of the genitalia.

Three types of evidence were adduced in favor of the castration-anxiety hypothesis: (1) literary and mythological; (2) historical; and (3) clinical.

Regarding the first source, reference was made to a variety of fictional characters, such as Oedipus, Tiresias, and Samson, for whom blinding is directly connected with sexual transgression. In the next chapter, which deals with the theme of blindness in the arts, the reader will note the great frequency with which visual disability accompanies sexual abnormality or, as a punishment, follows some form of sexual behavior. Indeed, the castration motif is not always merely symbolic but is sometimes expressed quite openly. For example, Milton's Samson (of the epic poem *Samson Agonistes*), likens himself to a "castrated ram." This is only one of many similar instances.

By way of historical evidence, Chevigny and Braverman indicated the common use of blinding as a means of punishment during antiquity and the Middle Ages and pointed out that this sentence was usually executed for crimes of a sexual nature. Blindness was thus a symbolic castration. It was considered the ultimate in chastisement, for it presumably meant a "living death," a fate worse than actual death. Real castration was practiced much less frequently than blinding, probably because it provoked greater anxiety in the agents of punishment and at the same time was less practically frustrating than blindness. Although the authors dealt less with recent history, it likewise offers confirmation for the castration-anxiety hypothesis. For example, early in the present century, in Western societies, masturbation was widely thought inimical to health, and countless teen-age boys were admonished by parents to shun it lest they suffer insanity, sterility, impotence, blindness, or a generalized physical decline. Even in our own day appreciable remnants of this superstition persist, particularly among rustics and the poorly educated. Also, the old ideas are still apparent in the fantasy life of more sophisticated people, as exemplified by an association of masturbation with blindness in certain contemporary popular jokes. One of these, for instance, deals with several little boys whom a preacher apprehends in the act of masturbation. He orders them to desist immediately and warns them never to masturbate again, for if they resume the habit, they will eventually go blind. This ominous consequence frightens the boys, who are much subdued when the preacher leaves. Their unhappiness continues until one of their number suggests a solution to the problem: "Well, let's just do it till we need glasses." However, unlike most jokes about blindness, this contains an element of genuine humor in that it illustrates a fundamental characteristic of the sex drive, viz., its insistent need for expression, regardless of the nature of the obstacles that act to frustrate it.

From the quarter of psychopathology, Chevigny and Braverman cited cases similar to those discussed by Schauer, i.e., neurotic patients with visual disturbances who are at the same time unable to accept certain sexual tendencies in themselves or who retain an infantile need of punishment for assumed sexual misdeeds. Also mentioned were those occasional schizophrenic patients who attempt or actually carry out self-mutilation of the eyes in order to atone for some imagined sexual sin. In this connection, it is interesting to note that the Greek philosopher Democritus, who was to all appearances a manic-depressive, blinded himself during a psychotic attack, though the symbolic significance of self-blinding in this case is not clear.

In the view of Chevigny and Braverman, the Freudian hypothesis assists immeasurably in accounting for many of the peculiar traits prejudicially ascribed to the sightless, for a number of these characteristics are equivalent to those imputed to eunuchs. Both the blind man and the castrate are often perceived as victims of the direst of calamities, creatures robbed of all physical power and inexorably walled off from any possibility of pleasure in life. Both are thought to be characterized by a blank, unsmiling face, by a grievous absence of normal emotions, as well as a plethora of affects alien to the sexually potent man. Social intercourse with the blind man and the eunuch is perforce strange and abnormal, owing to this lack of shared experience. They constitute types so radically different from the normal that the average person is confused as to how he should respond to them, even in relatively trivial, impersonal social situations. Similarly, the blind man and the eunuch are both often adjudged mentally or morally deficient, e.g., in fiction each is frequently depicted as dull, and if intelligence is present, it often consists in some low form of cunning.

These investigators also related pity for the blind to castration anxiety. To the average person, the sight or thought of blindness engenders a feeling of repugnance, which, in turn, is likely to set off guilt and hence pity. For Chevigny and Braverman, such pity is compulsive since it stems from guilt over the wish to avoid the blind stimulus-object. The avoidance tendency is ultimately an outgrowth of the castration anxiety mobilized by the stimulus. The authors referred to the fact that the pitier frequently offers the blind person pseudo-aid, viz., help the latter neither wishes nor requires. The pitier is both selfish and unrealistic. His true concern is not the well-being of the pitied blind person. He is primarily desirous of reducing his own guilt and asserting his superiority over the pitied, for pity is always patronizing. If the sightless individual does not appreciate the proffered pity, its bestower becomes offended, for his ego has been made to suffer a narcissistic wound, however slight. The everyday lives of blind people are replete with experiences illustrative of this point. For example, on a city street I once observed a woman trying to force a dime into the hand of a sightless teen-age boy. The boy politely withdrew his hand and declined her offer, which incensed the woman, who then accused him of ingratitude and disrespect. Unfortunately, cases like this are fairly common. Chevigny and Braverman rightly asserted that pity is destructive in that it tends to make the pitied feel inferior to the pitier. Kindness, on the other hand, is realistic and attends to the actual situation and need. They went on to contend that the social and economic condition of the blind could be greatly improved, despite the irrational attitudes of the seeing community. To assist in forwarding this goal, they recommended that agencies for the blind totally abstain from the employment of pity-seeking devices when soliciting monetary contributions. It is deplorable that just such a strategy is still sometimes practiced, a circumstance that only serves to reinforce the idea that the blind are helpless and inferior and thereby retards the aim of genuine cultural integration.

Though Chevigny and Braverman dealt primarily with negative attitudes toward the blind, especially those of males, the castration-anxiety hypothesis applies equally to the positive stereotype of blindness, as well as to female reactions. On this view, exaggerated favorable attitudes, such as those embodied in the legends of Homer and St. Hervaeus, would arise, like pity, out of a reaction formation against guilt over avoiding or aggressive tendencies toward the blind. These latter reactions, in turn, are released by the sexual anxiety associated with ideas or perceptions of blindness. As to the attitudes of women, they, along with men in our culture, are developmentally exposed to the same prevailing overestimation of visual sexuality. Both sexes grow up with the same symbolic frame of reference with respect to the eyes and eye disorders. Thus, women are also inclined to equate blindness with ideas of castration or sexual debility, though in them the condition provokes no castration anxiety as such, unless, of course, they happen to be psychologically abnormal. Moreover, in the next chapter it will be noted that in literature blind women are often portrayed as undesirable love objects, unfit for motherhood or conventional wifely duties. In this symbolic sense, they, too, are castrated or, at the very least, sexually devalued.

On the other hand, Chevigny and Braverman believed that the castration-anxiety hypothesis alone is insufficient to explain the entire range of misconceptions about blindness. For example, they suggested that the frequent ascription of mental inferiority proceeds much less from excessive visual eroticism than from the overrating of the visual function in cognition. However, they still argued for the general superiority of the Freudian hypothesis, finding it quite adequate to account for the bulk of irrational attitudes concerning the blind.

Within my own psychological experience, instances of the symbolic affinity between blindness and castration have been numerous. A blind teen-age boy, for example, reported open ridicule in connection with his sexuality. A male peer, supposedly his friend, habitually addressed him as "sexless" and, on the occasion of the blind boy's birthday, presented him with a miniature condom, of the sort sold in novelty shops. Enclosed in the box with the condom was a note that read: "Try this on for size. If it doesn't fit, I'll get you a smaller one that does." Another sightless youth described comparable experiences. His emotionally disturbed father, when angry at his son, was wont to indulge in verbal flagellation, referring to the boy by such appellations as "cunt, pussy-boy, dickless wonder" and "blind freak." Later, as a young man, this same individual, while smoking marijuana, once experienced acute anxiety states in association with vivid images of attacking, castrating weapons, e.g., a knife, then a pair of scissors, flew through the air toward his penis, threatening to cut it off (Kirtley, 1971). Likewise, a blind man, who had attended a residential school for the visually handicapped during his teens, related other cases of sexual devaluation. For example, the male students jokingly called the school's sightless superintendent "rubber balls" because, though married for many years, he had never fathered any children. A few of the more naive boys took the fantasy seriously, believing in a literal castration with a subsequent transplantation of artificial testes. Although a number of the institution's sighted male teachers and dormitory supervisors were also married and without offspring, they were not referred to as "rubber balls." The only apparent reason for the epithet was the superintendent's blindness. The boys were projecting their own feelings of castration upon the older man. Cases like these are by no means rare or isolated occurrences. Castration (or more generally, sexual inferiority) is, indeed, one major unconscious meaning of blindness.

Blank (1957) has extensively observed blind children and adults, usually as patients undergoing psychoanalysis. In his discussion of eye symbolism, he considered factors akin to those cited by Schauer and Chevigny and Braverman but, in addition, emphasized the aggressive-phallic meaning that often attaches to vision. Looking sometimes possesses a piercing or probing quality, analogous to penile penetration of the vagina.

This phallic significance of the eyes is evident in such common expressions as: "He ravished her with his eyes," "He looked right through her," "She melted under his gaze." Also, certain standard meanings of the word *eye* entail a connection between vision and projectile weaponry, e.g., "to eye" means to aim at, while the aggressive implication in "eyeshot" is obvious. Similarly, in dreams the penis is often represented as a pistol, rifle, knife, spear, or the like, whereas in the symbolism of sexual slang, sadistic coitus is designated by such verbs as "bang", "cut" and "shaft". The symbolic interchangeability of eye and phallus is pointedly illustrated in the following sonnet, penned by a twenty-four-year-old man, blinded through a shooting accident that occurred shortly before his pubescence.

The Eye of the Penis

Long since, when I was young and knew nothing
Of sexual maneuver save its bliss,
Which came alone from fancy's conjuring,
I feared the precious target I would miss
Ere moment to make the foray had come.
I trembled lest first shot should go awry,
With heart pounding like an Indian's drum.
No magic telescope with which to spy
The sleek quarry—and naked eye too weak!
But then my marksman's instinct made me try,
And with the nether organ I did peek
Along the rosy frontiers of her thigh,
Till in perfect fornication we twined.
Ah, the Eye of the Penis—never blind!

The above poem was written while its author was a patient in psychotherapy. During his virgin adolescence, he had been obsessed with the fear that his blindness would render him sexually clumsy and ineffectual. His initial heterosexual experiences had been characterized by marked anxiety and occasional erectile impotence, which was one of his chief reasons for seeking therapeutic assistance. The poem was composed at a time of therapeutic progress, when his impotence, as well as other neurotic symptoms, was beginning to abate. Early in the treatment, he reported that since his blinding, he had felt "unmanned" and sexually undesirable to women. This feeling persisted even after he had met a number of blind men who were sexually well adjusted. He was obsessed with the idea that sighted people, especially women, perceived him as a eunuch, largely a projection of his own identification of blindness with castration. In his case, the emotional aftermath of blindness was unduly severe, owing partly to the timing of the physical trauma and partly to the neuroses of his parents, both of whom hampered rather than facilitated the patient's rehabilitation through an admixture of rejection and overprotection. In his sonnet he parodies the eye-penis symbol and disavows any real connection between blindness and castration. Thus, the sonnet signaled the emergence of a new and healthier sexual identity.

A similar humorous reversal of the blindness-castration equation occurs in Steinbeck's *The Grapes of Wrath* (1939), when Tom and Al Joad encounter a one-eyed garage mechanic who has been weeping over his lost organ. The man's empty eye-socket is exposed to open view, revealing the raw flesh within. He is despondent because he feels that women no longer want to have anything to do with him. Tom advises him to cover the offensive socket with a patch, as it looks like a "cow's ass" and would naturally repel women. When the mechanic asks Tom if he thinks any woman could genuinely like a one-eyed man, Tom replies in the affirmative, suggesting: "Tell them your dong growed longer."

As is apparent from the foregoing, the ocular orbit may be identified with the anus. In fact, any aperture of the body is susceptible to such representation in dreams and fantasies. For example, a college student in psychotherapy once painted a picture of a hated professor, depicting the latter's eyes, mouth, nostrils, and ear openings as feces-smeared or defecating anuses.

The eye socket may also be used to symbolize the vagina. For instance, at the school for the blind previously mentioned, an adolescent boy with one glass eye was sometimes teased by two of his dorm-mates about the vacuous orbit. On one occasion, his taunters christened him "fuckface" and laughingly threatened to insert their penises into his "eyehole". A second boy who had been blinded by a brain tumor was likewise hazed by this pair over the surgical incision at the back of his skull. Sometimes the two sadistic jokers would also say: "Let's fuck his brains out through that hole in his head." These victims of sexual disparagement were, like the school superintendent, merely scapegoats for their detractors' projected castration anxiety and self-hate. As can be seen above, a diversity of body openings, in addition to the eye socket, may come to serve as symbolic substitutes for the vagina, just as is the case with the anus.

Blindness in Ordinary Language

Famous Quotations

In *Bartlett's Familiar Quotations* (1968), I counted fifty-six entries specifically pertaining to blindness. These fall fairly naturally into the following broad categories: (1) blindness as ignorance or impaired understanding, spiritual or affective deficiency, purposelessness or caprice—thirty-nine entries; (2) blindness implying wretchedness, inferiority, and chronic depression—eighteen references; (3) the blind as objects of condescending pity—three references; (4) blindness as akin to death—six entries; (5) blindness in association with compensation—three entries; (6) religion as the only remedy for the suffering of the blind—eight references; (7) undisguised ridicule of blind persons or creatures—three entries; and (8) blindness as hampered physical vision—two entries. These categories overlap considerably since many of the quotations are equally appropriate to two or more classifications. As the vast majority of Bartlett's quotations were derived from well-known poems, aphorisms, and rhetorical prose, they provide a representative sampling of what blindness has meant to artists of metaphor and simile down through the centuries.

■*Category 1*—This category comprises almost seventy percent of the entries. Consequently, the most pervasive symbolic meanings of blindness in imaginative language link it to intellectual, emotional, or spiritual lack and to natural or moral fortuity. Some examples are as follows: "blind folly, blind desire, blind ecstasy, blind tradition, blind obedience." Also, "fortune", "justice", and "love" are said to be blind. Moreover, blindness sometimes implies a state of sin. One reference from John Godfrey Saxe's poem *The Blind Men and the Elephant* clearly implies that physical blindness inherently prevents one from adequately understanding the nature of the objective environment. In it, six learned blind men of Hindustan try, through touch, to form a concept of an elephant, but each fails miserably, owing to the limitations of this sensory modality. Although the poem seems to be intended mainly as a satire on the frequent vanity of intellectual man, it nonetheless suggests much about its author's attitude toward the physically-blind.

■*Category 2*—Nearly a third of the quotations belong under this category. Thus, the second most frequent use of the blindness symbol highlights misery and degradation. The blind are indiscriminately lumped together with the poor, the maimed, the lame, and the deaf, and they are also associated with mendicancy. A line from Ralph Hodgson refers to "wretched blind pit ponies and little hunted hares." Such ponies may, indeed, be wretched, yet at the same time the image conveys the idea that blindness necessarily means misery and helplessness. The famous line from Matthew, "If the blind lead the blind, both shall fall into the ditch," says, in effect, that the sightless are incompetent to get about or help one another in any way. In a quote from Robert Green Ingersoll, we find one of the most glaring instances of the blindness-inferiority equation: "The superior man is the providence of the inferior. He is eyes for the blind, strength for the weak and a shield for the defenseless." The least opprobrious entry is perhaps Shakespeare's line: "He that is stricken blind cannot forget the precious treasure of his eyesight lost." My experience with individuals blinded later in life confirms this idea, to the extent that visual loss is always regretted—sometimes merely abstractly, at other times with a poignant nostalgia. However, Shakespeare's words may also be interpreted to mean that the blinded person lives from day to day in a state of mourning over his loss, which of course is not the typical case. While deep depression inevitably follows blinding, in the healthy person it disappears with the passage of time. He may continue to feel sorrowful over his loss, but this sorrow is seldom intense or frequent. Though it may linger after many years of blindness, it does so in the manner of any other basic human grief. Mourning over lost vision is an experience akin to grieving over the death of a loved one. We may always miss the deceased, but nevertheless we go on living, eventually to regain a reasonable degree of happiness.

■*Category 3*—Within this category we find about five percent of the references. Pity for the blind does not appear to be an important theme in famous quotations. In everyday life this emotion tends to mask feelings of contempt or devaluation for the one being pitied. It almost never involves constructive empathy or compassion. The same is true in regard to pity of the blind in figurative language. However, a quote from Harry Kemp is not entirely disparaging: "I pitied him in his blindness, but can I boast I see?

Perhaps there walks a spirit close by who pities me." The blind man is pitiable, but the poet, to some extent, identifies with him, though the latter implicitly remains below the poet on the pity (or inferiority) hierarchy.

■*Category 4*—This group, which concerns death, contains a little over ten percent of the entries. As previously mentioned, the association between blindness and death was prevalent during antiquity. Furthermore, it has continued to be important up to the present day. Gutheil (1951), among others, discussed blindness as a common death symbol in dreams, while in Chapter 3 we shall examine its significant place in literature, mythology, legend, folklore, music, and the graphic arts. However, within the present context, the feelings of Samuel Pepys are typical: "And so I betake myself to that course which is almost as much as to see myself go into my grave, for which and all the discomforts that will accompany my being blind the good God prepare me." In Blake, blindness appears in the sense of death and brute, tragic fate: "I dance and drink and sing till some blind hand shall brush my wing." In the following lines by Swinburne, vision is made the quintessence of life, while blindness represents meaninglessness and death: "In his heart is a blind desire, in his eyes foreknowledge of death. . .His life is a watch or a vision between a sleep and a sleep." By implication, blindness entails a state of nothingness, a personal vacuum. In usages of this ilk, the death meaning is scarcely ever restricted to the defective (viz., "dead") eyes, a symbolization that would make some sense; instead, the "death of vision" is generalized to the whole personality of the blind individual. For the sightless, this is indeed the most obnoxious symbol of their condition ever conceived by man.

■*Category 5*—Approximately five percent of the quotations fall under this category, which deals with compensatory gifts stemming from blindness. The anonymous medieval ballad *The Blind Beggar of Bethnall Green* contains the line, "A fairer lady there never was seen than the blind beggar's daughter of Bethnall Green," suggesting that the mendicant's beautiful daughter was a natural compensation for his blindness. Of Milton's artistic gift, Donald Robert Perry Marquis says, "Poetry is what Milton saw when he went blind." Of Homer, Sir John Denham writes the following:

I can no more believe old Homer blind
Than those who say the sun hath never shined.
The age wherein he lived was dark; but he
Could not want sight, who taught the world to see.

Though Homer is praised, blindness is viewed as being incompatible with great achievement. Either Homer was sighted or, if actually blind, he possessed some mysterious psychic vision that enabled him to see more fully than human beings with normal eyes. Regardless of which meaning is intended, it is obvious that the poet does not want to think of Homer as a blind man. He cannot accept Homer unless the latter can somehow be rendered visual.

■*Category 6*—This category (religion) covers about fourteen percent of the entries. Some examples are as follows: from Vachel Lindsay: "Booth died blind, and still by faith he trod, eyes still dazzled by the ways of God." And from Giles Fletcher:

If any chance to hunger, He is bread. . .
If any be but weak, how strong is He.
To dead men life is He, to sick men health,
To blind men sight, and to the needy wealth.

■*Category 7*—Approximately five percent of the quotes appear under this category, which focuses upon direct contempt. Most of the references thus far considered involve deprecation, but they do so implicitly, while the statements in the present group are quite openly disparaging. Here the most blatantly defamatory instance is that of the anonymous nursery rhyme *Three Blind Mice*. The mice, on account of their blindness, are characterized as running about in a laughably ridiculous manner. By cutting off their tails, the farmer's wife makes them even more absurd. The amputation of the tails may be interpreted as a symbolic castration. Unquestionably, the behavior of the mice is ineffectual simply by virtue of their visual defect.

■*Category 8*—This category, dealing with blindness as visual impairment, comprises only about four percent of the total entries. One of the quotes, that of Christopher Codrington, states: "Thou hast no faults, or I no faults can spy. Thou art all built beauty, or all blindness, I." If one could not see the beauty in question, perhaps he would indeed be blind. However, the lines suggest that the sightless, because of their handicap, cannot know physical beauty, that only through sight can such beauty be appreciated. The second and final quotation in this class, from Browning, refers to God's "blinding fireballs," where blinding is used in the sense of dazzling. This is the only reference in Bartlett that is completely free of negative attitudinal overtones.

Thus, we see that blindness has been an ample source of symbolic meanings in both verse and poetic prose, albeit generally unflattering meanings as far as blind people are concerned.

Dictionary Definitions

We encounter a similar picture for blindness when we turn to *Webster's Third New International Dictionary*(1966), unabridged.

The word *blind* derives from Old English and is directly related etymologically to (A) *blend* (i.e., to mix so that discrete constituents cannot be distinguished; to darken the hairs of a fur with dye; archaically, to bedazzle, blind, or deceive, etc.) and less directly to (B) *bland* (i.e., dull, insipid, wishy-washy, etc.) and (C) *blunder* (i.e., to move awkwardly, to stumble, to make a stupid mistake, etc.).

In Webster, I found 155 citations under *blind* and its grammatical variants, including nouns compounded of *blind* and another term. Among these, it is possible to identify at least ten broad meaning clusters, which are enumerated below. My classification is only approximate, for, again, categories are not mutually exclusive, there being extensive overlapping in some cases.

■ *Category 1*—Concealment, screening, deception and the like (forty-eight entries, thirty-one percent of the total): "blind advertisement," an advertisement that does not reveal the name of the advertiser; "blind bridle," a bridle with blinders; "blind date"; "blind" in the sense of a decoy; "blindman's buff" in the sense of something accomplished through trickery or done without awareness of pertinent facts or issues; "blind pig" or "blind tiger," a speakeasy; "blind set," an unbaited trap concealed in the runway or burrow of an animal; "blindage" in the sense of an overhead protection.

It can be seen that Thass-Thienemann's previously mentioned emphasis of dissimulation in connection with window shades is amply exemplified by many other usages of the word *blind.*

■ *Category 2*—Closed or closed at one end, passing only partially through, filled, empty, plugged up, blocked, covered, etc. (thirty-three references, twenty-one percent): "blind attic," a closed, unfinished dead space immediately beneath the roof of a building; "blind baggage," a railway, baggage, express, or postal car that has no door or opening at one end; "blinding" in the sense of the sand and fine gravel used to cover or fill in a road; "blind mortise," a mortise that does not extend completely through the material where it is cut; "blind flange," a cover plate bolted or otherwise fastened across a pipe flange to seal the pipe; "blind P," the paragraph mark, so labeled because the loop is inked in.

Such meanings are, no doubt, related to fantasies that interpret blindness as a condition characterized by psychic emptiness, incompleteness of personality, obstructed potential, and isolating encapsulation of the ego.

■ *Category 3*—Defective, abortive, diseased, incapacitated, stupefied, dead, sterile, worthless, poisonous, pestiferous, and so on—excluding literal anomaly of the visual organs per se (twenty-seven definitions, eighteen percent): "taste" or "smell blindness"; "blind nettle," white dead nettle; "blind pocket," a phase of psorosis of citrus trees; "blind seed," a disease of forage grasses resulting in abortion of the seed; "blind shell" in the sense of dud; "blind drunk"; "blind staggers," a disease of the central nervous system; "blind teat," a teat that does not allow the passage of milk; "blind tire," a bald tire; "Blind-Your-Eyes," an Australian tree with volatile juice, believed to be poisonous; "Blind-Eyes," a scarlet-flowered poppy, often occurring as a weed in cultivated fields or waste ground; "blind plant," failing to produce a growing tip or flowers or to develop vegetative parts.

The preceding meanings are connected with fantasies that construe the blind person as dangerous, repulsive, lifeless, and sexually disabled. The various references to plant infertility, the milkless teat, and defective ammunition support the Freudian interpretation of blindness as symbolic castration. The equivalence of these two conditions in the irrational unconscious appears to have influenced ordinary linguistic usage as well as folk belief and imaginative literature.

■ *Category 4*—Animals (eight entries, five percent): "blindfish"; "blind rat," mole rat; "blindworm," defined as "a small, burrowing, limbless lizard with minute eyes, especially a small-scaled European lizard that feeds on grubs and worms and popularly is believed to be blind."

Many of the species in this class are commonly regarded as lowly or in some way unpleasant or unattractive. Like the blindworm, not all of the animals cited are actually blind. The "sightlessness" of the blindworm may originally have been suggested by the blindness-impotence fantasy as well as by that organism's tiny eyes. In this connection, Shakespeare, in *A Midsummer Night's Dream* (Bartlett, 1968), refers to blindworms as follows: "You spotted snakes with doubled tongue . . . newts and blindworms do no wrong. Come not near our fairy queen." The snake or worm, a well-established phallic symbol, seems here to be assuming its traditional function—in other words, the fairy queen is safe because a blindworm (i.e., an impotent penis) can do no harm.

■ *Category 5*—Lacking intensity, luster, coloring, or gilding, etc. (ten citations, six percent): "blind stamping," stamping the cover of a book without coloring or gilding; "blind" in the sense of a dull finish to paneling.

This usage may bear upon the attitude that sees drabness of personality as a natural consequence of blindness.

■ *Category 6*—Ignorance, lacking mental vision, judgment, or plausibility, carelessness (fourteen citations, nine percent): "blind rage"; "blind faith"; "blind choice."

Many seeing persons treat the sightless as though they are mentally, as well as visually, handicapped. This prejudicial tendency is strongly reinforced by ordinary language, as is apparent from the foregoing.

■ *Category 7*—Unintelligibility, indiscernibility, obscurity, and the like (sixteen entries, ten percent): "blind mail," illegibly addressed mail; "blind path," a dim or ill-defined path; "blind spot" in the sense of an obscure area in the environment.

The attitude associated with this usage would seem to be similar to that involved in the immediately preceding category.

■ *Category 8*—Purposeless, fortuitous, etc. (five references, three percent): "blind chance"; "blind fate."

Among the seeing, one frequently encounters the attitude that life without sight would be entirely meaningless. The blind person is viewed as being the helpless victim of circumstances. Because of his physical condition, he possesses no means of inner direction or control. He is totally at the mercy of those about him. Obviously, this attitude, too, is supported by linguistic usage.

■ *Category 9*—Profanity (two entries, one percent): "blinding," a slang expression meaning darned, blamed, or blasted.

This usage apparently stems from the horror and aversion generally associated with physical blindness. In view of the contemptuous reactions often elicited by sightless individuals, it should not be surprising that blinding has become part of the vocabulary of profanity.

■ *Category 10*—Literal visual impairment and circumstances or behavior associated with it (twenty-two citations, fourteen percent): "legal blindness"; "blind school"; "blindisms."

The latter term (which refers to certain meaningless, repetitive acts of self-stimulation, such as rocking, whirling, head jerking, and similar behavior) is unfortunate, in that these responses are not characteristic of all or probably even most blind people. When they occur, they are usually found among emotionally disturbed blind children. Moreover, similar behavior is typically observed among sighted autistic children. Consequently, *blindisms* do not appear to stem from blindness as such. The term is best regarded as a misnomer.

It is interesting to note that eighty-six percent of the above definitions pertain to matters other than actual physical blindness. The vast majority of usages are figurative, and among these, negative meanings predominate. It is clear that the anti-blind prejudices of society are built into our very language. In view of the adverse emotional loading of *blindness* and cognate terms, some might advocate that we should drop such words from our vocabulary and replace them with new, more impartial labels. However, it is doubtful that mere name changing would appreciably mitigate the negative attitudes in question. New terminology is not likely to be effective unless such attitudes have already improved, for without this change, the older, prejudicial meanings would simply become reattached to the liberalized vocabulary. The label *visually handicapped,* which many sightless people prefer to *blind* because of its prima facie neutrality, has, since its adoption, acquired much of the deprecatory aura of *blind.* For numerous prejudiced sighted persons, as well as self-rejecting blind people, calling an individual "visually handicapped" is merely a kindly or euphemistic way of saying what the word *blind* connotes quite bluntly, viz., that he is hopelessly helpless and inferior. Van Weelden (1967) has pointed out that other terms commonly used in connection with blindness similarly involve such negative connotations. For example, *incapacitated* and *disabled* intimate disqualification and incompetence; *defective* and *deficient*, faultiness and inadequacy; *infirm* and *invalid*, ill health or weakness; and *unfit*, unsuitability. All these terms suggest that the person has fallen in value and express the general prejudice against the blind. Van Weelden found *handicapped* the least opprobrious word of this class. In any case, new synonyms would probably not fare any better than those in current use; consequently, it would be rather quixotic to regard vocabulary revision as a problem worthy of serious attention.

A significant facet of the present problem (prejudice in relation to language) concerns the blind's use of verbalism, i.e., words that lack true experiential referents. I know many sightless persons who are often "corrected" by seeing friends, acquaintances, and sometimes even strangers merely for employing visual words, notwithstanding the fact that these frequently have appropriate referents. For example, the blind person who says, "I see" meaning "I understand" or "I'll see you tomorrow" meaning "I'll meet or converse with you tomorrow" may be challenged with: "Do you really mean *see*?" Here the figurative import of *see* is completely overlooked. The sightless person is implicitly charged with verbalism, though no verbalism has been committed. Reactions of this sort are difficult to understand, considering the multiplicity of age-old metaphorical meanings in the visual language. Words like *see, sight,* and vision have always possessed intellectual and imaginal referents as well as purely visual ones. Even the word *eye* does not always refer to literal attributes or acts of that organ: "to have in one's eye" can mean to have a mental picture of, to have in mind; "to set one's eyes by" means to have a great affection or esteem for; and "to see eye to eye" means to be in full agreement with. The sighted and blind alike utilize this language of visual metaphor. It does not depend upon physical vision for its efficacy and, therefore, is not the special property of anyone. Why, then, would the seeing person deny the sightless individual the metaphorical usage that he grants himself and other seeing people? Are such persons simply ignorant of the figurative component in the visual language? This seems unlikely, for even if conscious knowledge is lacking, one ordinarily possesses sufficient unconscious familiarity with the language to use it correctly. One is, therefore, likely to be at least intuitively cognizant of visual metaphors. The insistence that the sightless person should eschew these metaphors is tantamount to demanding that he extend his blindness from the purely organic realm to that of mentation, as if he were somehow not already blind enough. Not only is this misguided, it also belittles the blind person. The tendency seems to be motivated, at least partially, by a need for dichotomous conceptual classifications, with the blind and the visually normal being interpreted as two discrete, unrelated groups. In other words, the blind, as a class, possess no significant characteristics in common with the seeing, as a class. Insofar as the former manifest visual qualities (viz., visual memory and/or the use of visual metaphor), they overlap with the latter class, and the all-or-none, black-white distinctions break down, thus creating a threatening state of cognitive ambiguity. The resulting anxiety is then reduced through denial of the common element, i.e., visual imagery or visual metaphor. The blind are thereby kept in their "proper place," the sighted in theirs. Were the image or metaphor to be verbalized by another seeing person, it would be accepted, as such, since the latter would not be perceived as belonging to a different class. In this case, the figurative usage would not be confused with literal visual experience; the metaphor would simply be understood as metaphor, if only unconsciously. Another probable motive for the spurious attribution of verbalism is hostility toward the blind person. The evaluator, by criticizing the sightless individual's use of the common language, tacitly questions the latter's humanity and thus relegates him to a position of inferiority. This covert release of aggression is typically not directed against the victim for any particular behavior on his part, but against him as a symbolic substitute for the frustrating agent that originally engendered the motive of hostility. In other words, the victim, because of his imagined vulnerability and incapacity for retaliation, is assigned the role of displacement object or scapegoat. Incorrigible overgeneralizing, dichotomous thinking, intolerance of cognitive ambiguity, free-floating hostility, and the tendency to displace aggression are all basic constituents of the authoritarian personality (Adorno et al., 1950), which is characterized by a deep-seated, psychological need for prejudice. To the extent that such factors are relevant to the attitude that the blind should renounce all forms of visual language, the authoritarian syndrome is involved. On the other hand, ignorance of visual metaphor or the mental effects of blindness cannot be wholly ruled out as contributing determinants.

According to Van Weelden, the accusation of verbalism is frequently exaggerated or unfounded. The visual language is meaningful to the blind, for language possesses its own relatively autonomous visual qualities, viz., an image initially derived from the visible environment may obtain new value through the linguistic context in which it occurs; when verbally expressed, the image tends to acquire a life of its own. In his research Van Weelden found that for the congenitally blind, associations to color words were not significantly different from the associations of the partially seeing, the adventitiously blinded, or the normally sighted—to the extent that the color names possessed an unambiguous connotation in everyday speech. The colors that lacked such connotation (e.g., aquamarine) did not produce comparable associations. Van Weelden rightly stressed the point that the term *verbalism* should be confined to empty language, i.e., language that does not communicate a meaning. At present it is too often inappropriately applied to fully or adequately meaningful language, especially when the meanings are affective or figurative.

Conclusions

In language and everyday behavior, the idea of blindness is symbolically employed in a wide variety of ways, many of which suggest or clearly indicate negative prejudicial attitudes toward blind people as a class. In view of their prima facie diversity, these symbols (or the attitudes underlying them) would appear to be overdetermined, that is, no one isolated factor produces all or most of them. While castration anxiety is apparently a major determinant, perhaps more important than any other single antecedent, a number of additional variables probably operate in conjunction with it to create the total range of blindness symbols, e.g., fantasies of the kinds described by Thass-Thienemann, Schauer, and Blank, authoritarianism or dogmatic personality, as well as the more obvious part typically played by cultural conditioning in the formation of any prejudicial stereotype. This matter will be discussed at length toward the close of Chapter 3, particularly with respect to Jung's hypothesis of the collective unconscious.

References

Chapter 2/The Symbolism of the Eyes

Adorno, T., Frenkel-Brunswik, E., Levinson, D. & Sanford, R. 1950. *The authoritarian personality*. New York: Harper.

Bartlett, J. 1968. *Bartlett's familiar quotations*. E. Beck, ed. 14th ed. Boston: Little, Brown.

Blank, H. 1957. Psychoanalysis and blindness. *Psychoanalytic Quarterly* 26: 1-24.

Braverman, S. 1951. The psychological roots of attitudes toward the blind. In *Attitudes toward blindness*. New York: American Foundation for the Blind.

Chevigny, H. & Braverman, S. 1950. *The adjustment of the blind*. New Haven: Yale University Press.

Gutheil, E. 1951. *The handbook of dream analysis*. New York: Washington Square Press.

Kirtley, D. 1971. Effects of marijuana upon the imagery of a blind subject. Paper presented at annual convention of California State Psychological Assoc., San Diego.

Schauer, G. 1951. Motivation of attitudes toward blindness. *New Outlook for the Blind* 45: 39-42.

Steinbeck, J. 1939. *The grapes of wrath*. New York: Viking Press.

Thass-Thienemann, T. 1968. *Symbolic behavior.* New York: Washington Square Press.

Van Weelden, J. 1967. *On being blind: An ontological approach to the problem of blindness.* Amsterdam: Netherlands Society for the Blind.

Webster's third new international dictionary (unabridged). 1966. Springfield, Mass: G. and C. Merriam Co.

3

Blindness in
the Arts

From earliest times to the present, imaginative productions of all sorts reveal much concerning attitudes toward blindness but little regarding the objective nature of the condition. Though the sightless have elicited considerable interest among artists and storytellers, their depiction has generally been distorted, usually in a negative direction,—but sometimes in a positive one. Often the expressed attitudes are highly ambivalent, comprising a paradoxical mixture of both unrealistically favorable and unfavorable beliefs. According to Twersky (1955), the blind, during any given historical period, have scarcely ever exceeded a small fraction of one percent of the total world population, yet sightless characters have been very important in literature. In view of their extreme minority status, this role in creative writing is at first glance perplexing. However, further reflection suggests that the critical stimulus to such portrayals has typically been some abstract idea or fantasy about blindness and not actual experience with concrete blind individuals themselves. Man's thoughts on blindness have always been imbued with affective meaning far more potent than that associated with most other physical handicaps, including some that are equally, if not more, limiting, e.g., deafness, which appears much less frequently in literature than visual disability. This emotional impact, rather than the factual meaning of blindness, is the basis of its significance as a symbol in works of imagination. Some possible determinants of these exaggerated affects will be discussed at the end of the chapter.

The Sightless in Myth, Legend, Folklore, and Fairy Tales

Perhaps the most thorough study, to date, of the function of sightless characters in oral tradition, fairy tales, myths, and legends is that of the depth psychologist Von Schumann (1959). The many depictions that he discussed disclose at least eight recurring themes: (1) the healing of blindness through religious rites, dreams, and folk remedies; (2) blindness compensated by moral goodness, religious profundity, wisdom, genius, and supernatural powers of prophecy, divination, dream interpretation, and healing; (3) blindness as punishment for sins, often of a sexual nature; (4) blindness as involving sexual anomaly; (5) the blind as lowly, immoral pitiable creatures; (6) the eyes as possessing magical, radiating powers; (7) the eyes as vessels of the life force; and (8) blindness as entailing loss of discriminatory faculties other than vision.

During antiquity, visual disorders were generally treated by means of temple magic. In Greece, this approach dated back to the fifth century B.C. when blind patients had begun entering the temples of Aesculapius to participate in various holy ceremonies involving the use of soporific drugs following which they would fall asleep and dream of being cured, allegedly to awaken thus. Votive tablets later unearthed at the site of the Temple of Epidaurus describe a number of these miraculous recoveries. One man, for example, dreamed that his eyes were opened by the fingers of a god whereupon he saw the trees of the temple sanctuary; the next day he awoke to find the prophecy of his dream fulfilled. A warrior, blinded in battle by a spear thrust, dreamed that a deity removed the weapon from his head, so restoring his vision; the following day he left the temple once again sighted. In a dream sent by Aesculapius, the poetess Anyte was said to have learned how to heal Phalysius, who was going blind. Moreover, in old Egypt, as well as Greece, there existed a special god of the sightless, called Bes. The statues of this divinity were faceless and had eyes on their feet. Where Bes was worshiped, there were also temples for sleep-healing. Furthermore, archaeological records indicate that sleep therapy was practiced by both the North and South American Indians. For instance, under the Incas the Peruvians employed a form of temple magic very similar to that of the Greeks. However, the shaman often did the patient's sleeping and dreaming for him, a practice applied for the blind and sighted alike.

The role of dreams, as such, in the healing of blindness was quite important during the ancient period, as well as later. In a Babylonian-Assyrian text, a pious prince recounts how he was cured of his sightlessness through dreams visited upon him from the god Marduk. Another case of dream-healing occurs in the ancient Christian legend of Andreas and Matthias, according to which the latter was captured by the dread Anthropophagen and was blinded in their customary rite of torture. This practice consisted first of ripping out the victim's eyes, then administering to him an insanity-producing drug that would induce the eating of hay in the manner of cattle; thirty days later, the prisoner was slaughtered. After his blinding, however, Matthias saw God in a dream and was thereby healed.

References to the treatment of blindness in folklore stress the great value of dreams, prayer, herbs, and other substances credited with medicinal properties. For example, in an old German folktale, a woman dreams that an angel appears to her and explains how she could heal a child's sightless eye by means of dew and prayer. In the fairy tale "Rapunzel" (Scharl [Ed.], 1944), the blinded prince is cured by two tears from the eyes of his beloved, which fall upon his own thorn-stabbed orbs, clearing them of all defect. In Bavaria, the plant Teufelsabbiss was long used as a drug for the eyes, a custom connected with the legendary Dr. Abbissage, who sold his soul to Satan in exchange for knowledge of the therapeutic powers in weeds. Satan subsequently blinded the doctor, lest the latter's learning should render him too forceful a competitor. The doctor, however, retained his precious knowledge of weeds and was thereby able to heal himself.

Among primitive men, the ancients and unsophisticated peoples generally, the prevalence of unscientific beliefs concerning the healing of visual maladies attests to the all-engulfing horror with which blindness has been received down through history. As already indicated in previous chapters, early folklore regarded the eyes not only as a potent instrument of magic but also as the reservoir of man's vital essence. Blindness was thus the direst of all physical calamities because it implied death.

This point is well illustrated in "The Merchant and the Genie," a tale from *The Arabian Nights* (Lang [Ed.], 1946). Here the genie's son is killed when the merchant accidentally tosses a date pit into his eye.

This climate of belief was bound to spawn desperation in the blind and those close to them, thereby further encouraging extant magical practices (and consequently purely delusional tactics) for warding off visual disability, rather than constructive adjustment to the reality of visual loss.

The perennial fantasy attributing occult or unusual abilities to the sightless was earlier discussed in connection with Homer and St. Hervaeus, among others. However, the most illustrious mythological representative of this belief is the Greek prophet Tiresias. Indeed, until the time of Homer, Tiresias had no serious rivals among his fellow blind. He was characteristically portrayed as wise, virtuous, and parapsychologically endowed, a spiritual superman who knew all the secrets of life and death. The Eleventh Book of *The Odyssey* describes him continuing to prophesy, though dead in Hades. In one version of the myth, he receives his power from Zeus, after having been blinded by Hera. As the story goes, Hera and Zeus one day argue over which sex experiences the greatest enjoyment during the act of love. After much fruitless debate, they summon Tiresias, whose wise judgment should settle the question once and for all. He declares that the woman feels nine times more pleasure than the man. This candid verdict offends the falsely modest Hera so much that she blinds the noble Tiresias. Another version has Tiresias blinded for the impiety of watching the chaste Minerva at her bath.

In both accounts we see that blindness is a punishment for sexual knowledge or behavior, as was the case with Peeping Tom and Oedipus, previously mentioned. Also, the Hebrew Samson is shorn of his locks and blinded after consorting with the pagan Delilah, while in the German "Rapunzel," the prince is blinded at the hands of the witch for his liaison with the latter's forcibly adopted daughter. The punishment of blindness is, therefore, quite frequently the result of some type of erotic activity, a fact that lends clear support to the Freudian interpretation of the blindness symbol.

On the other hand, the penalty of visual deprivation is sometimes associated with nonsexual misconduct. Blindness is visited upon the mythical Thracian poet Thamyris after he has challenged the Muses to a contest of song and verse and lost. Here the chastisement is for arrogance. In another tale of *The Arabian Nights,* "The Blind Baba Abdullah," the rich merchant, Baba Abdullah, is blinded in punishment for his greed. Through a magic eye ointment provided by the well-meaning dervish, which the merchant applies to his left eye, he is able to see all the treasures of the world. He then requests additional ointment for the right eye, but his benefactor refuses, telling him this would cause blindness. Yet Baba Abdullah takes no heed of the warning, believing the dervish is trying to deceive him. He thinks that once the ointment is administered to the right eye, he will be able to see a way of procuring the riches beheld with the left eye. He presses the reluctant holy man until the magic substance is again presented. As soon as it touches the lids of his eye, he is stricken with total blindness. Now he begs the dervish to restore his sight. "Unhappy man," the dervish replies, "it is not my fault that this has befallen you, but it is a just chastisement. The blindness of your heart has wrought the blindness of your eyes."

Although other sightless prophets and sages appear in Western mythology—e.g., the Thracian King Phinius, a victim of the Harpies—Tiresias nonetheless remains the paramount figure in this class in that he alone has achieved true archetypal stature in the fine arts. We encounter him in Sophocles' *Oedipus Rex* and *Antigone*, where he is pictured as being led by a boy-guide, though in the original mythological account he gets about by himself through the aid of a magic staff. In 1679, he appears again in John Dryden's drama *Oedipus*, while in Corneille's play *Oedipe* of 1659, he is not physically present but is an important figure behind the scenes. In our own century Gide has employed Tiresias as a symbol of moral virtue in his *Oedipus*, a drama inspired by psychoanalytic and existential concepts. Here the ancient seer comes forth in monk's attire and proclaims that God rightly enlightens only the blind, and Jocasta says she will rely on the prophet as he knows the will of God. Igor Stravinsky's oratorio *Oedipus Rex* features Tiresias emerging from a grotto under bright lights, as the embodiment of the Spirit of Truth. In Act II of Hugo von Hofmannsthal's *Tragedy of Oedipus and the Sphinx*, Tiresias suddenly appears amid a group of ordinary mortals, who immediately fall back from him in reverential awe. In "The Wasteland" of T.S. Eliot, Tiresias returns as an interpreter of the spiritual devastation of modern life. Interestingly enough, he is here depicted with the breasts of a woman. Comparable hermaphroditic portrayals can also be found in earlier descriptions of

Tiresias, which, taken together, spotlight the persistent, irrational identification of visual loss with sexual abnormality, a further datum congruent with the psychoanalytic view.

Early in the thirteenth century, Hartmann von Aue, in his *Legend of Gregorius*, made use of the Oedipus saga but replaced Tiresias with a sly girl of low rank. However, such demeaning of Tiresias has been the exception rather than the rule. In Aue's poetry, the sightless are characteristically divested of all mystical powers, being represented exclusively as pitiful sinners cast down by God.

In "The Tale of the Blind Man and the Cripple" (Burton [Ed.], 1962), another of Scheherazade's Thousand-and-One, physical defect is also linked with immorality, blindness coupled with an exaggerated restriction of nonvisual sensorimotor functions. The blind man and the cripple are both rogues and companions in beggary. One day the master of a lovely garden allows them entrance, provided they promise not to despoil his trees. As soon as he departs, the cripple asks the blind man to pick him some fruit, which he cannot do himself owing to his disability. The other man says that since he is sightless, he could not possibly find the fruit. Alone, then, each man is quite powerless to pluck the desired fruit. However, together, they decide they might be successful. Accordingly, the cripple climbs upon the blind man's back and directs him from tree to tree, from each of which the cripple is now able to gather fruit. In this manner they go about the garden until, through their thoughtless avarice, they have stripped every tree. When the owner returns to find his once beautiful garden now in a shambles, the mendacious culprits attempt to excuse themselves via their handicaps, asserting that it would be impossible for a blind man and a cripple to wreak such havoc. Nevertheless, the owner is not deceived, for he has correctly surmised the pair's plundering technique. Consequently, he upbraids them for their misconduct and orders them out of the garden. Of course, in reality many blind people are able to climb trees and pick fruit quite independently. Thus, this depiction is a gross distortion of the extent to which blindness limits one's physical capability. Moreover, the immorality of the two men is implicitly ascribed to their handicaps. A similar attitude underlies the fairy tale "One-Eye, Two-Eyes and Three-Eyes" (Scharl [Ed.], 1944). Two-Eyes is good and beautiful, apparently because of her physical normality, whereas her sisters, One-Eye and Three-Eyes, are not only ugly but thoroughly evil as well, seemingly for no other reason than that of their anatomical deviations.

Further instances of unrealistic sensory constriction can be found in "The Seven Voyages of Sindbad, the Sailor" (Lang [Ed.], 1946) and Aesop's fable "The Mole and his Mother" (Townsend [Trans.], 1968). In the former, Sindbad and his comrades, during the third voyage, blind the one-eyed, cannibalistic giant who is their captor and thus render him entirely helpless. While attempting to flee the prison island on rafts, most of the band is killed with huge rocks hurled by the giant's sighted fellows, who now lead him after the fashion of the stereotypically dependent blind man. Because of his blindness, he cannot join his brothers in the attack on the sailors, for he is unable to aim the stones effectively, even by sound. In the example from Aesop, a young mole, blind from birth, announces to his mother that he can see, whereupon she places some grains of frankincense before him and asks him to identify them. He says they are pebbles. His mother then ridicules him for his inability to discriminate. The little mole is not only blind but also lacks a sense of smell.

The image of wretchedness, stressed by Aue, also occurs in "Rapunzel," where the prince, while blind, wanders for years through the forest, aimlessly stumbling and groping and surviving only by means of the crudest foods—namely, berries and roots. The portrayal obviously greatly exaggerates the limitations inherent in blindness. Furthermore, blindness relegates Baba Abdullah to a life of mendicancy, the misery of which is augmented by his masochistic need for punishment, as he regularly entreats passersby to beat him so that he might atone for his past sin. Likewise, the blind man and the cripple (previously mentioned), though they are charlatans of the pettiest ilk and in some ways stupidly awkward, are nonetheless somewhat pathetic by reason of their gloomy lot as beggars. During antiquity and the Middle Ages, the sightless, by and large, were certainly a wretched group, but this state of affairs was much more the product of adverse social conditions than of weaknesses peculiar to visual disability. As Twersky (1955) has pointed out, the natural consequences of blindness have always been minor compared with those which are man-made.

One of the most telling supernatural powers bestowed upon blind prophets like Tiresias is that of dream interpretation. From earliest times until fairly recently, this ability was ascribed to many of the sightless, to the humble as well as the exalted. For example, in the Greek story of Phormion, the blind fisherman of Erythrae, the fisherman correctly interprets a dream sent him by the gods, follows the dream's instructions, and thereby becomes instrumental in saving a holy picture of Heracles from a destructive attack by the neighboring Chier. Also, Publius Cornelius Rufus, a legendary Roman consul, dreamed he was blind and awakened so the following morning. According to another legend, Johann von Trozsnow, himself blind, dreamed of victory in battle, a prophecy subsequently realized in the Hussite war.

In fairy tales blindness is often associated with benevolent, magical powers: the blind characters typically being old, wise, and para-psychologically gifted. In the tales of the South Sea islanders, for example, an old blind woman with such abilities sits at the gateway to the underworld. In a Malay fairy tale, a congenitally blind boy is the bearer of healing. Similarly, in an old German saga, "Blind" is the name of a man whose prophetic warnings protect his king from danger. A parable (the origin of which I have not been able to determine) deals with a blind mountain hermit who is old and very wise. One day he is visited by a boy who attempts to make him the butt of a practical joke. In one hand the boy holds fast a small, still living bird. He asks the old man if the bird is alive or dead, intending to crush it if the answer is "alive" or let it be should the old man say "dead." Either way the latter would be proved wrong and his renowned wisdom thus mocked. However, the blind man at once detects the boy's purpose and simply replies: "As thou wilt, my son." And the mischievous boy goes away ashamed and humbled. Aesop's fable "The Blind Man and the Whelp" likewise links blindness with wisdom. The blind man is given a wolf whelp and asked to identify it, whereupon he says he cannot tell whether the animal is the whelp of a wolf or the cub of a fox, but in any case such a creature should not be admitted to the sheep fold. Also associated with uncanny powers of knowledge are the Blind Belien of Dutch folk belief. These are rather ominous beings that manifest themselves at night and reveal secret things.

Although the blind of old Israel were generally regarded as untouchables, social attitudes were not entirely negative. The Talmud refers to the sightless as "enlightened" and states that they need not direct their prayers to Jerusalem, like the seeing, but may communicate with God directly. In the Schiking of the seventh century B.C. (the Chinese book of folk art), the blind are mentioned as playing a special role at the ceremonies of the princes; while in India and Moslem countries, as already indicated, the sightless were often assigned important religious duties in mosques and other sacred places, for they were believed to be naturally suited for the holy life.

Unreasonably positive attitudes, such as the above, were the historical forerunners of the contemporary stereotype that connects blindness with automatic compensation by some extraordinary ability—characteristically sensory, artistic, or intellectual. Stevie Wonder, a currently popular, blind rock-and-roll singer, in his choice of a stage name exemplifies this tendency. It likewise manifests itself in the numerous, widely read stories about the marvelous exploits of blind detectives, of which television's "Longstreet" is the most recent example.

The Blind in Music and the Graphic Arts

Von Schumann (1959) also reviewed representations of the blind in classical music and the graphic arts. Although the theme of blindness occurs less frequently in these arts, its purport is essentially the same here as in verbal productions.

In music four dominant motifs appear: (1) the blind as sad, helpless, or socially rejected; (2) the blind person as mystic; (3) blindness as entailing the loss of discriminatory faculties other than sight; and (4) the blind as morally superior or inferior.

A Serbian beggar song about blind children, sung to the gusla (a one-stringed violin), emphasizes the melancholy of blindness. The song expresses the wish that sightless children in their dreams see light and color. A recent American popular song alludes to the helplessness of a blind man trying to cross the road, while a somewhat older American ballad deals with a blinded soldier at a railway depot where no one has come to meet him. He is utterly alone and rejected. The mice of "Three Blind Mice" are, on the other hand, incompetent to the point of absurdity and consequently convey no sense of unhappiness.

Mystical powers are attributed to the blind in Stravinsky's opera *Oedipus Rex* (mentioned earlier) and in Mussorgsky's *Boris Godunov*. In the latter, during Act IV, the supernatural dream of a blind shepherd is related to Boris by the wise old man Pimen.

In Eugen D'Aldert's opera *The Dead Eyes*, sightlessness is associated with an inability to perceive physical beauty or ugliness. An ugly but rich Roman city official marries Myrtocle, a poor blind girl. Her great happiness is disturbed only by the fact that she cannot see her tender beloved husband. She has no awareness of his bodily appearance and thinks him beautiful. She is exalted morally in that she responds to her husband's inner true nature, which is good, rather than to his unpleasant exterior, which is of no spiritual consequence.

This goodness-due-to-blindness is a fairly frequent theme in literature. As usually depicted, the blind must react to the "real spiritual person," for, by reason of sensory constriction, they cannot relate to the "superficial material person." Of course, in reality the sightless perceive aesthetic qualities through their remaining senses (mainly via aural and tactile stimulation) and on the basis of such information distinguish between the "beautiful" and the "ugly". There is no reason to believe that they are any less repelled by physical ugliness than the sighted; nor are they necessarily compassionate toward ugly persons, for many blind people are just as rejecting of the ugly as are the seeing. Thus, the alleged compensation of moral superiority is wholly spurious. On the other hand, moral inferiority, not superiority, is the more common trait associated with blindness in music. For example, in traditional Christian hymns, as well as popular religious songs (such as those of the contemporary country and western genre), mentions of blindness, whether figurative or physical, typically equate the condition with a state of sin, i.e., spiritual ignorance, separation from God, pathetic weakness, or degradation.

When we turn to the graphic arts, we see that they, too, disclose at least four central themes: (1) blindness in relation to mysticism and heightened religious awareness; (2) the curing of visual disorders; (3) the blind as social isolates; (4) visual deprivation as necessarily causing generalized cognitive impairment.

The religious motif appears, in *Inhalt Eines Traumes*, a German Renaissance drawing by Burgkmair, and in Ernst Barlach's lithograph *Der Blinde*. The former depicts the content of a blind man's dream, that credited to the Bishop Goericus von Metz during his youth, in which he saw an angel holding his eyes on a cloth. The dream presumably portended his future calling as a Prince of the Church. *Der Blinde* shows a blind man asleep on a bench. The heaviness of his body indicates his bondage to the dreary materialism of the earth, while his face is turned away from the earth as he talks to an angel hovering in front of him, suggesting that his vision has been directed inward to the realm of God. The attitude implicit here is that the blind can experience true joy and peace only in Heaven; this world is not for them. They can love only death because life offers them nothing but pain. Consequently, they would do well to renounce this world and prepare themselves wholeheartedly for that to come.

An artistically talented woman of my acquaintance, who associated blindness with mysticism, once painted the portrait of a sightless man, representing him in the dark void of outer space with tiny planets, stars, and snakes circling about his head and thereby symbolizing his sensitivity to the awesome mysteries of the cosmos.

The healing theme is suggested by Rembrandt's painting *Der Engel Verlaesst Tobias,* which depicts the blinded Tobias of the Apocrypha by the aid of much light and dark and an angel attired in oriental garb. In the Biblical story, Tobias is rendered sightless by falling bird dung. He is later cured through a treatment recommended by an angel to his son, which consists in an application of fish gall. This substance loosens Tobias's cataracts, which he is then able to remove. The treatment of blindness also appears in the pen-and-ink drawing of the sixteenth-century Peruvian artist, Felipe Guaman de Ayala. The drawing shows the handling of both the sick and the sightless via the temple magic of the Inca priests.

Both personal isolation and mental inadequacy are elements in the drawing *Autobahn* by the late nineteenth-century Norwegian artist Olaf Gulbransson. Here a blind man is portrayed with his face in the shape of a locomotive, symbolizing his concept of the cars he has never seen and, therefore, cannot picture, while his alienation is indicated by his being at the side of a highway. Implicit in his inability to picture objects is the idea that visual percepts and images constitute the only modus operandi whereby one can meaningfully conceptualize the external environment.

The subject of blindness crops up much less often in sculpture than in music, painting, or drawing. Perhaps the best examples here are the faceless statues of the ancient god Bes, referred to earlier. Since the human face has always been an important symbol of ego identity, the facelessness of Bes suggests that blindness was thought to eradicate such identity, viz., the continuity and stability of the personality. This notion is reflected in the widespread contemporary belief that visual loss automatically produces massive and permanent pathological changes in the basic personality structure or that the blind, by virtue of their handicap, manifest a certain form of personality that is profoundly different from any pattern to be observed among the seeing. In other words, there are no unique persons who also happen to be blind but only a class of the blind, one that possesses special characteristics, its members being amorphous as individuals. This old prejudice is connoted by the phrase "the blind" as it is generally used, and for this reason many visually handicapped persons dislike the term and would prefer some other, less value-laden designation.

The Sightless in Novels, Short Stories, Poetry, and Drama

Jacob Twersky's (1955) investigation of the meaning of blindness in Western literature stands as the most comprehensive piece of psychological research on this topic. This study covered nearly a hundred different writings, dating from antiquity to the present century, and included the works of minor as well as major authors. Its chief purpose was to describe the evolution of attitudes toward blindness in the West, viewing them both as expressions of particular periods and distal, if not proximal, determinants of social reactions to visually handicapped persons. Twersky divided this evolutionary process into four distinct phases, based upon important historical developments in educational and rehabilitative services for the blind. The initial stage encompasses the centuries from antiquity to 1784, when the first Western school for the blind was founded in Paris. The next period extends from this point to 1873, the date marking the incipient, general adoption of Braille by educational institutions for the sightless. The third phase begins here and continues to 1914, with the advent of rehabilitative programs for the blind of World War I—an event that brought beneficial results for the visually disabled as a whole, through positive publicity and improved vocational opportunities. During World War II, such services were reinstituted and considerably augmented. This last stage embraces the decades from 1914 to 1955. Below I shall point out representative instances from each of these periods, emphasizing important material omitted in the Twersky review. In addition, I shall consider a typical sample of depictions for the years following 1955.

Antiquity to 1784

This period's literature manifests the same themes regarding blindness as do its concomitant mythology, legend, and folklore, with one critical exception: beginning with medieval literature, the blind are sometimes represented as comical.

In *The Canterbury Tales* (Nicholson [Ed.], 1934), we find a classic instance of this tendency. The old knight January of "The Merchant's Tale" is blind and regularly cuckolded by his young wife May. On one occasion, he even assists her into the branches of a pear tree where she and her lover Damian copulate, with the unsuspecting January standing beneath them. Suddenly King Pluto magically restores the old man's sight, and he beholds all. However, the clever May promptly denies her adultery, claiming that January has been dazzled by his newfound vision and thus has not seen correctly. The simple January accepts her explanation, and May is exonerated. January is as naive while sighted as while blind. This depiction is interesting because it links blindness with sexual impotence, stupidity, and the weakness of old age.

Although comic portrayals such as the above are demeaning to the blind, Twersky considered them an improvement over the uniformly somber attitudes expressed in ancient literature.

This emphasis upon the tragedy of blindness is best exemplified by Oedipus in the plays of Sophocles. In *Oedipus at Colonus,* the chorus suggests that Oedipus has lived in utmost despair since his blinding and will be freed from his wretchedness only after death. Twersky viewed Oedipus as the most helpless sightless character in classical literature, since his mobility and awareness of the external world appear to depend almost wholly upon the ministrations of his daughter Antigone. Once Oedipus is asked if he were born blind—an expression of the age-old misconception that assumes most blindness to be congenital. From earliest times to the present, only a small minority of the sightless have been so born. Twersky interpreted the error as an attempt by the seeing to ward off the fear that arises from the realization that they too are susceptible to blindness-inducing diseases and accidents. At the close of the play, Oedipus becomes a prophet and departs this life for Heaven or the Underworld. Thus, he is finally compensated supernaturally, but only at the time of death. In *Oedipus Rex,* the preferability of death to a sightless life is unequivocally stated. The old belief that mockery of the blind inevitably provokes divine punishment is also indicated here, for Oedipus, who mocks Tiresias, becomes blind himself. This taboo, according to Twersky, is related to that which forbade the mocking of the dead, since the blind were regarded as quasi-dead.

One of the most forlorn sightless figures in tragic drama is to be found in Shakespeare's *King Lear.* The blinded Earl of Gloucester is depicted as utterly helpless and disoriented. His son Edgar, posing as Mad Tom, leads his father to a supposed cliff in Dover, where the latter intends to commit suicide. Edgar, in fact, takes the old man up a small hill so that his jump will not be fatal. Though the Earl falls but a short distance, Edgar convinces him that he has leapt from a high cliff. Moreover, by changing his voice, Edgar deceives Gloucester into thinking he is different people. As Twersky pointed out, this depiction is most unrealistic, for even a newly blinded person, as Gloucester is, would not be likely to show such massive disorientation.

On the other hand, Shakespeare's attitude toward the blind is not entirely negative. For example, Lear says, "A man may see how this world goes with no eyes." Also, Shakespeare's twenty-seventh sonnet refers to a blind dreamer, stressing the vital quality of his imagination.

After *Oedipus Rex,* the most important tragic work dealing with blindness is unquestionably Milton's epic poem, *Samson Agonistes.* Although Milton's hero is dramatically superior to the Biblical Samson, the poem nonetheless contains some of the most negative and distorted evaluations of blindness to be encountered in all of literature. Samson describes his blindness as a living death, as necessarily entailing generalized incompetence, and as the worst possible spiritual and physical agony. Blindness renders one more lowly than the vilest of creatures. The blind man is imprisoned in himself and is almost always credulous before the sighted. In Line 538, Samson compares himself to a "castrated ram," indicating that Milton identified visual loss with emasculation.

Milton's famous nineteenth sonnet tells us much less about his attitude toward blindness, though its dominant tone is one of sadness and passive resignation.

In *Paradise Lost*, Milton also briefly refers to his blindness. Here, however, he mentions the great sightless poets and prophets of antiquity and expresses the hope that God will similarly compensate him. He wishes for an "inner light" to make up for the outer one that is lost so he may tell of things the carnal eyes cannot see. Nevertheless, this literary concern with compensation is a mere trifle alongside the immense emphasis upon negative characteristics in *Samson Agonistes*.

Considering his apparent self-contempt, Milton's literary achievement was even more remarkable than it otherwise would have been. Though never completely succumbing to the defamatory stereotype of the blind, he seems to have accepted it almost as fully as his political enemies, who ridiculed him by means of it.

In medieval German poetry, frequent mention is made of the dreams of the blind, typically within a context of sorrow. A poem by Reinfried von Braunschweig asserts that the sightless can see in their dreams, while Wolfram's *Parzival* suggests that dreams give the blind a feeling of seeing, but the actual degree of vision is small and short-lived, providing only momentary joy (von Schumann, 1959).

In summary, Western literature, from ancient times to the eighteenth century, is consistent in its attitudes toward the blind. These are preponderantly derogatory, with only a handful of characters being viewed positively, owing to supernatural compensation, e.g. Tiresias in the plays of Sophocles and the bard Demodocus in Homer's *Odyssey*. However, whether favorable or unfavorable, the depictions of the blind are always substantially unrealistic.

1784-1873

In the representations of this period, Twersky found some progress toward objectivity. This change was engendered largely by the humanitarian empiricism of the eighteenth-century French Enlightenment, which culminated in the creation of systematic education for the blind. Still, characters at this time are more clearly portrayed as good or evil merely by reason of blindness, and the proportion of helpless blind exceeds that of the preceding period.

Twersky located the most realistic depictions in the writings of Sir Walter Scott. For example, in *Old Mortality*, the sightless Elizabeth MacLur is self-sufficient, resourceful, satisfactorily mobile, and assesses the personalities of those about her by the traits they disclose in their speech. She is not depressed by her handicap and takes an active interest in both the physical and social environment. With the assistance of her young granddaughter, Elizabeth successfully manages an inn and enjoys a generally happy life.

Scott's unprejudiced attitude toward the blind was probably in large part the product of his relationship with Dr. Thomas Blacklock, the sightless Scottish scholar mentioned in Chapter 2. Nevertheless, such realism is exceptional for the period, as the vast majority of depictions continue to be stereotypic. Even Scott, as Twersky has indicated, was not wholly exempt from this tendency, for the blind characters in his works tend to be somewhat idealized.

One very revealing instance of this latter brand of distortion appears in Gustavo Adolfo Becquer's short story, "Master Perez, the Organist" (Flores [Ed.], 1956). The blind and aged Master Perez is poor but saintly. He has no family other than his devoted daughter, no friend except his organ, which he plays at the church of Santa Inez. He believes he will see God when he goes to Heaven, a faith so firm that it inspires his performances to angelic heights of beauty. His mysterious artistic gift is wholly supernatural, profoundly moving all appreciators who partake in it.

Then, one Christmas Eve, Master Perez is suddenly taken ill, and it seems he will not be able to officiate during the special Midnight Mass, as he has traditionally done in the past. However, nothing can keep this dauntless old man in bed on so holy an occasion. At last, in a chair supported by attendants, he has himself borne into church and placed before his organ. Knowing this night to be his final one, he executes a supremely powerful performance and dies at his beloved instrument.

Thereafter no one dares play the organ, not even the old man's daughter, who is a music teacher, until the next Christmas Eve when a former rival of Perez comes forth and announces that he can take the great musician's place. This new organist, however, is widely known to be inferior. In addition, he is quite ugly, being emaciated and cross-eyed—the latter deformity reflecting his evil nature, for Becquer refers to the face as "the mirror of the soul." The congregation finds him unforgivably presumptuous, and when he sits down to play, they try to drown him out with drums and other noisemakers. Yet much to everyone's astonishment, the organ begins to produce beautiful, even heavenly, music, and all within the church fall silent. The stupid organist, however, dislikes this music and says he will never play the organ again, as it is old and out of repair. The audience is mystified, for they are sure such artistic wonders could never spring from the hands of one so inept as this cross-eyed charlatan.

Some time later the mystery is solved. One night Señorita Perez sees the ghost of her father playing the organ, and subsequently during a Midnight Mass, she witnesses a repetition of the vision, while the congregation does not see the ghost of Master Perez but instead beholds the organ playing by itself.

Though ludicrous, the story is psychologically significant in that it juxtaposes two diametrically opposite concepts of visual defect. At one extreme we find the virtuous Master Perez, a divinely inspired genius; at the other, his bungling, cross-eyed rival. This paradoxical bipolarity of attitudes is by no means rare in literary accounts of the visually handicapped. We first observe it in *Oedipus Rex*, where Tiresias is exalted and Oedipus degraded; much later in two blind characters from the pen of Charles Dickens—the evil Stagg of *Barnaby Rudge* and his spiritual antithesis, the thoroughly innocent, morally pure Bertha Plummer in *The Cricket on the Hearth*. Thus, seemingly incompatible attitudes regarding visual disorder may exist side by side within one and the same individual. The incompatibility, however, is merely logical, a fact of which the emotional life notoriously takes no heed, for the ambivalence in question can and does occur among all species of human motivation and attitude. We should, therefore, be wary of those who display an ostentatiously accepting attitude toward the blind, as this is likely to mask an equally rejecting counterattitude.

This period's emphasis on the invalidism of the blind is, as Twersky noted, strikingly exemplified by Charlotte Brontë's *Jane Eyre*. After his accidental blinding in the burning mansion, Edward Rochester is profoundly frustrated in his efforts to develop independence and consequently becomes almost wholly dependent on Jane, who plays the part of the good nurse until his sight is restored. A symbolic castration theme is also pronounced here, for until his sight returns, Rochester's masculine vigor is largely held in abeyance, after the fashion of the defeated Samson, with whom Jane identifies her sightless lover.

A theme akin to that stressing helplessness and dependency appears in Holderlin's poem *The Blind Singer*, which highlights the alleged disorientation of the sightless. Here the blind's certainty in the spiritual world is contrasted with their uncertainty in the real world (von Schumann, 1959).

The sexual undesirability of the sightless woman is a central motif in Bulwer-Lytton's *The Last Days of Pompeii*, in which Nydia, the Thessalian blind girl, is hopelessly in love with the hero Glacus, who, in turn, cares only for the heroine Eione. At the close of the novel, the three are in Pompeii during the eruption of Vesuvius, which so darkens the atmosphere that neither Glacus nor Eione can see their way through the streets of the city. This, of course, is no obstacle to Nydia, who knows the city thoroughly without vision. She leads her friends to the sea and an awaiting boat. Glacus and Eione plan to return to their native Greece. In the boat Nydia lies, like a dog, at Glacus' feet, while the beloved Eione rests on his breast. When the two lovers are asleep, Nydia slips over the side and vanishes beneath the waves. Her drowning symbolizes a return to the womb, insofar as the sea is described as a great mother: "Century after century shall the mighty mother stretch forth her azure arms, and know them not." Though Nydia is intelligent, competent, and attractive, her blindness renders her essentially unlovable.

Such is also the case with Dickens's gullible Bertha, who loves her father Caleb's employer, though he regards her as an idiot. In examples like these, the woman tends to be viewed as sexless, after the manner of sightless male characters, such as Milton's Samson.

To sum up, these nine decades show the blind as less deviant and bizarre than the prior epoch. Nevertheless, the improvement in attitudes is not marked. Although some fairly realistic depictions can be found, they are much less frequent than irrational renditions, which tend to carry on the stereotypic images of the past, with only slight modification in some cases and none at all in many others.

1873-1914

According to Twersky, this period manifests more representations of the sightless as normal human beings, but at the same time there is a comparable increase in prejudicial portrayals. Some works reflect a growing knowledge of blindness, in that it alone is not perceived as a cause of helplessness, i.e., when blind characters are helpless, they tend to be multihandicapped. However, the literary themes involving blindness remain largely the same as those dominant during the previous periods.

The image of the blind as evil recurs in a number of writings. Robert Louis Stevenson's *Kidnapped* refers briefly to a sightless criminal, while *Treasure Island*'s blind Pew is the leader of a pirate gang. Twersky interpreted such depictions as an improvement over the earlier, more popular stress upon incapacitation, for to be successfully evil, one must be intelligent and self-sufficient. Pew, for example, is far from helpless; he is clever, highly mobile, and an effective leader.

The themes of helplessness, despair, and the preferability of death to blindness continue to be common during this period. "Die Blinde," Rainer Maria Rilke's sonnet about a blind woman, focuses upon the fear, loneliness, and bodily constriction of the blind (Von Schumann, 1959). In *The Black Arrow* by Stevenson, Sir Daniel Brackley poses as a blind leper, a wretched, fearful creature whose mere touch is death; he is both pitiable and disgusting. In Gabriele D'Annunzio's tragic play *The Dead City*, the sightless Anna in Act I dreams of becoming suddenly old. Her hair falls out, her skin grows wrinkled, her gums shrink, and her lips hang down flaccidly. All over she is formless and wilted. She likens herself to an old beggar woman as well as to a poor idiot. She feels she has lost all to achieve deep spiritual recognition (von Schumann, 1959).

One of the most defamatory depictions of the period is that of Rudyard Kipling's *The Light That Failed.* The blinded hero Dick Heldar, former artist and soldier, is portrayed as helpless, emasculated, and better off dead. At the end of the novel, however, he shows considerable independence in traveling from England to the Sudan, where he is killed in a military engagement, a death that he has sought deliberately. Among

Western writers, Kipling ranks as one of the most blatantly negative in his attitudes toward the sightless.

The blinded Wolf Larsen in Jack London's *The Sea Wolf,* though praiseworthy for his great courage and satanic cunning, is nonetheless described in accordance with various stereotypic images. Humpfrey regards him as: "utterly weak and broken . . . like a woman wringing her hands . . . blind and helpless . . . a straw"; as showing "the feebleness of the blind in his walk," as well as "that fabled sixth sense" in relation to nearby objects. Elsewhere, Humpfrey says of him: "I was only five feet away and directly in what should have been his line of vision. It was uncanny. I felt myself a ghost, what with my invisibility." Nevertheless, Wolf Larsen does not become completely helpless until his brain tumor affects him with additional physical disabilities. Were he only blind, he would remain a force to be reckoned with. In this connection Humpfrey says: "I shall never be able to trust him . . . and far less now that he is blind. The liability is that his part helplessness will make him more malignant than ever." Furthermore, this passage suggests an affinity between blindness and evildoing. Though Larsen is wicked while sighted, he is rendered even more demoniacal by visual loss.

The emphasis upon disorientation reappears in Strindberg's drama *A Dream Play,* in which the experience of a blind man is represented as dreamlike and totally unrealistic in regard to time and space. Moreover, his predominant feeling is that of loneliness (von Schumann, 1959).

Supernatural compensation also continues as an important theme. In Arthur Conan Doyle's "Sir Nigel," a blind man is compensated with wonderful, mystical powers. In Barlach's drama *Der Tote Tag,* the devout blind man Kule courageously views his suffering and moves closer to God by reason of his blindness (von Schumann, 1959).

On the other hand, Korolenko's novel *The Blind Musician* handles its subject quite realistically. The protagonist Petrik, a congenitally blind boy, develops in a healthy manner, largely through the educational efforts of a sophisticated uncle. Petrik is psychologically stable, physically vigorous, and sexually competent. Owing to native ability and a supportive environment, he becomes a distinguished musician. His victory, however, does not come easily but only after great toil and frustration. The author's central point is that blindness in itself need not be an overwhelming handicap. Assuming satisfactory heredity and environment, the sightless can conduct essentially normal lives.

Also fairly favorable is the depiction in H. G. Wells's short story "The Country of the Blind." The blind characters here are efficient, independent, and happy. They successfully manage their totally blind society without the aid of a single seeing person. By their standards, it is the sighted intruder Nuñez who is made to appear maladjusted.

However, as Twersky indicated, the fact of their complete isolation from the seeing world suggests that Wells believed the blind could never truly be at home in that world. Furthermore, the blind group's conception of the external environment contains certain bizarre elements that would not necessarily result from a lack of vision. For example, they believe the sky is roofed a short distance above their heads, in the manner of a cave; also, they have no knowledge of birds, as such, and think them to be angels. In addition, the entire community is congenitally blind, a highly unlikely contingency. Twersky, in this connection, found a marked overrepresentation of the congenitally blind in the literature of every period studied. His previously stated hypothesis concerning the origin and persistence of the false belief in question is indeed cogent.

In conclusion, the literature of these four decades (1873-1914) reveals significant but meager progress toward realism regarding blindness. Accurate representations still constitute only a small minority within the relevant literary output.

1914 to the Present

For the literature of the period from 1914 to 1955, Twersky found a generally greater understanding of the blind with some diminution in the tendency to stereotype. Nonetheless, distorted portrayals persist in outnumbering those that are realistic or favorable. I, moreover, find the same to be true of the literature after 1955. All the irrational motifs of earlier fiction have not only survived but live on quite vigorously in works of the contemporary period.

The idea of the evil blind reasserts itself with unabashed bluntness in Thomas Wolfe's novel *You Can't Go Home Again.* On the train journey to his boyhood hometown in North Carolina, the hero George encounters a fellow-native of the area: the wicked Judge Bland, long since blinded by syphilis—a loathsome old man who for many years has been earning his living through the usurous exploitation of poor, ignorant blacks. The Judge inspires George with the utmost terror; indeed, Chapter 4, in which he appears, is entitled: "The Hidden Terror."

The following passage epitomizes George's perception of the blind man: "At the corners of the mouth he thought he also caught the shadow of a smile—faint, evil, ghostly—and at sight of it a sudden and unreasoning terror seized him. . . . He just sat quietly, gripping a heavy walnut walking-stick with a frail hand, the sightless eyes fixed in vacancy, the thin and sunken face listening with that terrible intent stillness that only the blind know, and around the mouth hovered that faint suggestion of a smile, which, hardly perceptible though it was, had in it a kind of terrible vitality and the mercurial attractiveness of a ruined angel."

George's near phobic anxiety in response to blindness seems akin to the common childhood fear of darkness. Blindness here symbolizes not only evil but also death and punishment for sexual immorality, for the Judge is called "ghostly," and his defect is described as the product of lascivious conduct. Moreover, the Judge's very name, "Bland," is not without its own special symbolic significance, as it suggests psychic dullness or an emptiness within the person. The great anxiety George feels in the Judge's presence stems from these associations, perhaps more directly from a reactivation of repressed castration anxiety stimulated by the symbolic castration of the old man's blinding.

Such gross prejudice is especially deplorable in a writer of Wolfe's intelligence and artistic stature. On the other hand, its existence should not be too surprising since Wolfe was similarly prejudiced against Negroes and Jews, and his works, though lyrically magnificent, are replete with exaggerations and unfounded generalizations on numerous other subjects as well. Unfortunately, even creative genius is no guarantee against the jaundiced eye of bigotry.

In Richard Wright's *Native Son*, blindness is connected with death, unacknowledged evil, invisibility, relative physical incompetence, and general ignorance. When accepting a job as chauffeur with the wealthy white Dalton family in Chicago, Bigger Thomas, the black protagonist, meets the sightless mistress of the house and feels as if he is in the company of a dead person. Her face is described as "still," "tilted," and "waiting."

She has a "stony stare" and never looks at people when addressing them. Her face reminds Bigger of a dead man's face he has once seen. He feels that talking to a blind person is like talking to someone he himself can scarcely see. Furthermore, though long blind, Mrs. Dalton cannot get about her house except by feeling her way along the walls. Also, her exclusive wearing of white makes her a patent symbol of the oppressive, white American power structure, if not the entire Caucasian race. Accordingly, the white world is blind in that it cannot see the true life of the American black, viz., the immense depth of his frustration and anger. The Daltons are philanthropic liberals and wish to help Bigger by giving him a decent job, yet Mr. Dalton, without recognizing the fact, is, by virtue of certain business interests, just another cog in the wheel of racist-capitalist exploitation. Consequently, even if well-intentioned, the whites can see only the surface problems of the Negro community, because, to varying degrees, all or most of them are enmeshed within the general system that oppresses Negroes. The white liberal assuages his guilt through paltry, condescending acts of benevolence, and thus remains *blind* to the grave evil his bourgeois position necessarily perpetrates against the black man. Indeed, during the course of the novel, Bigger refers to many people as "blind," in the sense of being ignorant—not only the Dalton family and other white people but also his own mother, sister, brother, and girl friend Bessie. These black persons are "blind" in that all are naive and passive before the social and economic conditions that constantly act to degrade them.

Although one may justifiably concur with Wright's assessment of the American race problem, his literary use of blindness clearly performs a disservice to another minority group, for it implies that the sightless in general are characterized by the same undesirable traits as those assigned to Mrs. Dalton and the world of ignorant, superficial mortals at large.

Blindness as a death symbol also occurs in Tennessee Williams's *Streetcar Named Desire*, in which a blind Mexican woman, selling flowers for the dead, appears toward the close of the play. Finally, she offers her wares to the unhappy Blanche, foreshadowing the latter's impending destruction via rape and insanity.

We meet with another instance of the death-blindness theme in Dylan Thomas's poem *Under Milk Wood.* Here the blind Captain Cat, a retired sea captain, dreams of a descent into "Davy Dark," where the fish "nibble him

down to his wish bone" and the "long drowned nuzzle up" and talk to him
He lives in his memories of the sea and weeps for what is lost, including hi
former girlfriend Rosie Probert; for the Captain was also a "tom cat" in hi
younger, sighted days. During the day he is the town bell-ringer, an
through his still normal sense of hearing, he continues to be aware of th
nature of the community life about him. Even so, he remains a lonely isolat
whose sadness is known only to the local children, as they alone have spie
him in his solitary weeping. Then with the fall of night: "Blind Captain Ca
climbs into his bunk. Like a cat, he sees in the dark. Through the voyages o
his tears, he sails to see the dead. . . ."

Though the Captain is not represented as entirely helpless o
dependent, his modest, if not minimal, assets are dwarfed into utte
obscurity by the overpowering burden of his losses. The vision of deatr
and with it social alienation, and the inexorable despair and impotence o
old age and infirmity are the critical features of blindness, as here depicted

In Jenny Hobbs's short story "The Last Bushman" hopeles
dependency is the chief ingredient of blindness. The young heroine Jessic
has a sightless grandfather, who is described as good-natured
affectionate, understanding, spiritedly blasphemous and an able singer, bu
he is also helplessly dependent on Jessica's father, Donald (the old man
son). He abhors the evil in his son, who without reason hunts down an
murders a defenseless Bushman, a sadistic sport he has already enjoyed o
numerous occasions in the past. But the present killing is particularly tragi
since the victim is the last of his kind. The old man wishes to stop Donald'
cruelty but is powerless to do so. When he disapproves of his son'
behavior, the latter calls him a "parasite." His only show of strength occur
when Donald is bitterly reprimanding Jessica for her denunciation of him a
a wanton killer, and the old man intercedes in order to draw Donald'
aggression away from Jessica and against himself instead. Though he i
thus successful in protecting his granddaughter, the victory is meager i
contrast with the steady diet of humiliation at his son's hands.

A similar association of blindness with incompetence is briefl
manifested in Saul Bellow's novel *Mr. Sammler's Planet.* At the very outset o
the story, the hero Sammler describes a blind beggar on Seventy-secon
Street in New York who shakes pennies in a cup and pulls at his "Seeing Ey
dog" while singing "What a Friend We Have in Jesus."

The depiction is purely stereotypic. Bellow is obviously ignorant of th fact that the Seeing Eye organization does not and never has sold dogs to beggars, as their policy is to promote independence, not dependence, in their clients. Indeed, the Seeing Eye has always posed relatively strict prerequisites to dog-guide ownership, involving the blind applicant's emotional stability, physical health, and vocational or practical need. Moreover, other legitimate dog agencies employ comparable criteria, and certainly none of them would knowingly sell or donate a dog-guide to a beggar.

Bellow, in addition, seems to connect blindness with a special secrecy-endowing capacity; for Sammler wears smoked glasses in order to pass as a blind man, thereby hoping to avoid a certain Negro pickpocket.

Why does Sammler choose this particular disguise rather than some other? In such a situation the possible alternatives would, of course, be innumerable. A serious street criminal is not likely to spare a blind man simply out of charity, but only if he suspects the latter of possessing little or no money or anything else worth stealing. Sammler could just as well have played the part of a humble sighted man. Bellow's use here of the disguise of blindness seems to rest on the invisibility fantasy, discussed in Chapter 2.

In fact, as it turns out a bit later in the story, a different facade could easily have been more effective, since Sammler does not have the "look of blindness" and fears the pickpocket will detect the disguise, which indeed he does.

References to the alleged "look of blindness" are frequent in literature and imply that it is universal. They ignore the fact that many blind persons do not immediately appear blind, even at close quarters. Among individuals who are on familiar ground, and who have good mobility, voice contact, and no visual disfigurement, blindness often goes unnoticed. A blank, staring face, immobility of the head, and awkward, rigid posture or movements are by no means necessary concomitants of blindness, though such characteristics are certainly popular components of the negative stereotype of the blind.

Sammler is actually sightless in the left eye. The author's selection of "left" instead of "right" eye may be symbolically significant. In this regard, Stekel (1943), in his exhaustive study of dreams, found the left position to be a common symbol of evil. Consequently, Sammler's blind eye suggests that Bellow perhaps equates sightlessness with immorality.

Another blind beggar appears in *The King's General* by du Maurier.

The story is set in seventeenth-century England, during the time of the Puritan revolt against Charles I. The blind man is an old harper to whom an aristocratic family gives shelter on Christmas Eve. He is one of many such homeless wayfarers produced by the war, and his class is generally scorned. He is ragged, wears a black shade over his eyes, and sits in a far corner of the gallery where he plays and sings for his hosts. Despite his wretchedness, the old man is a good musician.

Considering the historical period, this depiction is realistic. During the late Middle Ages and early Renaissance, mendicancy abounded among the European blind, and their plight was, without doubt, most grievous because of widespread public antipathy.

Other references to a historically more recent group of sightless mendicants will be found in Jorge Amado's novel *Gabriela, Clove and Cinnamon*. The individuals here described are traveling folk singers, guitarists, and rhymesters of the cacao region in southern Brazil during the 1920s. This portrayal is also basically accurate, for at that time such blind beggars were apparently numerous in Brazil.

Mystical or extraordinary compensation attendant to blindness continues to be a popular theme in contemporary literature. However, as Twersky also observed, unusual ability is often intermingled with equally unusual inability.

Beckett's play *Waiting for Godot* furnishes an excellent example of such mixed depiction. By Act II, the cruel Pozzo has become blind. He is awkward and bumps into Lucky, his mistreated servant. Both fall and lie helplessly on the ground, Pozzo begging for help and pity. He cannot get up by himself; he does not even know where he is, nor does he recognize the two vagabonds, Vladimir and Estragon, though he recently knew them when sighted. Finally this pair helps him to stand, whereupon he tells them he is blind, which leads Estragon to wonder if he can see into the future. In answer Pozzo says: "The blind have no notion of time. The things of time are hidden from them too." Then Vladimir notices that Lucky has become dumb, and asks Pozzo when this fate befell the poor man. Pozzo angrily replies: "Have you not done with tormenting me with your accursed time? It's abominable! When! When! One day, is that not enough for you, one day he went dumb, one day I went blind, one day we'll go deaf, one day we were born, one day we shall die, the same day, the same second, is that not enough for you? . . . They give birth astride of a grave, the light gleams an instant, then it's night once more." Later Vladimir asks Estragon if Pozzo was really blind, for he thinks that Pozzo may have seen them.

Pozzo's physical debility and disorientation are obvious comic exaggerations. In his ludicrous blundering, he reminds one of the myopic Mr. Magoo, the animated-cartoon character so popular during the 1950s. Of course, no blinded person, in reality, would be so utterly incapacitated, unless he were multihandicapped. On the other hand, Pozzo's blindness gives him insight into the ultimate meaning of life, at least from the existentialist's viewpoint—i.e., life is essentially tragic owing to its absurd purposelessness. Time is of no consequence because all temporal things are doomed to end in the same timeless nothingness of death. It is in the sense of this revelation that Pozzo sees, and this is why Vladimir questions his blindness. Nevertheless, Pozzo is not truly compensated, since he remains miserable, his existence being as futile as the cosmos itself. Also, though blindness is here a vehicle for philosophical truth, it acquires this symbolic function largely through its fantasied affinity with the vacuity of death.

Another mystical blind figure, but one much less wretched than Pozzo, appears in Tennessee Williams's *Camino Real.* The character is an old woman who is compassionately attuned to the suffering humanity about her. She seems to symbolize the tragic nature of life, both the inevitability of human misery and the ultimate pain-erasing power of death.

A further instance of mental compensation, together with certain negative traits, occurs in James Hilton's novel *Random Harvest.* The hero Smith meets an old retired actor who is sightless. The old man has been reading *The Merchant of Venice* in Braille and remarks that one cannot skip passages when reading by touch and, therefore, obtains more information than he would from visual reading, where scanning would be too easy to resist. He says this increased learning makes the blind think more than the sighted.

While it is true that Braille is comparatively difficult to peruse, the reader can nonetheless omit material without sacrificing understanding. Likewise, there is, of course, no evidence to indicate that the blind are any more or less inclined to the contemplative life than are the seeing.

Although the old man knows his room well, he seems needlessly clumsy in other respects. He bumps into Smith several times, and when Paula,

Smith's girl friend, introduces him to the blind man, the latter does not offer to shake hands. In addition, he is rather odd looking, with a dome-shaped head.

What is significant here is not that the character's physical attributes and behavior are unrealistic, for in themselves they are credible. The important point is simply that Hilton emphasizes negative physical characteristics, when he might just as well have done the reverse or been neutral.

In William Golding's *Lord of the Flies* visual defect, though not associated with compensation, appears as part of an essentially favorable symbolization. The myopic boy Piggy becomes functionally blind when Jack, the sadistic leader of the Hunters, steals his glasses. Later one of the boys in Jack's group kills Piggy by knocking him over a cliff with a boulder.

E.M. Forster, in his introduction to the novel, interprets Piggy as a symbol of man's rational, civilized strivings and Jack as a representation of our base instinctual nature. Throughout the novel, Piggy is unique among the island-marooned group of boys in being consistently conscientious and reasonable. When the other boys talk unrealistically of rescue, want to play, loaf, or hunt wild pigs for the mere fun of killing them, Piggy is practical and points out the possibility of their permanent isolation from adult protection and their consequent pressing need for rules of conduct, shelters against the elements, and so on. His visual handicap, his fatness, asthma, and general awkwardness suggest the frustrations inherent in a life of reason. Rational problem solving requires self-control, patience, and foresight; like Piggy, the way of reason is slow, circuitous, and painstaking. Jack, by contrast, is stong, lean, agile, and boisterous. Impulsive action, like Jack, is thoughtless, spontaneous, and exciting. The killing of Piggy by the Hunters symbolizes the threatening power of man's animal instincts, his ever-ready tendency toward atavism—or in Freudian terms, the ceaseless warring of the id, ego, and superego.

An uncommonly believable portrayal of a sightless character appears in Leonard Gershe's dramatic comedy *Butterflies Are Free*, a recent Broadway hit that has subsequently been produced as a motion picture. The young hero, Don Baker, is congenitally blind. He is bright, independent, good-natured, witty, artistic, and sexually healthy. At his urging, his overprotective mother has allowed him to live alone in New York City on a

rief trial basis. If by the end of this period he has not made a successful
djustment, he will have to resume residence with her. She has agreed to
ie experiment only reluctantly and unconsciously hopes it will fail.
lthough Don no longer needs his mother and wishes to start his own life,
ie retains a strong emotional need for him and wants to keep him under
er control. In a Bohemian manner, he lives simply but quite adequately in a
nall apartment, knows the surrounding neighborhood well, and is just
eginning to earn a little money as a coffee house guitarist. His rapid
daptation to the new environment does not impress his mother, who still
ears he will perish without her. He counters her exaggerated anxiety with a
riendly but firm insistence that she stick to the terms of their original
argain. During the New York sojourn, he meets Jill Tanner, an attractive
oung woman who lives next door, and promptly initiates an affair with
er. This development greatly distresses his mother, who attempts to
abotage the relationship by admonishing Jill that Don's blindness forces
pon him a special need for love and security, one that a carefree,
nmature girl like Jill could not possibly understand or gratify. Jill then
egins to doubt her initial perception of Don as essentially normal and
inally decides that she would be bad for him. She becomes convinced that
)on does, in fact, need the nurselike care of his mother, and consequently
erminates her involvement with him. Later, however, Don's mother realizes
ier mistake, including the selfishness of her own motivation, and,
accordingly, removes herself from her son's private life. Though frightened
off for a time, Jill soon returns to Don, and the play closes with their
eunion.

There is only one decidedly inaccurate element in Gershe's depiction,
and it concerns the blind's characteristic techniques of mobility. More
pecifically, Don Baker, in walking about his neighborhood, has to count
teps in order to be sure of arrival at the desired destination. Actually,
experienced blind travelers do not, as a rule, employ this method, but
nstead rely chiefly upon auditory cues, unconscious motor memory, and
:ognitive maps.

Three other features of this production, though not intrinsically
Jnrealistic, seem likely to facilitate stereotypic interpretations on the part of
audiences already long naive about the blind.

First, Don reacts to Jill's apparent rejection not only with a normal depression but also with marked regression. He loses his self-confidence, questions his capacity to live alone, and wishes to return home with his mother. She, however, owing to her recent enlightenment, persuades him to continue what he has started, and he remains in his apartment. Though the regression is short-lived, the playwright nevertheless implies that sexual rejection is far more painful for the sightless than for the seeing. While such rebuffs may, in fact, be traumatic for emotionally immature blind persons, the same is also true of many underdeveloped sighted people. The notion that the blind in general are psychologically devastated by these commonplace rejections is certainly unfounded. Moreover, if Don's newly won independence were as real as initially depicted, it should not have been jeopardized by his one bad experience. Nor should he have required bolstering up from his mother, for a truly competent young man would have taken such a disappointment in stride, without parental support. Don's behavior here suggests that the blind are more psychologically vulnerable than the sighted.

The second element conducive to misunderstanding centers about Jill's character. She is energetic, extroverted, and sexually liberated, if not promiscuous. She has never been able to commit herself to a meaningful emotional relationship with a man. The author intimates that Don, because of his blindness, cannot be happy without such a commitment. He differs from the seeing men who enjoy Jill's company without any need for serious emotional involvement; he must have lasting love. His desire for a committed relationship is artistically meant to reflect an admirable sensitivity of character, but this worthiness of purpose merely veils Don's emotional weakness. The urgent nature of his striving after commitment highlights his inordinate emotional dependency. Were he more self-sufficient, he would be less pushed toward romantic symbiosis and probably more inclined to sexual hedonism, after the fashion of most young men. Gershe thus unintentionally repeats the old theme of the overdependent blind.

Thirdly, the relationship between Don and Jill involves obvious abnormality on both sides. His deviation is physical, while hers is psychological. He is blind, while she is emotionally unstable and sexually indiscriminate. Many men, if not most, would not wish to become seriously involved with such a woman. Jill and Don seem to be thrown together by virtue of their respective deficiencies, the implication being that no normal person could relate meaningfully to either. This aspect of the depiction appears to be another instance of the common tendency to equate blindness stereotypically with all other types of abnormality, whether physical, psychological, or social.

On the other hand, Gershe's overriding aim is to represent the blind objectively, divested of their traditional strangeness, gloom, helplessness, physical repulsiveness, and sexual inadequacy. On the whole, he achieves his goal, for despite the shortcomings of his depiction of Don Baker, the character rings true, emerging as a basically normal human being minus his vision.

A somewhat more authentic portrayal can be found in Gary Adelman's lyric novel *Honey out of Stone*. The author is himself blind, his story being a fictional autobiography. The protagonist Ben Storch, a thirty-year-old English professor and poet, loses his sight through a complication of diabetes. His wife Alice is unable to accept his physical condition, particularly his blindness, and divorces him. The inescapable depressive aftermath of traumatic blinding, augmented by this crushing rejection, is described with poignantly ruthless realism. Ben feels castrated; blindness has rendered him "ancient," "womanly," and "laden to death with the wish to die." In time, he finds Eve, a young woman who is herself unhappily married. Through their mutual love, he again experiences meaning in life. Later he is imprisoned for aiding Vietnam draft resisters. In his cell, he thinks: "I am blind, yes, but that coffin had its key." Incarceration for him is a fate far worse than blindness. Only through memories of Eve is he able to endure the hell of his daily confinement. Through her, he has once more become a man, and the current of his fantasy consists largely in a romantic celebration of her restorative powers.

Still, one wonders what would have become of Ben had Eve not entered his life. Ben, like Don Baker, apparently requires permanent emotional intimacy with a given woman in order to be happy. Surely, many persons, including a number of blind people, are able to lead relatively contented lives apart from such lifelong romantic relationships. Thus, Ben's overpowering need to be loved must be understood as a matter of individual orientation; though to the unsophisticated reader of this novel, what is actual for Ben may also appear to have universal applicability to all who are sightless. However, in all fairness to the author, it should be pointed out that his purpose is merely to tell a personal story, the story of one blind man and not that of the blind in general. This purpose Adelman fulfills with commendable objectivity.

Another unprejudiced reference to blindness occurs in Horace Julian Bond's "The Bishop of Atlanta: Ray Charles" (Bontemps [Ed.], 1963), a poem eulogizing the great black entertainer. Unlike the typical poetic handling of blindness, this verse is free of disparaging projection, maudlin pity, or mystical overvaluation. It simply expresses the poet's admiration of a highly talented blind musician in warm, enthusiastic terms, which the latter surely deserves by virtue of his artistic accomplishment.

In summary, Western literature during the last six decades reveals definite but minor alterations in attitudes toward blindness. Depictions tend to be more empirically valid than during any preceding historical period. Nevertheless, stereotypic representations are still the rule rather than the exception. Twersky found that European and American fiction from 1784 to 1955 shows a gradual but consistent increase in concern for the factual nature of blindness, though the overall amelioration of attitudes has been small. In addition, my own survey of present-day literature indicates no appreciable attitudinal changes during the last generation, and, indeed, one would not expect any radical improvement in so short a time. Furthermore, basically the same descriptive trends are manifest in contemporary television, the cinema, comic strips, and popular jokes, with the emphasis upon stereotypic images being perhaps even stronger here than in current literature.

The Blindness Stereotypes and the Collective Unconscious

In this and the preceding chapter we have examined the meaning of blindness in language and imaginative productions and have found that the condition is seldom interpreted dispassionately or objectively. Instead, we have encountered numerous irrational conceptions, drawn largely or entirely from fantasies about blindness. Furthermore, from earliest times to the present, the images in question manifest striking consistency in content. Indeed, two distinct fantasy constellations may be identified as both universal and perennial. I refer here to the previously mentioned positive and negative stereotypes of the sightless—viz., the various images clustering about unrealistically favorable interpretations and those involved in unwarranted attitudes of devaluation. The former group sees the blind as superhuman or at least as extraordinary, owing to psychological or physical compensation following visual loss. The latter type views the sightless as subhuman or at best as inferior (either physically, spiritually, cognitively, or ethically), merely because of visual disability.

In Chapter 2 these two contrary pictures of the blind were explained largely in terms of psychoanalytic concepts, though the applicability of Jungian theory was also suggested; therefore, let us now turn to that subject. Both the positive and negative stereotypes appear to contain certain elements that Jung might justifiably have designated as archetypal, i.e., arising from the collective or racial unconscious. Both have existed in Eastern as well as Western cultures, essentially unchanged in form since remotest antiquity. Even today, notwithstanding our era of scientific rationalism, they endure with remarkable tenacity and, moreover, show no signs of disappearing, at least not in the foreseeable future. Nor has either stereotype developed out of any appreciable direct experience with real blind people; instead, they are basically pre-empirical. Jung's archetypes are likewise pre-empirical. While it is true that Jung based his hypothesis of the collective unconscious on the Lamarckian theory of evolution, one may nonetheless employ the archetype concept without presupposing the dubious doctrine of acquired characteristics. Thus, as I construe them, the archetypes consist of mental predispositions inherent in the human psyche, which arise not from unique individual experience or cultural conditioning but rather from the predetermined nature of the brain, within the context of certain universal constants of the natural world. As human beings, we share in countless ways a common environment by virtue of our inhabiting the same planet, regardless of differences in culture or individual life experience; and granting the presence of unique variations, our brains are anatomically and physiologically nearly identical. From this shared nature emanate a myriad of universal patterns of thought that spring up in response to certain recurring stimuli from the external environment. These thought-forms are the archetypes; they may be regarded as a kind of psychic a priori, analogous to the Kantian synthetic a priori. No genetic transmission based on ancestral or phylogenetic experience need be posited as a necessary condition for the existence of the archetypes. The nature of man's brain and world is, in itself, sufficient to give rise to such cognitive modes. According to Jung, our conscious behavior and attitudes are, to a large extent, under the direction of these unconscious archetypes. Though they may embody wisdom, as well as irrationality, they are best regarded as nonrational, for they do not necessarily represent objective reality. For example, Jung considered the god-concept archetypal because men have always been inclined to explain being by means of such an idea. Whether any god or gods exist objectively or not is irrelevant to the fact that the great bulk of mankind has, since the primeval past, believed in the existence of these supreme supernatural beings. Similarly, the archetypes of blindness mirror customary human thought without regard to validating empirical referents anchored in the lives of actual blind persons.

Several objections will no doubt be raised against the present position. First, the traditional conceptions of blindness may have originated wholly or primarily through cultural conditioning, for since the dawn of recorded history, they have obviously received potent reinforcement from culture. However, while one cannot rule out the importance of cultural influences, one may still legitimately question their alleged role as *prima causa.* The fact that the two stereotypes emerged so early in history in so many diverse and widely separated cultures (e.g., the Middle East, Europe, India, China, Malaya, the South Seas, and the Americas) in itself suggests that culture was not their sole or even central determinant.

Second, my nativistic emphasis might be considered pessimistic and inimical to the eradication of a prejudice through public education. Even so, I do not find my view incompatible with the goals of social reformers. Although man's nature may lead him to many irrational, inhumane modes of thought and behavior, such weaknesses can nonetheless be controlled extensively through conscious insight, appropriate education, and the enactment and enforcement of liberal egalitarian laws. While our primitive propensities may always be with us, in a truly sane scientifically managed society, they would be rendered virtually ineffectual. However, we are yet far removed from any such utopia. Also, whether one accepts the present hypothesis or that of cultural determinism, it must be admitted that harmful prejudices against the sightless continue to be intense and widespread. Regardless of their origin, they have been extremely resistant to change; this fact alone makes a degree of pessimism unavoidable.

Third, though my dichotomous classification of positive and negative fantasy modes leaves less room for disagreement, one might, of course, justifiably prefer further taxonomical divisions, as the present scheme is essentially a matter of conceptual convenience, simply the most parsimonious classification congruent with the facts at hand.

For want of any better terms, I shall label these positive and negative constellations (or more precisely, their archetypal constituents) as the "Tiresian" and "Oedipal" archetypes respectively. These designations would seem appropriate insofar as Tiresias and Oedipus constitute near-perfect bipolar opposites, at least within the dramas of Sophocles, where they embody the first important simultaneous pairing of positive and negative images of blindness to occur in Western literature. Moreover, with few exceptions, each of these characters includes the core elements of the major stereotype he represents, and those elements that are not manifest are at least implicitly present. For instance, mental deficiency is one ingredient of the negative stereotype, and Oedipus is obviously not mentally deficient. On the other hand, he is superfluously impaired with respect to mobility and knowledge of the immediate external environment, and it is but a short step from such impairment to a condition of outright stupidity.

The Tiresian archetype, as it exists today, is no longer primarily concerned with supernatural endowment, though spiritual and moral compensation remain as central as ever. The main focus is now upon sensory, intellectual, and artistic compensation. The blind are believed to possess uncanny powers of hearing and touch. Some people, for example, think the sightless can discriminate facial features by means of voice sounds or the colors of objects through touching them. Others believe that blindness leads to genius. Many think the blind are naturally inclined toward superior performance in the arts, especially in music. Though the exact powers of Tiresias are nowadays seldom imputed to the sightless, those who believe in extrasensory perception and psychokinesis (not to mention the occult in general) tend to credit the blind with an unusual proclivity for such abilities. Also, in the sphere of religion, the notion that blindness makes one a better person or more attuned to the will of God is still quite prevalent.

The Oedipal archetype stresses images of pathetic or ridiculous helplessness, profound and chronic depression, lifelessness, mental defect, sexual abnormality, deliberate or unintentional evildoing, and blindness as punishment for sin. Current expressions of it differ little from those prominent during the distant past, except that presently negative evaluations of the blind are more likely to be stated indirectly, merely as innuendo or under the camouflage of various rationalizations to justify social or vocational rejection.

These two archetypes, as previously suggested, reflect bipolar attitudes, having simultaneous existence within every individual. When one is conscious, the other is likely to be unconscious. They are, in other words, two sides of the same coin. It may be speculated that these distorted pictures of the blind originated out of the spontaneous fantasizing of prehistoric man and continue to be maintained today via similar fantasies in modern man. Moreover, these naturally occurring fantasies appear traceable to certain universal experiences of everyday life—experiences that were certainly as typical of early, primitive man as they now are of his living descendants.

Let us first consider the fantasies generated by the Oedipal archetype.

One environmental stimulus patently relevant to such fantasizing is the darkness of night. While both the seen and the unseen environments are potentially dangerous, one is naturally more vulnerable in darkness than in broad daylight. Mishaps of all sorts—burglaries, muggings, murders, and other aggressive attacks—occur most often at night. For primitive man in the primal wilderness, night must have been especially frightening, since his enemies were legion—at any moment death could spring forth from the shadows. To guard against roaming predators as well as physical accidents, he, no doubt, had to stay in or near his place of shelter. Night was thus a time of uneasy confinement, of comparative helplessness in the face of the unknown, of evildoing because the darkness threatened mutilation and death. From time immemorial, the subjective experience of blindness has been identified with the phenomenon of darkness. Though many blind people deny any awareness of darkness, claiming instead a visual neutrality that is neither dark nor light, the fact remains that most people associate visual loss with darkness. If the average sighted person is asked what he sees on closing his eyes, he will almost invariably say darkness. Early man was surely no different. Blindness to him was a visual night, and he projected onto the blind all he feared from that night. Thus, the blind were perceived as helpless, castrated, living dead, evil, and so on. They became objects of the same fear and suspicion as the night itself. Although nocturnal existence is now much less foreboding, it still involves increased susceptibility to peril and, as of old, spawns a multitude of infantile projections concerning monsters, demons, death, and the like. Consequently, in large measure the blind remain "creatures of the night."

Another critical stimulus to the Oedipal fantasies is, of course, the very real disability necessarily entailed by blindness. For primitive man, visual loss was, indeed, a terrible fate, for it tremendously heightened one's vulnerability to natural mishaps and aggressors—human as well as animal—and, in addition, virtually eliminated his effectiveness as a hunter or forager. Blindness was then almost death itself, literally bringing the individual to the brink of annihilation. Hobbes described normal life in the state of nature as "nasty," "brutish," and "short." For the blind of prehistory, we can safely imagine a life that was even nastier, more brutish, and far, far shorter. While blindness is no longer an unmitigated disaster, the fact still remains that life with vision is much easier than life without it. Even in that far-distant, ideal society, unencumbered by prejudice and discrimination, only a fool, masochist, or psychotic would prefer being blind to being sighted, had one the opportunity to make such a choice.

A further factor that seems basic to the equation of blindness with death involves the great importance of vision in environmental adaptation. Though the sightless in general appear to make better social and educational adjustments than the deaf, the vast majority of seeing people regard vision as their most valuable sense; certainly in the perception of objects and spatial relations it is superior to audition. In this connection, death is usually imagined as a state of sensory nothingness. In contemplating death, the sighted person is likely to imagine himself first blind, then deaf, and so on. Even were one to value hearing over sight, the closing of the eyelids will block visual awareness more readily and completely than fingers over the ears can impede sound; of course, the tactual and kinesthetic modalities cannot be shut off at all but can only be dulled somewhat through motor inactivity or consistently monotonous stimulation. The closing of the eyes is thus more immediately associated with ideas of death; therefore, within the context of the senses, visual lack becomes the primary death symbol.

So far we have dealt only with the origin of the Oedipal archetype. What of its Tiresian counterpart? It seems likely that the two have undergone a similar line of development.

Nocturnal fears instigate fantasies of beneficent supernatural beings and forces as readily and naturally as they produce images of real or fancied hazards. The association of darkness with the supernatural thus appears to be at least one source of the Tiresian archetype. In this connection, it should be noted that darkness has traditionally had positive as well as negative symbolic value. For example, in fiction, mythology, legend, and folklore, night is often said to have the power to evoke a sense of mystery or an awe of being, even creative thought, as well as benign rest for a careworn mind. Also, the well-known Chinese Yin symbol (viz., the abiding feminine principle of the cosmos) is linked to darkness, in addition to earth, receptivity, and generativity. Darkness likewise plays a positive role in the myth of Psyche and Eros. As the story goes, Eros visits Psyche each night and makes love to her in the dark, so that she never actually sees him. Eventually, Psyche's relatives persuade her that she should try to see her lover, despite the fact that the latter wishes his identity to be kept a secret. Consequently, when the first opportunity arises—one night while Eros is in bed sleeping—she looks at him by the light of a candle. Eros, however, immediately awakens in a fury and reproves Psyche for her violation of their trust. He says love should not have to be seen in order to be believed. According to one version of the myth, he punishes Psyche by turning her into an owl. Another has her transformed into a bat. In a third version, she and Eros reconcile and live happily ever after, devoting themselves to the aid of ordinary mortals in domestic conflict. The moral of the story is that faith in one's beloved is prerequisite to the capacity for true love. In other words, for love, seeing is not believing. Rather, the situation is exactly the reverse; for love, believing is seeing. Thus, symbolizations centering on darkness are by no means always concerned with the undesirable.

A further possible starting point for the Tiresian pattern involves the age-old intuition of a relationship between visual deprivation and introspective perspicacity. Though grossly overgeneralized, this notion, if only indirectly, has some basis in fact, insofar as recent research on the effects of sensory deprivation has demonstrated marked fantasizing and even hallucinations in normal subjects experimentally deprived of visual and other types of sensory input. Also, certain studies have shown the blind to have a propensity for fantasy (Cutsforth, 1933), while others have indicated that dreams are more important to the blind than to the sighted (McCartney, 1913; Blank, 1958; von Schumann, 1959). These findings, though probably much less typical of the total blind population than the investigators in question supposed, are nonetheless apparently true of many blind people. Of the various kinds of intrapsychic processes known to psychology, dreams seem to be of central importance in the formation of the Tiresian archetype. Since prehistoric times, man has recognized the bizarre, dramatic, and uncanny verisimilitude of dream life. Indeed, these cardinal characteristics led early man to endow dreams with oracular import, a superstition that, even in the present period of relative enlightenment, has not yet altogether vanished. With this frame of reference, it makes perfectly good sense to ascribe recondite powers of dream interpretation to the sightless, who, by virtue of their handicap and the consequent curtailment of exteroceptive input, would reasonably be expected to have greater than normal access to their own dreams and, via the knowledge thereby gained, superior insight into the dreams of other human beings as well. As already indicated, just such powers have traditionally been an integral part of the positive blindness stereotype. In this connection, the supernatural status of dreams appears, to a considerable extent, to have been the original inspiration for the legendary belief in the general parapsychological prowess of the blind, e.g., the blind's alleged powers of divination and clairvoyance, which could operate apart from dreams as well as in association with them. Indeed, it is tempting to conjecture that this old attitude toward the dream constitutes the chief root of the Tiresian archetype, an even more important determinant than the darkness fantasies discussed earlier. Thus, primarily by way of imaginative extrapolation from dream power, primitive man and the ancients may gradually have bestowed on the blind person his time-honored position as sage and seer.

In any case, this view of blindness is apparently less fundamental than the Oedipal, which appears older and more deeply embedded in human thought. As pointed out previously, early primitive man did not honor the blind. The available evidence indicates that their typical fate was a speedy death that sometimes involved torture. The Tiresian constellation seems to have been much more strongly influenced by culture than its Oedipal opposite. To a large degree, it may have arisen out of a reaction formation against guilt over aggressive feelings toward the sightless. Ancient Israel affords a clear instance of a culture in which the negative stereotype substantially predated the positive. The Old Testament picture of the blind is thoroughly disdainful, with the Tiresian pattern making its first appearance in the subsequent Talmud. Similarly, in our own time, the negative stereotype obviously continues to be the most popular of the two.

In conclusion, then, the traditional stereotypes seem to be composed of elements derived both from cultural conditioning and archetypally induced fantasies, with the latter contributing the skeletal ideas (viz., the universal images) and the former the flesh and sinew of specific imaginal elaborations in different societies and historical epochs. On the present interpretation, the fantasy modes earlier discussed in connection with Freudian theory (including the castration motif) may also be regarded as products of the collective unconscious.

While the multitudes of abject blind over the centuries approximated the negative stereotype in various ways—and the exploits of a few blind geniuses no doubt encouraged the positive stereotype—it would be a serious oversimplification to impute the genesis of these conceptions solely or mainly to the behavior of the sightless themselves; for when social conditions were not too oppressive, healthy, productive adjustments were made by individuals of humble background and average mental ability. Even in an age devoid of technological aids—such as Braille, the typewriter, electronic recording devices, etc.—the blind person did not require the great talent of a Homer or a Milton in order to conduct a reasonably normal life. Countries such as Egypt and China, where useful occupations were early found for the sightless, unequivocally demonstrate this fact. In less favorably disposed civilizations (e.g., Rome), there was a smaller but still sufficient number of such cases to show the injustice of the conventional overgeneralizations (or projections); nevertheless, they persisted. At any time in history, unbiased observation would clearly have evealed that blindness is neither an asset nor a curse but, to the contrary, a major handicap which can be overcome, for all practical purposes, through patient, intelligent action despite its intrinsically stress-provoking nature.

References

Chapter 3/Blindness in the Arts

Adelman, G. 1970. *Honey out of stone.* Garden City, N.Y.: Doubleday.

Amado, J. 1962. *Gabriela, clove and cinnamon.* New York: Alfred Knopf.

Beckett, S. 1954. *Waiting for Godot.* New York: Grove Press.

Bellow, S. 1969. *Mr. Sammler's planet.* New York: Viking Press.

Blank, H. 1958. Dreams of the blind. *Psychoanalytic Quarterly* 27: 58-174.

Bontemps, A.,ed. 1963. *American Negro poetry.* New York: Hill and Wang Publications.

Burton, R., ed. 1962. *Arabian nights entertainments.* New York: Heritage Press.

Cutsforth, T. 1933. *The blind in school and society.* New York: American Foundation for the Blind.

du Maurier, D. 1946. *The king's general.* Garden City, N.Y.: Doubleday.

Eliot. T.S. 1936. *Collected poems 1909-1935.* New York: Harcourt Brace and Co.

Flores, A., ed. 1956. *Great Spanish stories.* New York: Random House.

Gershe, L. 1970. *Butterflies are free.* New York: Random House.

Golding, W. 1968. *Lord of the flies.* New York: Coward-McCann.

Hilton, J. 1941. *Random harvest.* Boston: Little, Brown.

Hobbs, J. October, 1970. The last bushman. *Argosy.* London: Fleetway Publications.

Hughes, M., ed. 1957. *John Milton: Complete poems and major prose.* New York: Odyssey Press.

Lang, A., ed. 1946. *Arabian nights.* New York: David McKay Co.

London, J. 1948. *The sea wolf.* New York: Macmillan.

Lytton, E. 1854. *The last days of Pompeii.* London: Routledge and Co.

McCartney, F. 1913. A comparative study of the dreams of the blind and the sighted with special reference to Freud's theory. Unpublished M.A. thesis, Indiana University.

Nicholson, J. U., ed. *Geoffrey Chaucer: The Canterbury Tales.* Garden City, N.Y.: International Collectors Library.

Scharl, J., ed. 1944. *Grimms' fairy tales.* New York: Pantheon Books.

Stekel, W. 1943. *Interpretation of dreams.* New York: Liveright.

Wright, W. A., ed. 1936. *The complete works of Shakespeare.* Garden City, N.Y.: Garden City Books.

Stevenson, R. 1954. *The black arrow.* Garden City, N.Y.: Doubleday.

Thomas, D. 1954. *Under milk wood.* New York: New Directions.

Townsend, G., trans. 1968. *Aesop's fables.* Garden City, N.Y.: Doubleday.

Twersky, J. 1955. *Blindness in literature: Examples of depictions and attitudes.* New York: American Foundation for the Blind.

Von Schümann, H. 1959. *Träume der Blinden.* Basel: S. Karger Co.

Williams, T. 1947. *A streetcar named desire.* New York: Random House.

Williams, T. 1964. *Three plays: The rose tatoo, camino real and sweet bird of youth.* New York: New Directions.

Wolfe, T. 1940. *You can't go home again.* New York: New American Library.

Wright, R. 1966. *Native son.* New York: Harper and Row.

4

Research on Attitudes
toward Blindness

Although the preceding historical, linguistic, and literary surveys have already disclosed much about the nature of attitudes toward blindness, we have as yet examined only three empirical investigations directly concerned with this problem, viz., Twersky's qualitative content analysis of Western literature and the psychoanalytically oriented observations of Schauer and those of Chevigny and Braverman. Consequently, in the present chapter I shall review a representative sampling of contemporary work on this topic. The published studies fall into two relatively distinct categories: (1) those employing purely qualitative methods, typically phenomenological or clinical; and (2) those utilizing quantitative measurement, e.g., questionnaires, rating scales, and standardized personality tests. Though the latter class also includes experimental investigations, it should be pointed out that in this field there exists a paucity of genuine experiments, i.e., controlled research involving manipulated independent variables. The available qualitative studies (of which the three cited above are outstanding examples), while lacking scientific rigor, tend nevertheless to be far richer in observational content and theoretical explanation than their quantitative counterparts, which are much too often marred by a failure to take adequate account of the possible role of unconscious processes, not to mention conscious or semiconscious distortive trends, in the persons under investigation. The questionnaire studies, in particular, are likely to be highly deficient in controlling answers faked in the direction of socially approved values, especially when the subjects are comparatively well-educated or intelligent. Such studies tend to use too little item disguise to overcome confounding effects of this type. Thus, at the current stage of research development, the potentially more informative quantitative techniques cannot claim any unequivocal superiority to their inherently less precise qualitative brethren. For this reason, my overview shall focus upon typical research findings rather than methodological criticism. Toward the end of the chapter, these results will also be compared with those derived from investigations of attitudes toward physical disability groups other than the blind.

Characteristic Research

Attitudes of the Sighted toward the Blind

Most studies of attitudes toward the sightless are similar to those of Twersky, Schauer, and Chevigny and Braverman in emphasizing the prevalence of negative preconceptions. Barker et al. (1952), on questioning blind people and workers for the blind, noted nearly unanimous agreement that the blind are widely viewed as helpless and dependent and are, therefore, likely to be forced into a lifestyle of socioeconomic deprivation and inferiority. Researchers tend to agree that the seeing have little understanding of the capacities of the sightless. For example, Bateman (1965) found that her sample of sighted children believed their blind peers to be quite incapable of telling time, swimming, or enjoying television. A number of studies attest to the lingering power of certain ancient superstitions regarding blindness. In an early investigation, Simmons (1949) reported that seven percent of his visually normal subjects actually believed blindness to be a punishment for sin, and twenty-four percent stated the conviction that the blind could never be happy. Bauman (1954) interviewed sightless subjects regarding their attitudes toward visual disability and found that twenty-two percent then interpreted (or had once interpreted) their handicap as a punishment. Moreover, in conferences with the professional personnel of an agency for the blind, Bauman learned that several of these workers had encountered seeing persons who were openly and markedly fearful of tactual contact with the blind out of the belief that the latter might infect them with some disease.

In my own field and clinical work, I have met with at least a dozen instances of the foregoing. For example, two syphilophobic patients, manifesting the compulsive-avoidance pattern in question, regarded the blind at large as both victims and carriers of the dreaded disease. Another sighted individual, with pronounced traits of antisocial personality but the same "blindman phobia," considered the sightless to be potentially very dangerous. This man explained his reaction thus: "They look so mean, so full of hate. I've never seen a blind guy who didn't look that way—I mean just boiling mad, like a volcano ready to explode. A few months ago, I had to buy a sandwich from one of them—you know, one of those vending stand guys. God, it was all I could do to put the money in his hand! Kept thinking he was going to haul off and punch me in the nose or maybe even try to stick a knife in me. I got even with him, though. I gave him a one and told him it was a five. So the dumb bastard gave me change for a five. Hell, he didn't know his ass from a hole in the ground." The dynamics underlying this person's fear of the blind are too blatantly obvious to require elucidation here. On the other hand, a newly blinded, adolescent neurotic characteristically experienced strong discomfort in diverse social situations entailing some form of close physical contact with seeing people, even when the contact was merely of the conventional sort—such as that involved in handshaking or dancing with the opposite sex at school parties. Before losing his vision, this boy had thought of sightless persons as "slimy creeps who are always going around trying to feel everybody's face." In his fantasies, he imagined the blind person both as "an octopus with big greasy hands at the ends of its tentacles" and as "a stupid stumblebum who never even knows where he is." In addition, several normal visually handicapped individuals have apprised me of their encounters with analogous irrational reactions on the part of sighted people.

In this connection, a young graduate student in psychology reported an occasion on which he had just begun to shake hands with a sighted woman (a dean's secretary), when quite suddenly and unexpectedly she jerked loose her hand and moved quickly away from him, as if his mere touch had been intensely aversive—even electrifying. In another situation he was about to be led through an unfamiliar university building by a seeing professor who very awkwardly seized him by the end of a little finger and, in this manner, started tugging him forward—as though the guide wished to touch as little of the blind man's body as possible, for the latter distinctly felt he was being touched after the fashion in which one handles an unclean object. After a cumbersome step or two, the young man succeeded in disengaging his finger and explained that he could be led more efficiently were he simply to take his guide by the arm. In placing his hand on the professor's arm, he noticed that the latter's body immediately stiffened, his arm, in particular, becoming as straight and rigid as a board. This extreme muscular tension again suggested to the blind man that his touch was highly unpleasant to the sighted man. My respondent further informed me that in numerous similar interpersonal situations he had experienced comparable motor reactions in seeing strangers, sometimes when shaking hands or exchanging objects by hand but more often when taking the arm of a guide. Since all of these instances involved unfamiliar people, mere ignorance regarding the blind may have produced uneasy confusion and hence the inappropriate behavior described. In fact, the blind man himself believed that such naiveté was usually, if not always, a significant contributing factor to the incidents in question. However, the pronounced peculiarity of the two cases just related convinced him that they entailed more than the commonplace naiveté about blindness, and this added element consisted of a perception of the sightless as noxious tactual objects. The above professor and secretary were appreciably beyond the average in intelligence and education and therefore should not have responded in so grossly stupid a fashion without some irrational emotional factor providing the critical stimulus to their behavior.

In his now classic study of the war blind, Gowman (1957) also stressed the extensive influence of the negative stereotype. His observations indicated that the sightless occupy a marginal status in society, in the manner of other oppressed minority groups, such as Negroes and Latin-Americans. Furthermore, their visual disorder acts upon the unenlightened seeing population as a simultaneously strange and repellent social stimulus, one tending to ignite feelings of threat, conflict, and basic impotence. The sighted are likely to avoid the blind entirely or to be unwilling to enter intimate personal relations with them. According to Gowman, such avoidance reactions are common at all class levels in our society.

In a related questionnaire investigation conducted with a group of high school seniors, Gowman found a preponderance of negative attitudes concerning the blind. The subjects ranked five disabilities relative to assumed deleterious effects upon the self and a prospective mate. Blindness was designated by eighty percent as the most personally damaging handicap. As to impact upon one's anticipated spouse, agreement was less striking, though visual loss was still viewed as the injury most threatening to marital stability. On this dimension all subjects, except middle-class males, placed blindness at the first rung of severity, while the latter group gave blindness the second position. In addition, the questionnaire contained a number of agree-disagree items pertaining to the sightless, as well as a set of multiple-choice items describing a variety of social situations involving such persons. The lower-class subjects attended chiefly to alleged inabilities of the blind, relying heavily on stereotypic projections. On the other hand, the middle-class group demonstrated a greater tendency toward acceptance of the blind, no doubt because of the stronger emphasis on humanitarian values in customary middle-class socialization. Thus, notwithstanding the fact that unfavorable evaluations of the blind occur frequently in all social classes, it appears that the better educated and economically more comfortable members of our society are somewhat less given to prejudicial rejection than are those individuals living amid the constant frustrations of an underprivileged environment.

Some investigators contend that the importance of the negative blindness stereotype has been exaggerated. For example, Rusalem (1950) found generally favorable attitudes among his 103 subjects. The latter were graduate students in a social psychology class who were administered a questionnaire enumerating a variety of physical, sociological, and psychological characteristics commonly attributed to the sightless and asking which of these were most truly typical. For the three dimensions under study, item responses stressed the following traits: (1) "physical"—use cane or dog-guide, wear dark glasses, lack facial expression; (2) "sociological"—attend separate schools, rarely work in industry, economically dependent; and (3) "psychological"—superior senses of touch and hearing, above average memory. Of these subjects, fifty-nine had formerly experienced some degree of interaction with the visually handicapped; however, their answers did not differ from those of the subjects who lacked such contacts. As can be seen, the favorable attitudes pertained exclusively to the psychological dimension and are a part of what I have called the positive blindness stereotype. On the whole, the physical attitudes are only mildly negative, while the sociological are more noticeably so.

It should be pointed out that Rusalem himself recognized certain serious methodological weaknesses in his investigation: (1) conscious answers may not have corresponded with unconscious attitudes; (2) the selection of subjects was biased; and (3) the given set of items did not permit a free expression of attitudes. Regarding the blind as well as other minority groups, one would, of course, expect graduate students, particularly in social psychology, to state more liberal beliefs than the general population, and about the latter Rusalem's findings can tell us nothing.

Lukoff and Whiteman (1961) believed that both the positive and negative stereotypes of the blind have been overemphasized. Their investigation involved the questioning of 500 blind people from New York State and three groups of sighted subjects, comprising graduate students in social work, undergraduate college students, and a noncollege sample of lower-middle-class individuals. The results suggested four important variables underlying the attitudes of the seeing toward the blind: (1) the extent to which blindness is perceived as personally frustrating; (2) the conception of blindness as distinct from attitudes toward sightless persons; (3) the degree of readiness to interact with the sightless; and (4) individual differences in intensity of feelings regarding thoughts about or interactions with the blind. The most important attitudes of the blind subjects toward the sighted may be paraphrased as follows: (1) the sighted know almost nothing about the blind and are astonished when the latter show competence of any kind; (2) the sighted tend to pity the blind and at the same time think them more courageous than the average seeing person. In addition, Lukoff and Whiteman found that their sightless subjects tended to be submissive in interpersonal relations with the seeing. These investigators concluded that the sightless were realistic in viewing the seeing as pitying and deficient in understanding of blindness, but that they were unrealistic in assigning positive and negative stereotypes to the seeing, for among the latter, approximately half of the subjects gave no indication of such tendencies and even stated that the sightless could do almost anything without aid.

The assertion that the blind greatly exaggerate stereotypic thinking among the sighted runs directly counter to the observations of most workers for the blind and many researchers in this area, not to mention the everyday life experience of countless intelligent, well-adjusted sightless persons. It would appear that Lukoff and Whiteman assumed the blind to be more paranoid than the normal population; however, hard evidence in support of such a proposition is entirely lacking. On the other hand, the methodology here employed is notorious for its susceptibility to conscious faking as well as unwitting distortion. A biasing trend toward socially desirable responses may account for the relative absence of extreme attitudes among the seeing subjects. Nevertheless, these investigators demonstrated the significance of social attitudes in relation to the psychological health of the blind person and the critical role of the family and sighted friends in promoting his self-sufficiency.

Other observers have given considerable attention to the positive, as well as the negative, stereotype. Himes (1950), for instance, distinguished between three major stereotypes of the blind in American culture: (1) "the blind beggar;" (2) "the blind genius;" and (3) "the superstition of sensory compensation." Of these, the latter two are positive. This classification is similar to mine, except that for the sake of parsimony I have combined all favorable attitudes under one category. According to Himes, such stereotypes (which he labels "cultural constructs") are practically useful, perhaps even necessary, functions of culture, in that they enable its members to organize their thoughts for reactions in relation to the myriad complexities of daily life, particularly to unusual phenomena like blindness. Despite their prejudicial or detrimental qualities, these constructs provide, at the very least, an adaptive modus operandi for coping with the environment.

Himes seems to be saying that since stereotypes have a function—viz., offering easy cognitive frames of reference that, owing to their success, become highly rigid and resistant to change—they should not be challenged too strongly because to do so would be to threaten adjustmental mechanisms of culture and be largely futile as well. Indeed, his very substitution of the term "construct" (one ordinarily applied only to specific philosophical or scientific abstractions, at least within academic parlance) dignifies stereotypic behavior by raising it from the level of unwarranted emotionalism and overgeneralization to that of a lofty, intellectual concept. This attitude strikes me as cynical. Simply by virtue of their workability and pertinacious longevity, stereotypes, for Himes, almost seem to have acquired the status of moral goodness. Regardless of any pragmatic utility or the improbability of an eventual utopia in which all men think only rationally, such modes of thought are unrealistic and often harmful to those individuals who happen to fall within the firing range of interpretation. Hime's blindness constructs may be useful to culture, but they certainly are not useful to the blind.

At this point it should be noted that most investigators in this field acknowledge a wide variety of unreasoning positive and negative attitudes toward the blind. Relatively few have concentrated upon the former, apparently because the unfavorable attitudes are considered more basic, at least in the sense that they constitute the greater social and personal problem for the blind. Indeed, some might argue that the positive stereotype is no problem at all, except, of course, as a scientific puzzle or, practically, to the extent that it impedes authentic communication and hence mutual understanding between the blind and the sighted.

Attitudes of the Blind toward Blindness

In one of the few methodologically outstanding studies in this field (to be described at length in Chapter 6) Bauman (1954) found successful social and economic adjustment in the blind to be associated with attitudes involving a realistic emotional acceptance of blindness in the blind person and his family, together with intelligence and general psychological stability in the former. The well-adjusted blind subjects, unlike those who were unsuccessful, showed a relative freedom from attitudes entailing suspicion of others, the conviction that blindness necessarily puts one at a disadvantage to the seeing, and the belief that blindness may be a punishment for sin.

Regarding adjustment to blindness, other researchers interested in attitudes have generally tended to discover similar findings. As might well be expected, those sightless individuals who nurture in themselves a belief in miraculous cure (either medical or religious) in the face of unalterable visual loss are much less likely to make satisfactory personal and vocational adjustments than those whose attitudes toward blindness are constructive (Blank, 1957; Bauman and Yoder, 1966).

Attitudes of Parents

A number of researchers have spotlighted the effects of parental attitudes upon the adjustment of blind children. In a pioneering investigation, Sommers (1944) administered the California Test of Personality to 143 sightless adolescents, along with a specially constructed questionnaire for blind youth answered by 120 members of this group. Seventy-two of the parents received an additional questionnaire, while controlled interviews were conducted with fifty of the teenagers and their parents.

Sommers's data disclosed no consistent pattern of reactions among the visually disabled, even when maladjustment existed. She found that blindness per se was not a primary cause of psychopathology. Personality deviations, when present, were generally traceable to the influence of adverse attitudes deriving from the social environment. The sightless subjects were most conscious of their defect in those social situations in which sighted persons paid particular attention to it, were over solicitous, or pitying; in sports or games demanding vision; when crossing streets, window-shopping, visiting unfamiliar places or eating with strangers. For these subjects, the chief regrets induced by blindness centered about inability or frustration regarding the following: sports, games, driving, travel, reading, movies, exhibitions, independence, normal social experience (including home life), and the appreciation of natural beauty and facial expressions. Sommers found that the blind worried considerably more about future economic security than did a comparable group of sighted youngsters. However, the major apprehensions of both groups focused upon performance in school and teachers' evaluations.

Her interviews with parents revealed a chronic sense of frustration, arising from the offspring's blindness. The case studies suggested four sources of dissatisfaction: (1) the handicapped child was perceived as evidence of divine disfavor; (2) anxiety of society's possible suspicions of parental disease; (3) guilt emanating from personal negligence or deviations from social norms, i.e., unwanted pregnancy, attempted abortion, marital conflict, and the like; and (4) the child's sightlessness was interpreted as a personal disgrace. On the other hand, parental reactions to blindness were of five types: (1) realistic acceptance of the child and his disability—such parents were loving and made out as well as they could in the patently unfortunate situation; (2) denial of the handicap and its unavoidable impact—these parents denied having suffered any painful repercussions from their child's blindness and, furthermore, would not accept the idea that he was, in fact, handicapped—their vocational and educational plans for the child indicated no recognition of his limitations, with the result that unrealistically high achievement was demanded of him; (3) maternal overprotection—such mothers were inordinately affectionate and attentive, owing to engulfing feelings of guilt or pity—in many cases the mother generally blocked the child's efforts for independence because of her unusual need for retention of the love object; (4) disguised rejection—parents in this group regarded the child's handicap as a disgrace, but aversive tendencies were masked by means of reaction formations involving an excessive, anxious concern for parental duty and the child's well being; and (5) open rejection—such parents were admittedly, though defensively, hostile, tending to project their own devaluation of the child onto teachers, doctors, or society at large. Though the foregoing reaction patterns overlapped to some degree, eighty-two percent of the parents were clearly characterized by the negative orientations, while only eighteen percent were classifiable as rationally caring and accepting. Owing to the small size of her sample, Sommers made no generalizations concerning typical patterns of parental behavior in our culture as a whole; nevertheless, her findings strongly suggested a preponderance of negative and ambivalent reactions in the majority of parents with visually handicapped children.

Sommers ascribed the adjustmental status of the sightless child very largely to the operation of maternal attitudes. In turn, the character of these attitudes was seen to stem mainly from the unique personality organization of the individual, together with the quality of her social and marital adjustment. Sommers's findings, both quantitative and qualitative, indicate that the most appropriate therapy for the disturbed blind child would be one stressing constructive attitude change on the part of his parents.

Although Sommers's study is widely recognized by authorities in this field as one of the most important investigations of its kind (e.g., Lowenfeld, 1963), critics have nonetheless pointed out serious methodological shortcomings, perhaps the most telling of which concerns an absence of independence in the ratings of parental and child attitudes. Her qualitative evidence is generally considered to be of much greater significance than her statistical findings.

Attitudes of Teachers

A comparatively recent research interest focuses on the attitudes of teachers toward visually handicapped children. In an early exploration of this problem, Murphy (1960) asked 309 instructional personnel (including special educators as well as ordinary teachers) to rate eight types of exceptional children with respect to their attractiveness as pupils and the rater's knowledgeability concerning them. The eight groups were the visually handicapped, mental retardates, the emotionally disturbed, the aurally handicapped, the gifted, the delinquent, children with speech disorders, and those otherwise physically handicapped. Barring juvenile delinquents, the visually imparied were adjudged the least preferable and the group about whom raters were most ignorant. However, special educators were inclined to rank the visually handicapped more positively than did the subjects generally. In Murphy's view, these results constituted a tentative confirmation of the proposition that favorable attitudes about teaching any given exceptional group depend largely upon knowledge of that group.

A major criticism of this study emphasizes the possibility of incongruence between the ranking of a particular group and the actual attitudes felt toward it, i.e., a teacher may rate some group low, owing to the anticipation of certain practical problems in connection with it; for instance, a teacher may not wish to make Braille a part of the instructional repertory on account of its assumed complexity and, therefore, give prospective blind pupils a low rating. Since most of Murphy's testees were poorly informed regarding the blind, such misconceptions might have been a critical determinant of scale behavior.

Attitudes of Professional Workers for the Blind.

Another important little studied topic deals with attitudes of workers for the blind (especially rehabilitation counselors) toward their clientele.

Based upon psychoanalytic experience in this area, Blank (1958)
pointed out that the work of such professionals is too often impeded by
serious unconscious conflicts and designated the following patterns as
among the most salient: (1) excessive identification with the blind client; (2)
subjective "blind spots" regarding the nature of physical blindness; (3)
repressed sadistic urges toward the client; and (4) sexually toned
countertransference reactions. To mitigate problems of this sort, Blank
recommended that psychoanalytic consultation be made accessible to
rehabilitation counselors and other professionals intimately involved with
the welfare of the blind.

In a more recent study, Janicki (1970) asked fifty-four health
professionals (involved in work with the various disability groups) to rank
twelve disabilities as to severity of impact. Blindness was considered the
most disturbing condition on the list, with motor handicaps occupying the
next position down. Findings such as these remind one of the ancient belief
that blindness is the worst of all possible physical defects (including some
that obviously entail greater practical limitations) and suggest that workers
for the blind not infrequently share a similar prejudice against those they
allegedly seek to rehabilitate.

Changing Attitudes toward Blindness

A number of observers have discussed the contemporary movement
toward increasing objectivity in public attitudes about blindness. As already
indicated, the improvement has been meaningful but by no means
dramatic or profound. Pascal (1954) has referred to the fact that the old
notion that the blind are virtually dead is *in the process of changing* to the
new attitude that, in most cases, blindness is a handicap not incompatible
with a productive, emotionally rewarding life. Likewise, as evidence of the
growing integration of the visually handicapped into sighted society,
Lowenfeld (1964) contrasted present educational, training, and vocational
opportunities with the rather bleak state of affairs that existed early in the
century. On the other hand, he also noted that society's acceptance of the
sightless is as yet far from complete, for powerful prejudices, analogous to

those inflicted upon other minorities, continue to frustrate the progress of the blind. In this connection, Lowenfeld stressed the fact that bigoted attitudes toward the blind are highly correlated with similar attitudes toward Negroes and Jews as well as with the authoritarian personality. Thus, historically, the changes in question are part of a long transitional phase—with our culture now being somewhere between the gross cruelty and superstition of the past and the true egalitarianism of a still merely fantasized future.

Recent studies designed to test various techniques for producing constructive changes in attitudes toward the disabled have met with ambiguous results.

Concentrating upon employers' attitudes, Fletcher (1970) used a direct confrontation technique involving one group of well-experienced rehabilitation counselors and two representative employer groups, one of which was generally uninformed concerning the work capacities of the disabled, while the other was comparatively knowledgeable and progressive in its employment practices. The counselor-employer discussions focused on six types of handicap: paralysis, epilepsy, cardiac disorder, facial scar, blindness, and deafness. Regarding the employment suitability of individuals thus impaired, employers' rankings gave the least favorable position to the first three categories, the most favorable to the last three. The employers did not show any generalized reaction pattern toward all six of the disability groups but tended to express specific attitudes and concerns about each. For two kinds of jobs (those of clerk-typist and desk sales), the discussions appeared to culminate in at least moderate positive change, with attitudes of hiring reluctance being generally reduced, as all the handicapped groups were finally adjudged equally capable. Fletcher considered these findings as evidence of the utility of the small group discussion technique for educating the public on the true nature of physical disability.

Investigations like the above are, however, always suspect to the extent that verbalized attitude improvement is by no means necessarily associated with a similar change in actual employment practices. Therefore, in the absence of appropriate follow-up research, it is difficult, if not impossible, to ascertain the practical implications of studies such as Fletcher's. The latter's own review of previous research on this topic indicated that employers' attitudes toward the disabled are generall negative. If such attitudes are in fact as widespread and deeply ingraine as they sometimes seem to be, then Fletcher's conclusions regarding th value of the encounter group approach may well be overoptimistic.

In an experiment dealing with the attitudes of seeing college studen toward the blind, Cole (1971) also utilized the small group methc and found it to be only mildly effective in inducing positive attitude chang The experimental and control groups, which contained an equal number (males and females and met for six weekly fifty-minute discussion sessior in child psychology, differed chiefly in the fact that the former include three blind male accomplices, and the latter did not. All subjects we administered the California Personality Inventory both before and after th experiment, while their attitudinal behavior in the group discussic situations was assessed via the Bales' Interaction Process Analys procedure. In addition, each subject described the nature of his experienc with blind people prior to the experiment. An overall comparison of th experimental contact and control noncontact groups revealed little in th way of statistically significant differences. However, when the subjects we examined with respect to presence versus absence of previous contacts, th group interaction data clearly showed that those claiming no suc encounters tended to express strong stereotypic responses, either positive (negative, with the latter's attitudes, moreover, changing significantly to th positive as a result of experimental contact. On the other hand, r meaningful results were obtained from subjects' scores on the Californ Personality Inventory. Also, the subjects who reported prior experience wi the blind (both favorable and unfavorable) were not measurably affecte (neither in a more positive nor a more negative direction) by th programmed contact. The investigator concluded that the original conta with a blind person or group is crucial to attitude formation or alteration the sighted.

Cole's results are fairly pessimistic, in that they imply very sever limitations for all efforts to improve attitudes toward the blind by means (public education techniques. They suggest that this approach is likely influence only those seeing persons who are thoroughly naive about th sightless, for negative attitudes among the more experienced of the sighte would tend to be largely impervious to amelioration, even when th

periences in question were narrow and distorted and the subsequent
dactic information is comprehensive and objective. In this connection,
any blind people, as well as workers for the blind, have long since
come disillusioned with the hortatory instructional strategy (the latter
ing best exemplified by the numerous brief messages, programs, and
ticles in the mass media concerning the capacities of the handicapped)
d urge, instead, all blind to unite for the purpose of constructive political
tion. As indicated earlier, the National Federation of the Blind, through its
stematic lobbying campaigns, has been notably successful in bringing
out needed civil rights legislation on behalf of the blind of this country.
le's experiment suggests at least one major reason for the weakness of
lucational devices to enlarge objectivity in attitudes toward the blind.

titudes toward Other Disability Groups

Research findings in general indicate that attitudes toward the blind
d other disability groups are highly comparable. Wright (1960) found
at publicly verbalized attitudes toward the physically handicapped were,
the whole, mildly favorable, while McDaniel (1969), after reviewing
bsequent investigations in this area, has attested to the generality of
right's earlier observation. However, it should be pointed out that such
dies are typically plagued with the same methodological problems
eviously referred to in connection with research exclusively concerned
ith attitudes toward blindness. Thus, at the present time, we simply do not
ow to what extent the verbalized attitudes in question reflect actual
titudes or behavior toward the handicapped, though common-sense
servations, not to mention a number of empirical studies, suggest that
ue attitudes are more negative than positive—a condition that would
count for the fact that various forms of social and economic
scrimination constitute a nearly universal problem for the disabled in our
ciety.

McDaniel found the concepts of "devaluation" and "spread"
pecially applicable to the understanding of attitudes toward disabilities in
neral. Devaluation consists of disparaging social and personal attitudes
garding the given disability, involving heightened inferiority feelings in
e handicapped person and prejudicial reactions on the part of others—

the latter characteristically including imputations of dependency an
helplessness, as well as proclivities toward overprotection or rejectio
Spread occurs when the handicapped individual's self-devaluation i
generalized beyond the boundaries of his actual defect to encompa
unaffected organismic functions, so that he may come to regard himself o
more extensively disabled than he is in fact. Both spread and devaluatio
pose serious impediments to effective rehabilitation, regardless of th
disability under consideration.

According to McDaniel, the most trustworthy, empirical findings i
this field are as follows: (1) there is no single, universal stereotype of th
physically handicapped—McDaniel stressed the fact that people tend t
distort positive, as well as negative, attitudes; (2) prejudicial attitude
toward ethnic minorities and other social groups are associated with simil
prejudices toward the handicapped; and (3) the extent of favorabl
attitudes toward the handicapped varies with age, sex, maturity, an
perhaps level of education and intellectual sophistication.

Both individually and in collaboration, Lukoff and Whiteman (196
1965; 1967) distinguished between attitudes toward handicappin
conditions and those toward handicapped people, maintaining that th
given disorder is more negatively viewed than the person afflicted with i
Although their subjects generally thought blindness more disabling an
more frightening than other defects, these investigators also found that th
blind, as persons, were evaluated similarly to handicapped people at large

An obvious weakness of the above position is that it tends to overloo
the fact that abhorrence of disabling conditions is often generalized to th
persons possessing them. In our society that idealizes egalitarian value
few people are willing to admit to antihumanitarian prejudices of any kin
hence it is not at all surprising that most respondents evaluate handicappe
persons more favorably than handicapping conditions. The conditions a
patently undesirable, and one would be a fool not to regard them as suc
However, the persons in question, regardless of how they are tru
assessed, remain human beings and, qua human, are culturally dictated t
be of "inalienable worth"; to regard them as anything less would b
tantamount to a confession of poor sportsmanship—that is, failure to pla
by the rules of the cultural game. Until such propensities for dissimulatio
both conscious and unconscious, can be more effectively controlled, or

ould do well to take the findings of interview and questionnaire studies
ith a grain or two of salt. Common observation reveals widespread
ejudice against physically handicapped persons, yet Lukoff and
hiteman chose to trust their subjects' relatively positive verbal reports and
nsequently suggested that the negative attitudes in question mainly
ncern defects, not the people associated with defects. Thus, the role of
ejudice is gratuitously minimized, for the unfavorable attitudes about
efects per se are largely objective. This implication seems to me
avoidable, notwithstanding the fact that Lukoff and Whiteman
cognized the considerable frequency with which the damaging effects of
e various disabilities are exaggerated by the physically normal.

My study of the blind in artistic productions disclosed a plethora of
sitive and negative prejudicial depictions, not only in works of the remote
recent past but also in those of our own period. Though I did not consider
e handicapped in general, casual observation suggests highly similar
rtrayals for all major disability groups. For example, in D. H. Lawrence's
dy Chatterley's Lover, the crippled Clifford Chatterley is sexually
potent, selfish, irritable, childish, and spiritually shallow; in Hugo's *The
unchback of Notre Dame*, the deformed Quasimodo is pathetically
mple-minded, almost too grotesque a figure to play the sublime, tragic
rt for which he obviously is intended; in Gide's *La Symphonie Pastorale*,
e blind Gertrude has been irresponsibly raised by an ignorant, seclusive,
af grandmother. I could easily multiply such instances, but perhaps these
e sufficient to illustrate the point—namely, that here it is not only the
efect that is abominated but also the person having it. It is my conviction
at the arts, especially in their literary forms, often uncover deeper
ychological truths than do the traditional methods of modern behavioral
ience. At least in respect to attitudes about blindness, one will learn
mensely more from literature, folklore, and mythology than from any of
e more conventional brands of attitude research with their armamen-
rium of rating scales, standardized questionnaires, statistical analyses,
d so forth. Thus, it appears that Lukoff and Whiteman (as well as
cDaniel, who accepted their viewpoint) seriously underestimated the
tent to which negative attitudes toward physically deviant individuals
fluence the thought and behavior of the general population—though I
jree with McDaniel that unfavorable evaluations cannot be satisfactorily

explained solely on the basis of the "social prejudice" theory. As already pointed out, such tendencies are apparently overdetermined and involve potent intrapsychic factors (such as castration anxiety and primal fantasies), as well as ordinary, prejudicial attitudes based on authoritarianism, simple ignorance, or conformity to stereotypic cultural norms. Indeed, I would contend that the core component of antidisability prejudice arises chiefly from intrapsychic forces entailing images, preconceptions, and fantasies pertaining to one's own body integrity—with commonplace social pressures playing a merely secondary role.

In a fairly recent investigation focusing on attitudes of acceptance versus rejection, De-Levie (1966) found the latter type to be particularly characteristic of individuals who were comparatively uninformed concerning the limitations and capacities of disabled people generally. His 180 subjects fell into three groups, each containing thirty males and thirty females: (1) laymen; (2) untrained rehabilitation workers; and (3) trained rehabilitation professionals. All subjects were white. Attitudes toward the disabled were assessed by means of the Social Attitudes Picture Test and the Social Attitudes Picture Ratings. In addition, subjects were questioned about their previous contact, private or professional, with disabled persons. The central finding was that subjects preferred the nondisabled both as coworkers and as friends, regardless of the stimulus individual's race or sex, with the strongest such preference being expressed by laymen, the weakest by trained professionals, while a middle position was occupied by untrained rehabilitation workers. Furthermore, the disabled were generally more acceptable as co-workers than as friends, and females were more accepting of them than were males, regardless of prior degree of contact. This investigator found that the disabled were perceived as being profoundly different from physically normal people, solely by reason of disability; they were not seen as people *with disabilities* but as *disabled people*—the "spread phenomenon" applies as much to the physically normal's perception of the handicapped person as it does to the latter's self-perception. Regarding the shaping of attitudes toward the disabled, it was concluded that early, close, and extensive interaction with disabled individuals is of fundamental importance for the establishment of rational, accepting tendencies. Moreover, such experiences should be required of all persons who seek to become rehabilitation workers.

De-Levie's findings and conclusions are, of course, strikingly at variance with those of Lukoff and Whiteman.

Further empirical findings that run counter to the Lukoff-Whiteman interpretation are those of Noonan et al. (1968), who investigated attitudes concerning a variety of visible disabilities. While these researchers did not deal with blindness, their results were quite comparable to those obtained in analogous studies of attitudes about blindness. The physical conditions of interest were wheelchair confinement, amputation, and facial disfigurement. The subjects, who consisted of 240 college females drawn from elementary psychology courses, were administered the following assessment instruments: (1) the Bass Social Acquiescence Scale, to measure tendencies toward cultural conformity; (2) Barron's Ego-Strength Scale, to assess level of personality integration; (3) the California F Scale, for the measurement of authoritarianism; (4) the Barratt-Fruchter Chair Window Test, to evaluate field dependence versus independence; (5) Secord and Gourard's Body-Cathexis Scale and Secord's Homonym Test, for assessing extent of body satisfaction and concern; (6) the Marlowe-Crowne Social Desirability Scale, to ascertain degree of false-positive response bias; and (7) Granofsky's Pictures Test and a modified form of the Yuker, Block and Campbell Attitudes toward Disabled Persons Scale, to assess attitudes regarding visible disability.

A correlational analysis of the ensuing test scores revealed a number of significant relationships: (1) the F Scale correlated positively with both disability measures (significant at the 0.01 level of confidence)—moreover, the relationship between the F Scale and the Social Desirability Scale was slight and not statistically significant; (2) body satisfaction, though significantly related to both disability criteria (at the 0.05 level), was at the same time similarly correlated with social desirability response bias—hence body satisfaction, as here measured, was of dubious import for disability attitudes; (3) ego strength and field independence correlated at the 0.05 level of significance with one disability measure (viz., the Attitudes toward Disabled Persons Scale), but ego strength was also significantly related to social desirability and, therefore, cannot be ascribed any appreciable influence on attitudes toward visible disabilities—at least not ego strength as it is assessed by the Barron scale; and (4) cultural conformity, as measured in this study, was not associated with disability attitudes.

Thus, the most impressive result was the strong relationship between disability attitudes and authoritarianism, which, indeed, was the highest correlation of the study. The investigators regarded the handicapped at large as occupants of a minority group, equivalent to that of ethnic minorities, and suggested that both types of minority are customary targets of prejudicial attitudes arising from the same source, viz., authoritarian personality. Thus, authoritarianism was seen as the chief determinant of all irrational attitudes toward the disabled.

The meaningfulness of the foregoing results and conclusions rests primarily upon two considerations: (1) the conceptual and technical quality of the assessment procedures employed; and (2) the extent to which empirical dimensions relevant to disability attitudes were actually covered by the methodology of the study. Since the tests of ego strength and body satisfaction were contaminated by the presence of a socially desirable response bias, the instruments in question were apparently inadequate to tap the variables they purported to measure; consequently, one cannot legitimately conclude anything as to the influence of ego strength and body satisfaction on disability attitudes, though both, if properly measured, are conceivably important. Likewise, the lack of attitudinal relationship to cultural conformity may merely reflect the weakness of the Bass scale. While authoritarianism was the critical factor in this investigation, the conclusion that it is the major determinant of disability prejudice is unwarranted, since a number of possibly relevant variables (mainly intrapsychic ones, such as castration anxiety or the symbolic equation of disability with castration) were not even examined.

Some researchers have been primarily interested in taxonomy and test construction. For example, Siller et al. (1968), in a factor analysis study, attempted to identify the basic constituents in attitudes toward three classes of physical deviation: amputation, blindness, and cosmetic abnormality. Their 253 demographically varied subjects were given a series of exploratory questionnaires designed to tap attitudes to these physical conditions as well as certain variables not necessarily related to such attitudes, authoritarianism and physical health in particular. The resulting data, on statistical analysis, yielded eleven distinct factors, most of which were common only to blindness and amputation. These factors and the traits comprised by them are summarized below.

(1) Interaction strain (common to all three conditions): in diverse

social situations, pronounced anxiety, uncertainty, and embarrassment when in the presence of a disabled or disfigured person.

(2) Rejection of intimacy (applicable to each deviation): unwillingness to enter close, mainly familial, relations with such persons.

(3) Generalized rejection (pertinent only to amputation and blindness): a blanket negative orientation, including the advocacy of segregation and other practices detrimental to these individuals, viz., intense prejudice, hostility, aggression and revulsion.

(4) Reluctant aversion (cosmetic disfigurement alone): similar to "generalized rejection" above, but less massive, and involving guilt over the aversive reaction.

(5) Authoritarian virtuousness (blindness and amputation only): comprising authoritarianism together with superficially positive evaluations of the disabled, e.g., the attribution of valued gifts and personal traits, the recommendation of beneficial treatment, with the testee describing himself as highly warm and sympathetic to the disabled.

(6) Superficial empathy (cosmetic deviation only): paralleling "authoritarian virtuousness" to the extent that the individuals in question are assigned certain special characteristics, some of which are positive.

(7) Inferred emotional consequences (amputation and blindness): massively hostile assessment of the handicapped person's character and emotions, involving the ascription of self-consciousness, irritability, and hypersensitivity, with psychopathology considered a typical consequence.

(8) Distress identification (amputation and blindness): a degree of active identification with the disabled individual, largely representing him as a stimulus that triggers anxiety over one's own weaknesses.

(9) Functional overlimitation (amputation and blindness): the imputation of dependency and generalized organismic and economic limitations to the handicapped.

(10) Direct personal aversion (cosmetic disfigurement exclusively): open emotional repugnance to the conditions in question, which are of a type usually believed to be controllable.

(11) Proximate offensiveness (cosmetic condition): disgust over close body contact, involving moral indignation and stigmatization of the individual whose deviations are presumably controllable.

On the basis of these statistically derived factors, Siller et al. concluded that the disability attitude domain is multidimensional and not unidimensional, as other investigators have so frequently assumed.

It is here worth noting that the factor analysis method does not in itself invariably produce optimally appropriate taxonomies, since any given classification is perforce limited by the measuremental ingredients out of which it is constructed. If these incorporate too narrow a range of observations, the emerging taxonomy is bound to be inadequate. Despite its great classificatory utility, factor analysis often creates a merely factitious set of distinctions, statistically meaningful but largely irrelevant to the real world of everyday life behavior. The Siller et al. scheme may indeed possess greater merit than previous classifications (at least with respect to the three conditions studied); but, if so, this superiority would not arise simply by virtue of the quantitative rigor of their method.

Comments

Determining the extent to which verbalized attitudes accurately reflect ordinary, daily behavior is an old and, as yet, unremoved thorn in the side of social-psychological research. The same general problem, of course, continually crops up in studies specifically concerned with attitude toward the blind and the physically handicapped. Unfortunately, it is a problem that investigators in this field usually choose to ignore, owing to the practical methodological difficulties it necessarily entails. Consequently, until more systematic attention is devoted to characteristic behavior patterns in the natural social environment, the results of attitude studies will at best remain modest in value.

References

Chapter 4/Attitudes toward Blindness

Barker, R., Wright, B., Meyerson, L. & Gonick, M. 1952. *Adjustment to physical handicap and illness: A survey of the social psychology of physique and disability.* New York: Social Science Research Council, Bulletin no. 55.

Bateman, B. 1965. Sighted children's perceptions of blind children's abilities. New York: American Foundation for the Blind, *Research Bulletin,* no. 8.

Bauman, M. 1954. *Adjustment to blindness.* Commonwealth of Pennsylvania: Pennsylvania State Council for the Blind.

Bauman, M. & Yoder, N. 1966. *Adjustment to blindness reviewed.* Springfield, Ill. Charles C. Thomas.

Blank, H. 1958. Countertransference problems in the professional worker. *New Outlook for the Blind* 52: 185-188.

Blank, H. 1957. Psychoanalysis and blindness. *Psychoanalytic Quarterly* 26: 1-24.

Cole, F. 1971. Contact as a determinant of sighted persons' attitudes toward the blind. Unpublished Ph.D. dissertation, Florida State University.

De-Levie, A. 1966. Attitudes of laymen and professionals toward physical and social disability. Unpublished Ph.D. dissertation. Columbia University.

Fletcher, C. 1970. Employment and the disabled. Unpublished Ph.D. dissertation, University of Houston.

Gowman, A. 1957. *The war-blind in American social structure.* New York: American Foundation for the Blind.

Himes, J. 1950. Some concepts of blindness in American culture. *Social Casework* 31:416.

Janicki, M. 1970. Attitudes of health professionals toward twelve disabilities. *Perceptual and Motor Skills* 30: 77-78.

Lowenfeld, B. 1963. Psychological problems of children with impaired vision. In W. Cruickshank, ed. *Psychology of exceptional children and youth.* 2nd ed. Englewood Cliffs, N.J.: Prentice-Hall.

Lowenfeld, B. 1964. The social impact of blindness upon the individual. *New Outlook for the Blind* 58: 273-277.

Lukoff, I. 1967. *The social sources of adjustment to blindness: a study of role differentiation.* New York: Columbia University.

Lukoff, I. & Whiteman, M. 1961. Attitudes toward blindness: Preliminary findings. *New Outlook for the Blind* 55: 39-44.

Lukoff, I. & Whiteman, M. 1964. Attitudes toward blindness. Paper presented at convention of American Federation of Catholic Workers for the Blind, New York.

McDaniel, J. 1969. *Physical disability and human behavior.* Elmsford, N.Y.: Pergamon.

Murphy, A. 1960. Attitudes of educators toward the visually handicapped. *Sight-saving Review* 30: 157-161.

Noonan, J., Barry, J. & Davis, H. 1968. Personality determinants of attitudes toward visible disability. New York: American Foundation for the Blind.

Pascal, J. 1954. Changing attitudes toward the blind and partially sighted. *American Journal of Optometry* 31: 319-324.

Rusalem, H. 1950. The environmental supports of public attitudes toward the blind. *New Outlook for the Blind* 44: 277-288.

Siller, J., Ferguson, L., Vann, D. & Holland, B. 1968. Structure of attitudes toward the physically disabled: The Disability Factor Scale. *Proceedings of the 76th Annual Convention of the American Psychological Association* 3: 651-652.

Simmons, H. 1949. The attitudes of the sighted toward the blind. Paper presented at convention of American Association of Workers for the Blind, Washington.

Sommers, V. 1944. *The influence of parental attitudes and social environment on the personality development of the adolescent blind.* New York: American Foundation for the Blind.

Whiteman, M. & Lukoff, I. 1965. Attitudes toward blindness and other physical handicaps. *Journal of Social Psychology* 66: 135-145.

Wright, B. 1960. *Physical disability: A psychological approach.* New York: Harper.

II

**Blindness and
Personality**

5

Prominent Sightless Persons

From earliest times to the present, there have been innumerable instances of outstanding achievement on the part of blind persons. Most of this group were musicians, poets, and humanistic scholars; some were scientists, mathematicians, politicians, and lawyers. While the majority lost their vision adventitiously after a lengthy period of normal sight, many of them, including some of the most distinguished, were congenitally blind or became sightless during early childhood. That blindness, in itself, does not retard mental growth is amply proved by their success. The biographical sketches and notes that follow, though historically comprehensive, are by no means exhaustive, for I have focused upon the blind in Western civilization and have considered only those individuals who were known for reasons other than blindness or services rendered to the blind.

The Ancient Period

In early Greece, a number of gifted blind men attained prominence. For example, Timoleon, the eminent statesman of Syracuse, was sightless. His people considered him a prophet and saluted him when he entered their assemblies. His advice was sought on all public business, and on his death, he was given an elaborate state funeral. Timoleon was old when he lost his sight. Perhaps more important was the blind Stesichorus, who lived in the sixth century B.C. and won lasting distinction as an innovative lyric poet.

Moreover, the immortal Homer is said to have been blind. The facts of his life are obscure. Herodotus said he was an Asiatic Greek of the ninth century B.C. Other historians have located him as early as 1200 B.C. It is widely believed that he was born in Smyrna. According to tradition, he was a wayfaring bard, whose extensive journeying by land and sea filled him with the vast knowledge that was to issue in *The Iliad* and *The Odyssey*. In Ithaca he lost his vision through an eye disease. Much later he lived in Chios, where he founded a school of poetry and produced *The Odyssey*. In time, he set sail for Athens, but his ship was forced to land at Samos, where he passed the winter singing in the abodes of the wealthy. In the spring, he once more embarked for Athens, but while en route, he fell ill and died. He was buried at Ios, in a quiet spot near the sea. Thus runs the legend (Ross, 1951).

Homer is thought to have become blind rather early in life, before finishing *The Iliad* or beginning *The Odyssey*. Dionysius Cassius Longinus the third-century Platonist and teacher of philosophy in Athens, referred to *The Iliad* as Homer's "mid-day," *The Odyssey* as his "setting sun." Some historians regarded these poems as compilations from the works of numerous blind bards. On the other hand, Herodotus, Plutarch, Cicero, and other objective commentators believed that Homer had actually lived and that he created the great epics credited to his name, having, moreover been blind when he did so.

In Rome, too, there occasionally appeared a few outstanding sightless citizens. In the fourth century B.C., the still young Republic was governed by the blind Appius Claudius, functioning in the capacity of dictator. He inaugurated reforms that benefited the plebeians and promoted Latin prose and oratory. Cicero, Livy, Plutarch, and other praised his eloquence. It was said that no one should call him blind since his wisdom was the "eye of the state."

In Imperial Rome, Marcus Livius Drusus, Aemilius Paulus, and Pontius Lupus were all distinguished sightless lawyers. The litigations of the latter two habitually drew large audiences, while Drusus, in addition to interpreting the law, compiled legal records and was a respected author.

Among the more noteworthy blind Roman scholars were Asconius Pedianus and Cornelius Aufidius. The former, a historian, was an old man when his vision failed. However, after he became blind, he continued his work and spent twelve years writing commentaries on the masterpieces of Cicero. His own treatises on grammar were highly respected for their beauty of style. Aufidius, on the other hand, was young when blindness struck. Nevertheless, he became a senator and wrote a history of Greece.

In China, Tsoch'iuming, the historian and follower of Confucius, was perhaps the most important blind man of the ancient period. He compiled an elaborate narrative of China's feudal era, a work greatly esteemed by subsequent Chinese historians. Tsoch'iuming has been dubbed ''the father of Chinese prose.''

However, some authorities, like French (1932), have regarded Didymus of Alexandria (308-395 A.D.) as the greatest sightless scholar of antiquity. He became blind at the age of five. By means of an alphabet carved in wood, he learned to read and construct words and sentences. Yet the bulk of his studying was accomplished through hired readers. He was apparently more energetic than his numerous sighted assistants, as his enthusiasm for learning frequently exhausted them long before the master was ready to cease the day's work. In this manner, he accumulated vast knowledge in theology and Biblical literature and became one of the leading expositors of his time. The broad scope of his erudition encompassed pagan philosophy, mathematics, astronomy, and music. While a professor at the University of Alexandria, he grew famous as a theologian and teacher. He significantly influenced the early Christian church through his students, many of whom later became prominent ecclesiastics. The most important of these was St. Jerome. According to legend, St. Anthony, the first Christian monk, left his holy wilderness hermitage solely for the purpose of visiting Didymus, whose wisdom and immense education he revered.

The Middle Ages and the Renaissance

In Spain, during the early twelfth century, the blind Abul Hasan Rudezi was an immensely prolific creator of both secular and religious verse. He was also a physician and rabbi and eloquently defended Judaism in his major philosophical work. Rudezi owned 200 slaves and, consequently, led a life of luxurious ease.

Some noteworthy sightless monarchs were Bela II of twelfth-century Hungary, the scholarly King John of fourteenth-century Bohemia, and Basil II of Russia, who, during the fifteenth century, victoriously fought to establish the autonomy of the Russian church.

However, the most illustrious blind leader by far was Johann Ziska, the learned general of fifteenth-century Bohemia. His blindness resulted from wounds received in two separate battles, but this handicap did not diminish his fighting spirit. He loved to be with his troops in the thick of the action and was with them at the Battle of Kamnitz in 1442. On another, more dramatic occasion, Ziska, armed with a pole-axe, led his soldiers against the emperor Sigismund of Hungary. Owing to his prodigious geographical recall, he was able to plan military strategy without sighted assistance. His sightlessness inspired superstitious fear and awe among his enemies, who likened him to Samson. Despite his disability, Ziska was an exemplary leader, and his reputation soon spread throughout Europe. He was not only known for his military exploits but also for his enlightened social reforms and patronage of scholarship.

During this period, there also arose in Europe a number of outstanding professional scholars, some of whom had lost their sight in early life.

In Belgium, Nicaise de Voerda (1440-1492) was stricken with blindness at the age of three. Even so, he was later to teach canon and civil law at the University of Cologne. Because of his meritorious service, he was ordained as a priest by special dispensation from the pope. At the same time, Johannes Ferdinand, a Belgian blind since infancy, became a professor of fine arts in Paris and wrote several works in Latin. He gained distinction as a poet, musician, orator, and philosopher.

Also in Paris, Pierre Pontanus, during the early sixteenth century, dedicated himself to science and literature and produced treatises on rhetoric and poetry writing. Pontanus was three years old when he lost his vision. Jean Passerat (1534-1602), another Frenchman, was one of the most talented of these blind scholars. In honor of his accomplishments, he was awarded the Chair of Latin at the College de France in 1572. Later, in seventeenth-century France, Blaise François, Comte de Pagan (who had been blinded in adulthood), wrote what was adjudged at the time a military classic on the laws of attack and defense. In addition, the Comte was an astronomer, engineer, and mathematician. His astronomical tables and geometrical theorems were as much respected as his military treatise. He was also considered a brilliant conversationalist, with the result that his home in Paris was frequented by the educated citizenry of his day, as well as courtiers of Louis XIV. The blind Bourchenu de Valbonnais, a contemporary and fellow countryman of the Comte, was similarly revered as a literary historian.

In Italy, the most gifted sightless scholar during this period was Ludovigo Scapinelli (1585-1633). Though blind from infancy, he was to become an eminent philologist and poet. His erudition won him an appointment as Professor of Rhetoric at the University of Bologna, and in time he was to teach at other famous European universities. He translated a portion of Virgil and turned out numerous treatises on Livy, Horace, and Seneca, among others. In the Europe of his day, this man's scholarship was widely acclaimed.

In sixteenth-century Germany, Jacob Schegkius, without vision from early childhood, taught medicine and philosophy at Tubingen and wrote with distinction in these fields. Also in Germany, during the following century, the blind G.E. Rumpf taught physics at the University of Hanau. Moreover, he was a noted naturalist and authored a twelve-volume work on botany. Another recognized German scholar of this period was Uldrich Schonberg, blinded by smallpox when he was three years of age. Schonberg taught at several German universities and was well versed in mathematics and languages, as well as moral and natural philosophy. Furthermore, Johannes Kepler, the great German astronomer (whose work made possible the subsequent revolutionary discoveries of Sir Isaac Newton), was seriously handicapped visually, though not quite blind.

Of the sightless minstrels (whose number in Europe was legion during these centuries), the most famous was fourteenth-century Scotland's Blind Harry. Though congenitally blind, he composed poetry, sang, and traveled extensively. He was a beggar but reputedly possessed a smattering of knowledge in theology, languages, classical history, and astronomy. Blind Harry was well known throughout Europe. A further prominent bard was the seventeenth-century Irishman, Torlogh O'Carolan. At the age of fourteen, he suffered an attack of smallpox that completely destroyed his sight. O'Carolan wandered over the Irish countryside, performing for hospitality at private estates. He played the harp, sang, and composed. During his lifetime, he created at least 200 popular songs.

During the late medieval and Renaissance periods, there flourished among the blind a number of accomplished formal musicians. The Florentine Francisco Landino (1325-1397), a composer as well as performer, was one of the most notable members of this small, but honored, class. Yet still more important was Francisco Salinas (1513-1590), who ranked among the most talented of early musical scholars. He was born in Burgos, Spain, and lost his vision while an infant. During childhood, he sang well and showed great aptitude for the organ. A friend of the family taught him Latin in exchange for organ instruction. Later, his father, the city treasurer, sent him to the University of Salamanca, where he specialized in Greek, philosophy, and the arts. A powerful cardinal soon obtained patronage for him in Rome, where he played the organ for the church aristocracy and eventually was made an abbot by the pope. His masterpiece, *De Musica*, resulted from a thirty-year intensive investigation of the history of music. It was, for its day, an academic bombshell and affected musical scholarship all over Europe. On returning to Spain, Salinas was made a professor at the University of Salamanca. A German contemporary of this master, Casper Krumbhorn (sightless since the age of three), likewise achieved wide recognition for his compositions and prowess with the organ, flute, and violin. Krumbhorn also directed an important musical academy. He died in 1621.

Although music and poetry have always been the typical vocations of the artistic blind, history additionally reveals a few cases of successful blind sculptors. Probably the earliest such example was Giovanni da Gambasi in Renaissance Italy, who became sightless at the age of twenty. He then gave up sculpture but returned to it ten years later. His busts of the pope and other members of the nobility were well received and brought him a distinguished reputation among his fellow Italians. His method consisted in palpating the model, then working from memory. A similar approach has been employed by the respected contemporary French sculptor, Tourneau, who lost an arm, as well as his vision, during World War I.

The Modern Era

After Homer, the greatest of all gifted blind men was, without doubt, John Milton (1608-1674). Although Milton did not become totally blind until the age of forty-four, his major works (*Paradise Lost, Paradise Regained,* and *Samson Agonistes*) were composed after vision had failed. The exact cause of his sightlessness remains unknown. However, his political enemies ascribed it to divine retribution for his "sinful" support of the Puritan movement. One of his more articulate opponents referred to him as "a monster—hideous, misshapen, shriveled, and blind." Milton, in good humor, retorted that he was being equated with the Cyclops. However, such accusations must, to some extent, have been taken seriously, for he felt compelled to defend himself against them. In any event, his vision had always been weak. At the age of thirty-four, he lost all sight in the left eye, while the right (already impaired) gradually deteriorated to the point of complete blindness.

During his sighted period, Milton was an erudite champion of Puritanism and wrote numerous pamphlets in its behalf. The earliest of these, *On Reformation in England and the Causes that Hitherto Have Hindered It,* was published in 1641. Thereafter, he was a highly controversial figure, much hated by the Royalists and Catholics. He spoke out against decadence in church and state and argued for divorce and freedom of the press. He was the star propagandist of the approaching Commonwealth. Once in power, Cromwell named Milton Secretary of State for Foreign Tongues. Blindness, however, dampened his political ambitions and led him to concentrate his energies upon poetry, an art in which he had already demonstrated brilliance. By the time of the Restoration, he had entirely forsaken politics and was devoting himself exclusively to poetry.

In 1665, Milton dictated *Paradise Lost* to a Quaker secretary, Thomas Ellwood, as well as to his two daughters, who, incidentally, were not interested in their father's work and found both it and him irksome. The great epic was published in 1667, and by 1700 it was generally acknowledged as a classic. *Samson Agonistes* and *Paradise Regained* appeared in 1671. The former is of considerable psychological significance in that it throws much light on Milton's feelings about blindness, far more than do any of his other writings that also deal with this subject. (For more detailed information, see Chapter 3.)

Milton's private life was relatively tranquil. Although his first marriage ended in divorce and a second in the untimely death of his wife, the third was lasting and apparently happy. Despite his frequent attacks of gout and periodic depressions, Milton's friends usually saw him as cheerful. He was regarded as a first-rate conversationalist, owing to his immense learning and satirical turn of mind. He loved language and was fluent in eight. Also, he played the organ and viol and liked to sing madrigals. His blindness, though a tragedy for him, was perhaps a boon to world literature, for had he remained sighted, it seems likely that politics would have continued as his chief line of endeavor, with the result that his great poems would never have been written.

Another blind genius of this period was the distinguished English mathematician, Nicholas Saunderson (1682-1739). He was rendered sightless by smallpox when a year old. On the special recommendation of Isaac Newton, Saunderson was appointed Professor of Mathematics at Cambridge University. He was considered an outstanding teacher and lectured on optics, as well as mathematics. He became a fellow of the Royal Society in 1719, and in 1728 George II personally honored him with a doctorate of laws. In addition, Saunderson invented the first arithmetic board for the blind, the basis of contemporary mathematical equipment for the visually handicapped. His example attracted scientific attention to the mental capacities of the blind, as illustrated by the previously mentioned pioneering studies of Diderot.

Though Saunderson led a cloistered academic existence, he was known as a witty conversationalist and a bold, outspoken agnostic. However, his family life was fraught with frustration; mainly, it appears, because of irritability and self-centeredness on his part rather than any particular fault in his wife, son or daughter. He was often uncongenial toward all three, whom the community generally regarded to be unhappy.

The eminent Swiss mathematician and astronomer, Leonhard Euler (1707-1783)—who is said to have originated the calculus of variations—became blind at fifty-nine but continued to perform outstanding work. He was aided in his astronomical investigations by the observations of his son and two colleagues.

Another Swiss—the world-famous entomologist—François Huber (1750-1831) lost his sight through cataracts at the age of fifteen. His work on the behavior of bees was a landmark in the history of zoology. Aside from his empirical contributions to basic research (which included descriptions of the complex social organization of the hives and the process by which honey is made), Huber invented glass hives, a major technical innovation, to facilitate his observations. His wife, son, and manservant assisted him in his investigations.

Unlike the eccentric Saunderson, Huber experienced a happy domestic life. He enjoyed music and poetry and was considered urbane, affable, and compassionate. Moreover, his creativity was not limited to science. One of his inventions, a printing machine, was a primitive prototype of today's typewriter.

In some respects, the most unusual blind person of the eighteenth century was the comparatively humble Englishman, John Metcalf (1717-1810), otherwise known as Blind Jack of Knaresborough (Hogg, 1967). Metcalf was born of poor parents and lost his sight through smallpox at the age of six. He is of interest primarily on account of his remarkable physical development. Six months following the advent of blindness, he independently explored the streets around his home, and by the age of nine, he was traveling all over Knaresborough, his native town, without sighted assistance—not to mention climbing trees. As a teenager, he dived, swam, hunted, fiddled, and rode horses at a gallop. He grew to be quite tall and remained healthy, strong, and energetic throughout life. In 1745, he marched with the English against the Jacobite rebels of Scotland, inspiring the troops to bravery through the tunes of his fiddle. He boxed, wrestled, gambled on cockfights, and rode in horse races by the aid of a bell-ringing man stationed at each post along the track to give the signals that would keep him to his course. It is said that he rode at breakneck speed to the town of Harrowgate and absconded with his bride-to-be, just one hour before she was to marry another man. Their union was happy and lasted forty years, producing a great brood of children and grandchildren. Furthermore, Metcalf was a shrewd and prosperous businessman. For a time, he sold cotton and ran a stagecoach service, enterprises that necessitated considerable independent traveling on his part. He got about so well that he was not regarded as blind. Later, he made a large sum of

money as an engineer, planning and constructing roads and bridges in
north of England. He appears to have been of the first to use crushed sto
for the laying of road beds. On account of his ingenuity, joviality, a
immense vitality, he was well and widely liked and frequently played
fiddle at festive occasions and wakes. He loved the outdoors and, in 17
retired to a farm where he could live out his remaining years close
nature. Metcalf's life history dramatically demonstrates the gre
importance of constitutional determinants of personality, a source
behavior all too often ignored by contemporary environmentalis
psychology. To a large extent, this man's superior adjustment w
apparently the product of a powerful mesomorphic physique, coupled w
an equally lively somatotonic temperament (Sheldon et al., 1940; Sheld
and Stevens, 1942; Hall and Lindzey, 1970).

A respected contemporary of Metcalf was the Scottish scholar,
Thomas Blacklock, who was blinded by smallpox during infancy. He stud
for the ministry at the University of Edinburgh and soon gained recogniti
as a preacher but later gave up this calling for teaching and litera
pursuits. Blacklock wrote poetry and tutored in philosophy and languag
He associated with many of the socially, intellectually, and artistica
important people of his generation. For example, he promoted the poetry
Robert Burns, helping him to achieve fame. Also, he knew Samuel Johns
and was a friend of David Hume and Walter Scott. The latter was offer
the use of Blacklock's excellent library, a service for which he was alwc
grateful. Although Blacklock's poetry was not of enduring significance,
was financially successful during his day.

In addition, the eighteenth century gave birth to several high
distinguished blind concert musicians. Of these, the Englishman Jo
Stanley (1713-1786) was the most outstanding. His vision was destroyed
the age of two, when he accidentally fell on a hearth and shattered a piec
of chinaware which cut his eyes. At seven he was playing the organ, a
four years later he became a respected church organist. Through t
eventual relationship with Handel, Stanley grew famous as a conce
organist. In 1753, he participated in the first performance of Handel
Samson, and when the great master died six years thereafter, Stanle
played at his memorial concert. He was similarly gifted with the violin, flu

and harpsichord. Moreover, he produced numerous compositions of his own and was the leader of the king's personal band.

Incidentally, both Handel and Bach lost their vision in old age. However, their greatest work was done while they were sighted.

During the late eighteenth century, another noted concert performer, Maria Theresa Von Paradis (1759-1824), emerged in Vienna. She became sightless at the age of three. As a child, she manifested an extraordinary aptitude for the piano, which at age twelve led to a command performance for the empress Maria Theresa. In honor of the girl's talent, the empress granted her a pension. In time, the young Maria became an international celebrity, to whom the great Mozart was to dedicate a concerto.

There is reason to believe that this woman's blindness was, at least in part, hysterical, for Anton Mesmer, with magnetic treatments, was said to have increased her vision. This partial recovery, however, exerted an adverse influence on her art, as she became subject to violent, distracting emotions and began to lose interest in the piano. Maria's parents promptly removed her from Mesmer's hands, fearing that her returning sight would ruin her lucrative career. Thereupon, her vision quickly deteriorated to its former level. Interestingly enough, Maria's emotional disturbance appears to have resulted not from her newfound vision, as her parents claimed, but from an intense conflict engendered by sexual attraction to Mesmer. During her treatment, she lived for some time as a patient in Mesmer's house and apparently felt very close to him. Her parents seem to have been exploiting her blindness in the conviction that it rendered her greater public appeal than she would possess if sighted.

Among the noteworthy sightless scholars of the nineteenth century, William Hickling Prescott (1796-1859), the world-famous American historian, was unquestionably the most important. His blindness stemmed from an accident sustained during his junior year at Harvard. While leaving the university dining hall, he was hit in the left eye by a heedlessly thrown crust of bread, an episode which ruined that eye and eventually the right through an attack of sympathetic ophthalmia. Prescott's virtual sightlessness dissuaded him from his chosen career of law, and, in 1820, he turned his energies to literature. Through friends and hired readers, he conducted a comprehensive study of classical and European works an undertaking that resulted in the publication of a lengthy series of minor investigations. However, his interest soon shifted to history, and, in 1826, he began delving deeply into that science, a period of preparation that was to last ten years. He received a continuous flow of books and manuscripts from abroad and cultivated his capacity for memorization to a remarkable degree. In time, he could produce and recall up to sixty pages of composition before actually writing. He employed a wooden tablet with brass wires for lines, under which carbon paper over white enabled him to write by means of an ivory stylus. In 1843, Prescott published his magnum opus, *History of the Conquest of Mexico*, in three volumes and, in 1847, its renowned successor, the two-volume *History of the Conquest of Peru*. His approach to historical science was literary as well as objective, for he viewed history as inherently dramatic. Today, his two major works are generally acknowledged as both historical and literary classics (Cline et al., 1959).

During the nineteenth century, a few blind persons were in the political limelight.

George V, King of Hanover, was sightless when he assumed the throne in 1853. His handicap was caused by a playtime accident that had occurred during his tenth year. As sovereign, he supported both intellectual and artistic activities, being especially fond of music, while personally he was known to be friendly and of a lighthearted disposition. In 1866, a Prussian invasion forced George into exile. He later tried to regain his throne by leading an army against the Prussians but was once more vanquished.

Earlier in the century, the blind Alexander Rodenbach became an influential member of the Belgian Chamber of Deputies and a leader in the revolution that eventually established Belgium's national independence. He also successfully sponsored legislation in behalf of the blind and deaf of that country.

Yet the most important sightless political figure of this period was Henry Fawcett in England. In 1858, while still a young man, Fawcett was blinded suddenly in a hunting accident. He was defeated in his first race for a seat in the House of Commons but won the second time he ran. He was an independent liberal, a crusader for labor, the farmer, and the blind. He was a friend of John Stuart Mill, and, in 1863, his *Manual of Political Economy* secured him an appointment as Professor of Political Economics at Cambridge University, a position he retained throughout the remainder of his life. In 1880, under Gladstone, Fawcett was appointed Postmaster-General, in which capacity he inaugurated the parcel post in 1882.

Fawcett was also physically active and went about all over London unaided by guides. He grew vegetables, fished, and was an indefatigable debater on the topics of politics and biological evolution. He was esteemed highly by the public, and at his death, his contributions to the general good were praised by Gladstone.

In our own century, perhaps the most notable blind politician to date has been the well-known United States Senator, Thomas P. Gore. His blindness was brought on by two separate childhood accidents. At the age of eight, the vision of the left eye was impaired when a playmate threw a stick that struck him in the face. When eleven, he lost the right eye to an arrow shot from a crossbow. By the age of twenty, Gore was completely blind. In 1907, when Oklahoma was admitted to the Union, Gore was elected as one of her first pair of senators. He was a conservative Democrat, known for his independent turn of mind. He was much respected in both Oklahoma and Washington. After a long senatorial career, he successfully practiced law in the capital city (Billington, 1967).

In England, somewhat later, Sir Ian Fraser, a blinded veteran of World War I, was to become an effective member of Parliament. His political career began in 1921, when he joined the London County Council. During the next twenty years, he ran for the House of Commons six times and lost only one of these elections.

Fraser, like Metcalf, was physically strong and energetic. He rode horseback, rowed, and had his own skiff. He walked freely and independently through the streets of London and, in addition, was a frequent world traveler.

During the twentieth century, the foremost musical artist among the visually handicapped has been the wonderfully gifted composer, Frederick Delius. His fame grew out of works such as *The Magic Fountain, Koanga,* and *Appalachia.* Though eventually paralyzed, as well as blind, he continued to create music, dictating his compositions to a secretary. A memorial concert of his works is conducted every year in Florida, where he lived for a time during his youth, early in the century.

Later distinguished sightless musicians are Alec Templeton, the concert pianist, and still more recently the singer-guitarist, Jose Feliciano, and the very popular singer, piano-player, and bandleader, Ray Charles.

Among recently prominent writers, both Booth Tarkington and James Thurber continued to show considerable creativity following the onset of blindness in later life. Also, the presently eminent Argentinian writer, Jorge Luis Borges, is sightless.

The foregoing cases clearly indicate no adverse relationship between blindness, as such, and general intellectual or artistic abilities. Moreover, this appears to be true whether blindness is congenital or adventitious. Unfortunately, the present survey reveals nothing about physical development in the congenitally blind, though obviously such capacities are not necessarily retarded in the adventitiously blinded. Furthermore, these biographies tell us relatively little regarding the effects of either type of blindness upon emotional adjustment, although they certainly suggest that visual loss is not inherently deleterious. We will continue our discussion of these problems in Chapter 6, where both the physical and emotional adjustment of the blind are considered at length in the light of contemporary psychological research.

References

Chapter 5/Prominent Sightless Persons

Billington, M. 1967. *Thomas P. Gore.* Lawrence, Kansas: University of Kansas Press.

Cline, H., Gardiner, C. & Gibson, C., eds. 1959. *William Hickling Prescott: A memorial.* Durham, N.C.: Duke University Press.

French, R. 1932. *From Homer to Helen Keller: A social and educational study of the blind.* New York: American Foundation for the Blind.

Hall, C. & Lindzey, G. 1970. *Theories of personality.* 2nd ed. New York: John Wiley and Sons.

Hogg, G. 1967. *Blind Jack of Knaresborough: Road builder extraordinary.* London: Phoenix House.

Ross, I. 1951. *Journey into light.* New York: Appleton-Century-Crofts.

Sheldon, W. & Stevens, S. 1942. *The varieties of temperaments: A psychology of constitutional differences.* New York: Harper.

Sheldon, W., Stevens, S. & Tucker, W. 1940. *The varieties of human physique: An introduction to constitutional psychology.* New York: Harper.

6

Contemporary Investigations of Adjustment in the Visually Handicapped

Among blindness organizations and workers for the blind, one sometimes encounters two extreme views regarding the handicapping effects of blindness. On the one hand, there are those who see blindness as a virtual disaster. This group stresses the physical, psychological, and social limitations associated with blindness and considers it a tragic fate that can never be substantially overcome without superior ability and/or unusually favorable environmental circumstances. The blind person is seen as essentially different from the seeing individual; he is abnormal not merely in the sense of his statistical deviation from the norm of sight but also in the more fundamental sense of extensive behavioral restrictions or impaired personality functioning. At the opposite pole, there are others who assess blindness as nothing more than a physical nuisance or practical inconvenience. They contend that the problems traditionally linked to blindness are almost totally the product of social prejudice and discrimination, that blindness, in itself, is at most only a minor handicap. Indeed, the proponents of this view resent the very use of such words as *handicap, disability,* and *impairment* in connection with blindness. In support of their position, they point to the many sightless individuals of average ability who have clearly achieved successful levels of personal, social, and economic adjustment when given the necessary opportunities for doing so. The first view tends to be pessimistic and defeatist, fostering in those blind who accept it an unproductive orientation toward passivity, gloomy resignation, and childlike dependency on the seeing. On the other hand, the second position involves an unrealistic degree of optimism, for certain obvious handicapping effects of blindness are simply denied or ignored. This view also tends to impede optimal adjustment in the sightless, as those persons sharing it are frequently characterized by a self-frustrating bravado with respect to their handicap, by compulsive overcompensation, and by active aggressive dependency upon the sighted.

In the pages that follow I shall present the central findings of adjustment researchers regarding the question at issue: What is the nature of blindness as a handicap? It will be seen that the two approaches to blindness just described provide at best only simplistic or polemical answers to this question. Neither view objectively represents the truth about the role of blindness in the life of the blind individual.

Historical Beginnings

The first major scientific inquiry into the adjustmental status of the visually handicapped was conducted in 1933 by the psychologist Thomas Cutsforth. Based on clinical interviews and case studies of blind children, he concluded that the blind are generally neurotic. Blindness, he asserted profoundly alters and reorganizes the entire psychic life.

However, at the same time, Cutsforth believed that visual deficit by itself could not account for the great amount of disability observable among the blind, a condition he attributed primarily to unhealthy personal and social attitudes. Such attitudes tend to produce anxiety and feelings of isolation in the sightless person, and the latter will, as a rule, adopt one of two defensive mechanisms to reduce his sense of insecurity: (1) compulsive overcompensation, or (2) hysterical withdrawal. The former reaction is characterized by denial of the limitations intrinsic to blindness and engenders one-sided development, e.g., the talented blind scholar or musician who is socially inept and incapable of independent mobility. The second mechanism is typified by such trends as dependency, regression, and self-abasement. While any given sightless individual is likely to manifest both reactions to some extent, one will tend to predominate in his everyday behavior. In addition, Cutsforth stressed the prevalence among ne blind of such traits as passivity, egocentricity, submissiveness, sexual maladjustment, and chronic daydreaming.

The social forces thwarting mature adjustment were seen as consisting chiefly of parental overprotection and oversupervision of the blind child, the educational and social segregation of the blind from the sighted, and the tendency of blindness agencies to encourage dependency in their clients. Nevertheless, Cutsforth also maintained that internal psychological factors (such as distortions in the self-concept) are a far more serious problem for the sightless person than are the frustrations imposed on him by society. Indeed, unrealistic self-regarding attitudes constitute a more potent threat to healthy personality development than does blindness itself. In Cutsforth's view, the only remedy for the emotional pathology of the blind lies in responsible action on the part of the blind person himself, acting in behalf of his own self-growth. Reforming society will not solve his problems. "He must mature to accept himself as he is and to live in his social world as it is." (See Cutsforth, 1950.)

Although a number of Cutsforth's observations have been replicated by subsequent investigators, many others have not. Such discrepancies are not surprising in view of certain weaknesses inherent in the clinical method, viz., its qualitative, uncontrolled nature. The most rigorous research in the field (e.g., Cowen et al., 1961; Bauman, 1954) has generally failed to confirm Cutsforth's hypothesis of the "neurotic blind personality." Such studies indicate that Cutsforth's conclusions are, on the whole, excessively negative and overly general. Similarly, many authorities on blindness would now contend that, in identifying the causes of psychopathology among the blind, Cutsforth placed too much emphasis on the role of individual self-ate and far too little on social influences. In this connection, the same critics would find Cutsforth's position concerning the unsuitability of all attempts at social reform unwarrantedly conservative and pessimistic. Thus, appears that Cutsforth's contribution, though important, is primarily one of historical rather than contemporary relevance.

More recently, Lowenfeld (1963) has extensively reviewed the scientific literature on the adjustment of the visually handicapped, focusing mainly on studies of blind children and adolescents. This author classified the problems associated with blindness into three areas: (1) those involving alterations in cognitive functioning; (2) those connected with mobility; and

(3) those arising from psychosocial determinants. Lowenfeld concluded
blindness, by itself, produces problems only in cognition and mobility.

Below I shall discuss each of these problem areas, summarizing th
empirical findings and generalizations that seem to possess the grea
reliability—including, as well, conclusions from research conducted si
1963.

The Effects of Blindness on Cognitive Processes

Most research on this topic has been concerned with the follow
space perception, synesthesia, sensory acuity, memory, creative abili
intelligence, academic achievement, and speech and reading ability.

Space Perception

The nature of space perception in the blind has interested experime
psychologists since the late nineteenth century. However, the proce
involved in it are not as yet fully understood. The central problem b
concerns the mode of spatial awareness in the congenitally blind,
individuals losing their sight subsequent to the early childhood ye
appear to conceive of space primarily on the basis of visual memory.
among the congenitally blind, touch would seem to be the only orig
sense. While some investigators have concluded that tactile percepts do
result in awareness of space—i.e., the person born blind creates temp
schemata and verbal concepts that are a substitute for the spa
awareness he lacks—the fact remains that the congenitally blind are abl
reproduce all types of objects, large as well as small, in modeling
handwork, and can recognize objects on the basis of previous observati
This indicates that such persons must be able to integrate discrete ta
percepts into a single total concept of the object. Nonetheless, the ques
of how this integration takes place has not been answered, thoug
appears that senses other than touch also play a part in the process,
kinesthesis and cutaneous sensations of pressure, pain, and temperature

Synesthesia

Synesthesia (or the automatic tendency to associate particular color ima

ith various sounds, ideas, and affects) occurs fairly often in individuals
inded during later childhood or thereafter. Such experiences (sometimes
ferred to as photisms) vary considerably in nature from one person to the
xt. While they seem to possess emotional value for the individual through
riching imagination, they are apparently of little, if any, practical
gnificance in enhancing cognitive functioning.

Sensory Acuity, Memory, and Creative Abilities

he alleged natural superiority of the sightless with respect to certain
nsory, mental, and creative abilities is wholly mythical. The blind do not
rpass the seeing in sensory acuity, logical or rote memory, musical talent,
r the ability to interpret the human voice. On the other hand, the blind
ften learn to use such capacities more effectively than do the sighted, but
is compensation is not automatic; rather, it is the product of persistent
ractice. In most kinds of creative activity, including modeling, the blind
ppear to be neither superior nor inferior to the seeing.

Intelligence and Academic Achievement

general, research on intelligence indicates that blind youths have IQs
mparable to those of their sighted peers, though the percentage of blind
pils falling at the average level is somewhat smaller than that for the
eing, the percentage of superior scores slightly larger, and that of below
erage scores considerably larger. These deviations appear to arise from
variety of factors: inferior scores from unfavorable home environment
d neurological or physical handicaps other than blindness; and superior
ores from greater than average motivation for compensation through
tellectual channels. There is no correlation of intelligence with the age at
hich sight has been lost. Nor is the latter related to achievement in
fferent school subjects. On tests of academic achievement, the blind in
sidential schools perform similarly to comparable seeing groups, though
e blind generally score lower in knowledge of arithmetic. In regard to
hool achievement, Lowenfeld gave the following admonition to
searchers and professionals in the field of work for the blind: "It must, of
urse, be recognized that whatever is said about blind pupils as a group
oes not permit any conclusion concerning the achievement of individual
lind students."

Speech

The congenitally blind child cannot be aided in learning speech by imitation, although it plays a major role in the development of sighted children. He can only learn from hearing and touch; consequently, his progress in speech development may be slower than that of the seeing child. In addition, the congenitally blind are more likely to manifest verbalism than are individuals blinded later in life, though modern educational techniques are helping to correct this problem. Speech defects in blind children are usually remediable and their prognosis is better here than that of deaf children. Also, as to blind children, no study has actually demonstrated a connection between speech defects and any particular psychological reaction pattern. Studies concerned with the prevalence of various speech defects in the blind have produced highly contradictory results, with the blind sometimes appearing strikingly abnormal and at other times relatively normal. The following types of defect have been emphasized by some researchers: less than normal vocal variety, lack of modulation, comparatively loud talking, slower rate of speech, less effective use of gesture and body action, and less lip movement in articulation of sounds. However, other authorities have concluded that too frequently investigators are sensitive to minor speech defects in the blind, defects that they tend to exaggerate, judging the blind less favorably than they would the sighted with the same problems.

Reading Behavior

Touch reading appears to be at least three times slower than visual reading, but touch reading of words and sentences is accomplished by synthesizing word percepts and images, which is also the case in visual reading. So reliance on Braille reading means a relatively slow acquisition of knowledge. Even so, this weakness of the touch method can, for all practical purposes, be compensated through the supplementary use of tape and disc recordings, not to mention live readers. With respect to the use of the tactile modality in the education of blind children, Lowenfeld cautions that when models are employed, the child should be apprised of the differences between the real object and the model. This authority also concluded that our cultural taboo against touch experience poses a serious obstacle to the tactile education of the blind.

The Impact of Blindness on Mobility

For the totally blind or those with only light perception, the task of getting about the environment is one of the most difficult to carry out. At the time of Lowenfeld's review, virtually no research dealing with psychological factors involved in mobility was available, a situation that, to date, remains essentially the same. On the other hand, numerous studies of obstacle perception have been conducted over the last twenty-five years.

As Lowenfeld pointed out, obstacle perception is just one factor of importance in the ability to get about. Aural stimulation is both a necessary and sufficient condition for the perception of obstacles. The deaf-blind do not possess the obstacle sense and cannot learn it. Changes in loudness are neither necessary nor sufficient for this ability, yet changes in pitch are both. Moreover, approaching an object at relatively high speed does not necessarily impair obstacle perception.

Factors other than the obstacle sense have received only scant scientific attention. Certain children, including some who are congenitally blind, are surprisingly adroit in mobility, while others are quite poor. Why this is the case is as yet unknown.

According to Lowenfeld, two components underlie mobility in the blind: (1) mental orientation (viz., ability to recognize one's surroundings in their temporal or spatial relations to himself); and (2) physical locomotion (viz., movement of an organism from one place to another by means of bodily mechanisms). The first component entails a cognitive map that the individual must keep in mind while moving toward his destination. The experienced blind person will also rely on a wide variety of both internal and external cues, e.g., audible traffic sounds, air currents indicating an open space, changes in ground level at a given point, odors, the use of unconscious muscle memory so as not to have to count steps, and the use of the time sense to trace one's position on the cognitive map. He utilizes all his senses, not only in orientation but also in locomotion; he perceives distances in terms of time, movement, and sound. The more familiar the blind person is with any given route, the more mechanical and unconscious become such behaviors.

Many mobility instructors find that the adventitiously blind learn mobility skills more easily than do the congenitally blind, but there are occasionally striking exceptions to this rule. In short, visual memory can be

a major aid in the formation of cognitive maps, but it does not invariab[ly]
lead to superior environmental orientation.

The Relation of Blindness to Personal and Social Adjustment

Research in this area has focused upon the following: personal[ity]
structure and motivaion; the consequences of blindness at different a[ge]
levels; sexual adjustment; expressive behavior; motor abilities; the effects [of]
physical conditions other than blindness; and the adjustment of th[e]
physically handicapped in general (Cutsforth, 1933, 1950, 1951; Chevig[ny]
and Braverman, 1950; Cholden, 1954, 1958; Bauman, 1954; Bauman a[nd]
Yoder, 1966; Blank, 1957; Wright, 1960; Cowen et al., 1961; Davis, 196[;]
Cohen, 1966; Riffenburgh, 1967; Cohen, 1969; Saterbak, 1969; McDani[el]
1969).

Personality Traits

Of the various studies dealing with the effects of blindness on traits [of]
personality, some have shown differences between blind and sighted you[th]
and children in such characteristics as introversion, neuroticism, ment[al]
rigidity in problem solving, physiological response to frustratic[n,]
intropunitiveness versus impunitiveness, and general adequacy [of]
adjustment—with the blind typically revealing less favorable trai[ts.]
However, other investigations have found no significant differenc[e]
between the blind and the seeing in particular traits or overall adjustme[nt.]
In this connection, many investigators have questioned the validity of th[e]
personality inventories used in this research. Such tests are standardized o[n]
the seeing, whose life situation may be quite different from that of the blin[d,]
i.e., numerous test items will tend to have different interpretive meani[ng]
for the blind. Nor can any strong degree of confidence be placed in th[e]
results of research based on projective techniques specially constructed f[or]
the blind, as such devices are still in an experimental stage. Also, [as]
Lowenfeld observed, sampling problems and inadequate controls tend [to]
plague investigators in this area.

The Self-concept and the Body Image

Some clinical researchers have emphasized the role of the self-conce[pt]
(including the body image) in the adjustment of the visually handicapp[ed.]

particularly with respect to children and adolescents. For example, Davis (1964)—based on his counseling experience with youngsters at a residential school for the blind—concluded that the early developmental process of differentiation of self from environment is comparatively difficult for the blind child to achieve. The mother must assist him in this process by verbal communication and by encouraging his exploration of the immediate environment as well as his own body. Through this method, the child will more readily learn the cardinal features of his environment and their relation to himself, thus facilitating the process of differentiation. In other words, the mother should actively aid the child in locating important environmental objects and body parts. According to Davis, the process of differentiation and integration of an adequate body image proceeds more slowly for the sightless child than for the seeing child. The former needs touch experience, both of himself and other persons, but our cultural taboo on touch tends to be inimical to such learning. As a result, the blind child often does not know his body as well as he should, let alone the physical characteristics of others. In Davis's view, a healthy self-concept is impossible apart from a satisfactory body image.

The foregoing applies mainly to the early or congenitally blind child. What is the situation with individuals blinded in late childhood or thereafter, i.e., persons in whom a viable self-concept has already been established? According to Davis, such persons must learn a new self-image and body image, as the original ones have been destroyed by blindness. Furthermore, this relearning appears to take place more rapidly the earlier blindness occurs—barring, of course, onset during the first few years of life.

In addition, Davis found that partially sighted adolescents experience much greater difficulty in developing a stable self-concept than do either totally blind or seeing youngsters. The partially seeing person is sometimes regarded by society as sighted and at other times as blind, and he does, in fact, behave in this dual manner, that is, he is neither fish nor fowl. These conflicting identities impede the development of a stable body image and hence also the growth of a healthy self-concept. The partially sighted require more time to form a consistent, adaptive self-concept than do the completely blind or the visually normal. However, Davis also noted that most of his partially seeing counselees had, by the time of adulthood, finally resolved this serious problem of identity.

A fundamental assumption of studies such as the above is that the

self-concept and/or body image constitute critical determinants c
behavior, and that instability in either will lead to problems of adjustment i
areas such as sex, interpersonal relations, mobility, and independenc
Contrariwise, some observers, like McDaniel (1969), question the allege
centrality of the self-concept and the body image as causes of reactions t
physical disability; while Wright (1960) has concluded that somati
abnormality, as a physical fact, is not related in a direct or simple way t
covert or overt behavior. Moreover, it should be pointed out that in thi
particular field of blindness research, one is as likely to encounter glarin
contradictions among clinical or phenomenological investigators as amon
the previously discussed psychometric researchers.

Multidimensional, Longitudinal Studies

Of the many adjustment studies conducted over the last twenty years, thos
of Bauman (1954) and Cowen et al. (1961) are exceptional for thei
comparatively high degree of methodological rigor. Both were multidimen
sional, longitudinal investigations employing large, relatively representativ
samples of blind persons, as distinguished from most other researches i
this area, which have tended to be unidimensional and based on sma
samples with no follow-up inquiries.

■*The Bauman Study*—The purpose of Bauman's research was to ascertai
the major social and psychological characteristics making for adequate a
opposed to inadequate adjustment among blind adults. Her initia
investigation focused upon 443 visually handicapped persons in six state
of the Union. (All subjects were clients of agencies serving the blind.
Subjects were divided into three groups according to adequacy o
adjustment. Group A (the well-adjusted group) contained 162 individuals,
all of whom were self-supporting, relatively independent in mobility, with
satisfactory home life, recreational outlets, community contacts, grooming
and hygiene. Group C (the maladjusted group), comprising 131 subjects
was composed of persons who failed to meet the adjustment criteric
characterizing Group A, that is, C had not been self-supporting either fo
ten or more years or since the onset of blindness and, with respect to the
other characteristics mentioned above, was virtually opposite to A. One
hundred-fifty subjects made up Group B (an intermediate sample). These
individuals manifested most of the qualities of A, minus successfu

employment history. Though frequent attempts at job placement had been made on behalf of members of Group B, the end results were never wholly satisfactory—seemingly through no fault of the clients. All subjects, on the basis of a previously structured format, were interviewed at length regarding personal, educational, vocational, visual, and medical history, as well as on their attitudes about blindness—with such interviews being electronically recorded. Moreover, during the selection of the three groups, agency records were examined in depth for information in certain areas in which interview material might be inaccurate, e.g., with respect to ophthalmological and other medical details. In addition, subjects were administered the Wechsler verbal intelligence scale, manual dexterity measures, the Emotional Factors Inventory, and the Kuder Preference Record. The resulting interview and test data were analyzed both clinically and statistically.

On all measures, the different subject groups showed considerable overlap, with some unfavorably scoring individuals being, nonetheless, economically independent and socially successful. Even so, Group A was clearly superior to Group C in IQ, manual dexterity, and personality equilibrium. The two groups, however, did not differ in interests, as measured by the Kuder test. The interview data indicated that the families of A subjects tended to show realistic acceptance of blindness, as did the subjects themselves; whereas C families and subjects were more inclined to react irrationally and adversely. On the other hand, A and C did not differ significantly in ophthalmological diagnosis, nor in etiology of blindness, suddenness of onset, age at loss, or general health status before or during blindness. On the whole, A was better educated and academically more successful than C; also, more persons in A had received rehabilitative education with respect to their adjustment following visual loss. Still, some of A had little or no schooling of any kind, and for the group, generally, amount of education was only weakly related to IQ. When individuals in B and C, who had attempted but failed at professional or factory employment, were compared with A, it was found that the former two groups had significantly lower IQs than A as well as more unfavorable attitudes regarding blindness. With respect to mobility, the families of C were more overprotective and less likely to approve independent travel than were the families of A. As to recreation, A liked music, reading, and movies more than C, and were much less inclined to relinquish preblindness sources of pleasure because of present blindness. Furthermore, A's ha experienced less trouble with the law, were more certain people liked them had fewer fears and petty annoyances, were less prone to boredom revealed greater confidence about getting what they wanted out of life and were more likely to adjudge themselves as happy.

Further interesting findings emerged in regard to family attitudes These showed negligible relationship to amount of retained vision, as well as suddenness or etiology of loss. Blindness was more likely to be accepted in a simple unemotional way if the subject was young at the time of its onset. The subject who retained some useful vision was as likely to feel alienation from the family as was the totally blind subject.

As to the subjects themselves, it was not degree of visual impairment that produced pervasive feelings of isolation but emotional problems, such as hypersensitivity, depression, and distress over blindness. Neither intelligence nor emotional makeup disclosed any relation to diagnosis or etiology of visual defect. Nor was there any relationship between personality scores and gradualness or suddenness of blindness onset. Yet for successful adjustment, greater mental ability appeared to be required of the totally blind than of the partially sighted subjects. Similarly, relatively low intelligence characterized those who, even with some useful vision, were still unsuccessful. Suspiciousness of others, the sense of being at a disadvantage to the sighted, and the belief that blindness may be a punishment from the supernatural were related not to amount of vision but, instead, to personality traits, as measured by the Emotional Factors Inventory.

A third of the persons in Group A, the employed sample, were in blue-collar work, with professional people the second, and vending stand operators the third largest occupational groupings. Generally speaking, for these individuals, mental ability and educational background seemed appropriate to the kind of job held.

In summary: "No quality of vision, health, education, or family and social interaction has so much to do with adjustment as have the qualities measured by the intelligence quotient and personality inventory scores Each of the preceding may at times influence IQ and especially personality scores, but, regardless of what shaped it, that aspect of the client which is measured by these tests, in the end, most consistently shows relationship to adjustment, even when the most fundamental measure is economic adjustment.''

Fourteen years later Bauman carried out follow-up observations on approximately ninety-two percent of the original sample, and, on the whole, earlier predictions of continued adjustment or maladjustment were confirmed. However, the agency counselors who had participated in the original observations were more accurate in predicting continuing adjustment than continuing maladjustment. Of Group A, 85.2 percent remained well-adjusted; while in Group C, 57.3 percent persisted in maladjustment. On the other hand, a substantial portion of the individuals in the latter group, at this point deemed successful, were employed in sheltered workshops. Had this element been eliminated from the final tally, counselors' predictions of future poor adjustment would have been appreciably more precise.

No definite pattern emerged regarding the kinds of individuals who shift from one group to another. There were slight tendencies for younger persons and those with some usable sight to make positive moves, and for older people and those with no functional vision to make negative moves; but such tendencies were not statistically significant determinants of movement. Any sort of individual was apparently capable of moving. The chief sources of positive movement appeared to be effective rehabilitation counseling and job placement, reinforced by adjustmental or prevocational training with medical treatment or therapy where needed. Negative shifts were primarily the result of emotional instability and insufficient motivation for success. Though ill health played some part in the latter type of movement, personality problems remained the critical factor.

The adjustment of the subjects in this investigation could not be understood on the basis of any one social or psychological attribute; rather it clearly sprang from a combination of variables, some of greater and some of lesser moment. According to Bauman, adjustment, as here studied, was more complex than adjustment to blindness alone should have been. Personality trends, both healthy and unhealthy, were frequently present in the subjects prior to visual loss, and these acted either to mitigate or

exacerbate adjustment problems peculiar to blindness. As Bauman pointe
out, here one was not observing adjustment to blindness per se but overc
adjustment to life under the accidental stress of blindness.

In 1966, Bauman and Yoder, in reviewing a number of then rece
adjustment studies, cited evidence linking satisfactory adjustment
blindness to characteristics such as high ego strength, low manifest anxiet
constructive attitudes toward blindness, and realistic attitudes regardi
medicine and religion, with well-adjusted sightless persons uniform
rejecting belief in the possibility of magical cures for blindness. In the latt
investigations, poorly adjusted individuals revealed just the reverse of th
pattern. In another study, independent blind people, who were also social
and economically competent, were compared with two other groups
sightless adults—one unemployed and the second consisting of employe
from a sheltered workshop (i.e., minimally successful persons who cou
function only when their environment was externally structured for them k
seeing people)—in response to an auditory projective technique. On th
measure, the performance of the well-adjusted was superior to that of th
other groups, in that the former were more adroit in perceiving ar
integrating test stimuli—suggesting that the well-adjusted group possesse
greater awareness and comprehension of the world around them. On th
same test, the sheltered workers and the unemployed group, by contra:
were stimulus-bound and passively helpless respectively—behaviors th
were mirrored in their day-to-day relations to the environment. Still oth
investigations produced findings indicating better overall adjustment for th
totally or functionally blind than for individuals with some useful vision b
legally blind; e.g., the partially seeing were more likely to have jobs wi
lower status and responsibility than persons with less sight.

While acknowledging the contribution of studies such as the abov
Bauman and Yoder, at the same time, stressed the fact that most research
this field, including the foregoing, had tended to focus on relative
circumscribed elements of the total adjustment process, often utilizir
measuring devices of questionable validity or standardization c
unrepresentative samples of sightless individuals, a methodologic
situation that remains largely unchanged even today.

■*The Investigation of Cowen and Associates*—The next major stuc
to be discussed in the present section—that of Cowen, Underberg, Verill

and Benham—dealt with the adjustmental status of visually handicapped adolescents, as compared with that of their sighted peers. The entire investigation extended over a period of three years and was based on samples of 40 seeing and 127 blind and partially sighted youngsters, aged thirteen to eighteen, as well as the youths' parents, predominantly mothers. The study was conducted because of the contradictory findings and weak methodology of previous adjustment research—e.g., the unmodified application to the visually disabled of instruments designed for the seeing; the tendency to compare sighted youngsters living at home with visually handicapped adolescents living in residential schools for the blind; and the widespread inattention to the serious matter of cross-group matching on basic control variables.

The sighted teenagers provided a control group, against which two samples of visually disabled youths were compared—one of the latter being from a residential school setting, while the other lived at home and attended public schools. The seeing adolescents were demographically similar to the visually handicapped subjects, the three groups having been matched for age, sex, grade, IQ, and socioeconomic status. Level of adjustment was assessed by means of measures of self-concept, self-ideal discrepancy, teachers' behavior ratings, and various other measures of personality, attitudes, and understanding of blindness. In addition, parental attitudes and understanding of the child were examined in relation to child adjustment.

In overall adjustment, Group 1 (blind youngsters living at home and going to public schools), Group 2 (blind youngsters attending residential schools), and Group 3 (the sighted students) did not differ significantly. Though the differences were not marked, adjustment levels for males versus females in the three groups could be ranked from better to worse. When this was done, the following pattern emerged: Group 2 males best adjusted; then both males and females in Group 1; next males and females in Group 3; and finally Group 2 females, the least well-adjusted. Also, there was a tendency for the partially sighted to be more poorly adjusted than the functionally or totally blind. However, this difference was not statistically significant.

With respect to maternal attitudes, Group 1 and Group 3 mothers were essentially similar, but Group 2 mothers verbalized significantly more

positive attitudes toward their offspring than either of the foregoing
Likewise, mothers in Group 2 were significantly less overprotective the
Group 1 mothers and significantly less rejecting than Group 3 mothers. F
all three groups, correlations between maternal attitudes and chi
adjustment were generally low. On the measure of child understanding, tl
three groups of mothers did not differ, and in each group, heightene
understanding of the child was associated with better child adjustment. C
the whole, correlations between understanding of the child and the mother
attitudes to blindness were low and insignificant. Although few attitue
measures discriminated between mothers in the three groups, Group
mothers were appreciably lower in negative attitudes toward blindness the
either Group 1 or Group 3 mothers. In addition, high authoritarianism, o
measured by the California F Scale, was, for Group 2 mother
significantly related to child maladjustment on teachers' ratings a
measures of self-concept and perceived rejection on the part of the child.

As to paternal attitudes, there were relatively few statistica
significant findings. The relationship between child adjustment and paren
understanding of the child was weaker in the case of fathers than it ho
been for mothers. Also, with regard to fathers in Group 3, there exist
relatively high agreement between child perception of pity from others a
the father's prediction of the child's perception. Moreover, Group 3 fathe
were both more dominant and less rejecting of offspring than were fathe
in Group 1.

Yet the single most important conclusion to be derived from the Cowe
et al. study is that visual disability, in and of itself, does not predispose tl
young person to maladjustment.

Unconscious Factors

It will be recalled from Chapter 2 that Chevigny and Braverman (195(
considered castration anxiety the major determinant of attitudes to
ward blindness but focused upon this factor in regard to the attitudes o
the sighted toward the blind rather than those of the blind towar
themselves. My own research indicates that this can be just as important
variable in producing the blind person's self-attitudes. (In particular, se
Chapters 2 and 8). In addition, Chevigny and Braverman viewed society o
large as essentially neurotic. The average person is not able to express o

his aggression directly and so is always in need of displacement objects. Such targets—typically individuals belonging to certain minority groups who are incapable of effective retaliation—tend to be tacitly, but seldom openly, approved by one's society. Being just such a group, the blind make excellent scapegoats. In keeping with Freudian theory, Chevigny and Braverman see the aggression here as stemming, to a significant degree, from an innate destructive drive, which cannot be wholly eradicated through any particular type of energy discharge, for the biological ground of the aggressive drive is ever present to replenish all such expenditures of energy. Consequently, no utopia awaits the blind—or any other minority group, for that matter. Nevertheless, Chevigny and Braverman believed that social attitudes and reaction to the blind could still be ameliorated to some extent through appropriate public education. This position as to the basically neurotic nature of our society, not to mention others, is borne out by the fact that reform movements on behalf of the blind have, to date, met with relatively small success.

Blank (1957), also a psychoanalytic investigator, similarly concerned himself with the role of unconscious forces in the behavior of blind people, as well as in that of the seeing in relation to the blind. According to this researcher, psychoanalytic contributions to the understanding of the psychic life of the blind are scant, and psychoanalysts, Blank further contended, often have the same prejudices against the blind as do other people. Intrapsychic factors, which this author designated as underlying personality disturbance in the visually handicapped, have already been discussed in Chapter 2: viz., (1) the unconscious significance of the eye as a sexual organ, including the equation of eye with mouth and with genitals; (2) the unconscious significance of the eye as a hostile, destructive organ, including the equation of eye with piercing phallus and devouring mouth; and (3) the unconscious significance of blindness as castration, as punishment for sin.

In addition to the above, Blank has pointed out that there is not, nor need there be, any special psychology of the blind, for the principles of general psychology (in this case psychoanalytic principles) apply as much to the blind as to the sighted. Vision is not necessary to the healthy differentiation and development of the ego. In Blank's words: "The developmental, behavioral and emotional problems of the blind have essentially the same causes as similar problems in those who can see. These causes include (1) the disturbed relation between parent and child in infancy and childhood; (2) traumatic events; (3) organic disease of the central nervous system, which occurs more frequently in the congenitally blind than in the seeing; (4) constitutional factors; and (5) failure to provide economic, educational, medical, and other professional services needed by the blind child and its family." With respect to the latter point, Blank further indicated that ego development in the congenitally blind child depends primarily on "physical contacts, consistent communication, and other components of mother love. Psychotherapy with the mother and assistance to the whole family are important prerequisites for helping the child."

According to Blank, "certain conditions occur more frequently among the blind than among those with other physical defects, particularly the group of symptoms unfortunately labeled 'blindisms' "—including autistic conditions and severe disturbances of motility. Blindisms (e.g., rocking, twirling, and other similar repetitive, self-stimulating responses) are especially characteristic of the blind child. The behavior in question is essentially the same as that characterizing autistic children and is not a condition peculiar to blindness. Furthermore, in most blind children, such responses can eventually be eliminated with the help of consistent parental effort.

Reactions to blindness acquired later in life reveal a different behavioral pattern. If blinding happens at a time when ego functions are already well developed, the loss is inevitably traumatic. Blindness will then disrupt established patterns of communication, motility, work, recreation, self-attitudes, body image, and other aspects of self-awareness. The typical reactions of the healthy personality to sudden blinding can be divided into two stages: (1) immediate shock and (2) depression. (A similar classification of reactions to traumatic blindness was offered by Cholden 1954). The shock phase generally lasts from two to seven days and consists primarily of profound feelings of depersonalization, with virtually total immobility and blank facial expression. Also, there is usually a generalized hypoesthesia or anesthesia, together with mutism or speech that is meager, slow, and muted. "Superficially, the condition may resemble catatonia, but the patient does not utter the delusional or dissociated remarks of the schizophrenic." At such times (more frequently after the passing of the cute period), the patient is likely to state that he lacks feeling or that he eels as if he and/or the world were unreal. This depersonalization appears o be an emergency defense against the threat of ego dissolution via an ruption of overwhelmingly painful affects. Such affects are subsequently ermitted emergence bit by bit in order that they may be confronted and ssimilated by the ego, which, at such a critical time, is insufficiently strong o master these elements in any but a piecemeal fashion. The appearance f affects marks the beginning of the second stage, which follows nmediately upon the first. At this point, symptoms of depression gradually rise, which may blend imperceptibly with the initial feelings of epersonalization. Such depression is tantamount to any other acute eactive depression, though it may also involve symptoms of agitation. It is asically a "state of mourning" for the loss of the eyes. According to Blank, is mourning process is a prerequisite to optimal recovery from trauma. No sychotherapeutic or rehabilitative work should be initiated at this time, for uch efforts will serve only to prolong (and perhaps even exacerbate) the epression. Moreover, premature counseling or therapeutic intervention nds to foster negative attitudes toward readjustment, with such ounterproductive tendencies apparently being irremedial in some cases. he mourning process is natural and desirable and should simply be llowed to run its own course.

It should here be noted that by traumatic blindness Blank does not ean just that type of blindness that comes rapidly through accident or war jury but also kinds of visual loss resulting from protracted ocular disease or which the patient has not been prepared by his physician and family. Under these circumstances, the realization of blindness can be almost as uddenly traumatic as blindness due to an explosion." To the extent that the atient has been prepared for blindness by sound medical counseling, as ell as frank familial discussion, the shock phase is eliminated and the epressive phase reduced in severity. With respect to the latter, the iitigation of symptoms occurs because part of the work of mourning has een accomplished in advance of final blindness. Thus, adequate orewarning facilitates recovery from trauma by decreasing the emotional istress over blindness prior to the period of ultimate loss.

Regarding the period of depersonalization, Blank cautions as follows: One should not make any strong inference about psychiatric diagnosis

and ego-strength from the severity of the symptoms in the shock stage. Fo
a patient to seem little disturbed by the onset of his blindness is ominou
Such denial suggests the possibility of psychosis, latent psychosis c
gratification of a severe neurotic need for punishment."

Concerning the recovery period, Blank stated that: "The recover
phase is characterized by healthy resolution of the work of mourning
gradual resumption of object-relationships; direction of psychic energy t
the solution of real problems of living, re-education, communication an
motility, work and acceptance of blindness as a handicap rather tha
masochistic submission to the blindness or denial that blindness makes on
different from others."

Blank also pointed out that the more permanent maladaptiv
reactions to blindness include virtually every type of psychopatholog
Most frequently observed are these: "(1) prolongation of the depressiv
phase. . . .into a chronic state of masochistic depression with sel
recrimination and bitterness toward the world and God; these peopl
remain dependent and resentful of those on whom they are dependent; the
never accept the fact that they are permanently blind, frequently visitin
doctors hoping for cure; (2) character disorders which often are a
aggravation of pre-existing traits; most common is chronic dependency, th
individual expecting to be taken care of as a helpless person; (3) man
successful, adjusted and relatively productive blind people identif
themselves with other blind in a defensive, self-protective minority again
the 'hostile, inconsiderate, stupid world of those that see'; if the blin
person shows a relatively undiscriminating prejudice toward the seeing, w
may be certain that he unconsciously shares the hostile attitudes towar
himself that he attributes to those not blind." Blank regarded the latter typ
of behavior as much a matter of social as individual psychopathology, fo
the sighted are, in fact, very frequently prejudiced and ignorant abou
blindness; even so, the individual blind person may sometimes g
overboard in reacting against such group psychopathology.

As to blindness acquired during childhood, the most importan
variables affecting reaction to trauma and subsequent adjustment ar
according to Blank: "(1) the defects and resources of the child's ego; (2) th
phase of psychosexual development during which the blindness
acquired—all other factors equal, we expect blindness occurring at ag

nine or ten to be less traumatic to the ego than at age five or thirteen; (3) the quality of relationship between parent and child before his blindness; (4) the parents' reactions to the child's blindness as determined by a specific predisposition—e.g., a strong unconscious scoptophilic conflict in the parent; (5) the ophthalmologist's relationship with the parents and child—which often is a decisive factor.

Expressive Behavior

Research here suggests that the development of facial expressions in children born blind or blinded shortly after birth depends upon maturation, while in sighted children such development depends largely on mimicry. In general, sightless children and adolescents show less adequate facial expression of emotions than do their seeing peers. In the latter, adequacy of expression increases with age, but among the blind it tends to decrease.

Thus, vision is an important means of acquiring the ability to form appropriate facial expressions. Nonetheless, other manners of acquisition are possible, and these should be emphasized in the education of the blind.

Motor Ability

With respect to motor development, there is some evidence that the blind child is less severely hampered by parental neglect than by parental overprotection. In one study, overprotected visually handicapped children performed significantly less efficiently than neglected blind children in a variety of track and field sports.

Sexual Adjustment

Little is known about the sexual behavior of the sightless, as a group. To date, the most extensive research in this area has been that of Thomas Cutsforth (1933). This investigator stressed the prevalence of incest conflict, masturbation, and latent homosexual tendencies among the blind.

While a blind man intensively studied by Kirtley and Hall (see Chapter 8) revealed a pattern of sexual characteristics like the above, other researchers (e.g., Blank, 1958) have emphasized the fact that such deviations are by no means universal in the blind and probably not even typical, given that the blind person is satisfactorily mobile and has a sufficiently wide range of interpersonal contacts. Blank, in contrast with Cutsforth, has stressed the possibility for normal sexual life in the sightless.

The Effects of Physical Factors Other than Blindness

On this topic, research generally indicates that protracted hospitalizatic facial disfigurement caused by or connected with eye disorder, prolong medical treatment of eye diseases, or any blindness with onset after ＊ early childhood years will inevitably result in emotional trauma.

Child Development

According to Lowenfeld (1963), blindness per se does not retard ｃ velopment. For congenitally blind children, the sequence of developmｅ is generally comparable to that observable in normal children, with ＊ blind child progressing in basic patterns of posture, manipulatｉ locomotion, exploration, language, and social behavior—all indicating ＊ fundamental role of maturation in his development. Still, the blind chilｅ rate of development may be somewhat slower than that of the sightｔ child. Blindisms (including rolling or tilting of the head, thrusting the fingｅ into the eyes, and swaying of the body) are associated with a lack ｅ external stimulation in the child's environment. However, these automｃ acts of self-stimulation usually disappear as the child grows older. Childｒ of low mental ability, or those who are emotionally disturbed, frequenＴ continue to perform such behaviors for a longer period of time. As alreｃ indicated, responses of this sort are also characteristic of similarly affectＴ seeing children.

Some studies show more abnormal behavior and motility distｕ bance, with generally less normal development, in children blind frｏ retrolental fibroplasia (RLF) than in those congenitally blind throuｅ prematurity, as such, who, in turn, reveal more anomalies than tＨ nonpremature congenitally blind or children blinded during the first feｗ years of life. The latter two groups tend to do better in school than RLF premature congenitally blind children. RLF blindness is more likely to ｂ associated with some degree of brain damage than is nonprematｕ congenital blindness. The behavior of a considerable number of RＬ children has been observed to be similar or identical to that of childrｅ diagnosed with infantile autism. The etiology of such psychopathology ｉ typically explained either on the basis of psychological or neurologicｃ factors. Those favoring the psychogenic hypothesis stress evidence such ｓ maternal rejection of the infant, which tendency is likely to be greatly strengthened by the disrupted mother-infant relationship arising out of the premature offspring's necessarily prolonged hospitalization and the mother's reaction to this separation, as well as to the infant's blindness itself. Those holding the neurological hypothesis point to the fact that some RLF children are disturbed because of obvious neural damage. Some of these children are clearly multiply handicapped. Nevertheless, at the present stage of knowledge, the evidence is insufficient to permit justifiably selecting one of these explanatory alternatives over the other.

In general, research indicates that, within the broad range of possible parental responses to children born blind, two reactions tend to be typical: on the one hand, overprotection; and on the other, expecting too much of the child.

Likewise, a number of studies suggest certain characteristic personality differences between the congenitally blind child and children blinded during the first years of life or thereafter. For one thing, the person born blind never has to adjust to blindness as such; whereas the individual who loses his sight later obviously does have to make such an adjustment. Consequently, the latter is more likely to be plagued with emotional disturbances such as chronic anxiety or depression. Studies tend to show that congenital blindness has less impact on the self-concept than does acquired blindness. On the other hand, in contrast to the adventitiously blind, persons born without sight appear to be more strongly affected by what other people think of them.

For development, some vision is, of course, better than none at all. Partial sight, in itself, can objectively enhance adjustment potential; whereas total or functional blindness, in itself, is completely neutral, neither adding nor subtracting anything from potential. Nevertheless, most studies indicate that the partially seeing child tends to be more maladjusted than the blind child. Such maladjustment seems to emanate from the identity conflict discussed earlier in this chapter—and not from any factor peculiar to being partially sighted as such. However, regardless of whether one is considering the blind or the partially seeing, research generally suggests that the single most critical determinant of adjustment success is relatively high general intelligence.

With respect to the psychological functioning of RLF children in

comparison with other blind, as well as normal, children, Cohen (196
reported on the findings of a monumental, longitudinal, interdisciplina
investigation, conducted over approximately a twelve-year period, with tl
child subjects in question being observed at regular intervals from birth
about age twelve by both physicians and psychologists, as well as soci
workers. Altogether, fifty-seven subjects were studied. Forty-eight (
eighty-five percent) of these children were blind as a result of RLF, i.e., th
had been prematurely born and had suffered from the effects of ove
oxygenation during incubation. Between 1942 and 1955, this was tl
leading cause of blindness among neonates in the United States. Moreove
some of the subjects were only partially blind, while others were als
sightless from birth but not because of RLF. In this latter group, the caus
of blindness included optic atrophy, cataracts, and retinoblastoma (
absence of the retinal receptors). At least three-fourths of the subje
population had no vision at all or else only light perception.

Over half of the RLF children had weighed less than three pounds
birth. Still, most of these subjects had eventually caught up with the heig
and weight norms of their respective ages, though the lightest prematur
had tended to remain small for their ages. Like other premature infant
such individuals showed a high incidence of physical handicaps, that is,
this group handicaps other than blindness. Most significant among thes
were disorders of the central nervous system, viz., convulsive seizures ar
cerebral palsy, which were most pronounced in subjects who had weighe
three pounds or less at birth.

With respect to intellectual functioning, the group manifeste
extreme variability, with an IQ range of 45 to 160 on the Hayes-Binet Sca
(an intelligence test designed for use with blind children). Four of tl
subjects could not be tested reliably, and five were in institutions for tl
mentally retarded. The median IQ score for the group was 93. Of the fort
eight individuals tested, 12.5 percent scored over 120 and 37.5 perce
below 80. For the total group, a fourth of the children scored below 70 ar
half between 80 and 120. The distribution of scores was skewed toward tl
lower end, with a slight pileup at the higher level.

A significant relationship was found between the presence of ment
retardation and degree of vision during prematurity. Fourteen of tl
twenty-seven children who were totally blind or possessed only lig

reception (and who had weighed under 1500 grams on delivery) had IQs less than 70; while only about 25 percent of the other blind prematures with higher birth weights had such low IQs. Also, only two out of six partially sighted cases weighing below 1500 grams at birth had IQs lower than 70. None of the full-term children in the sample were similarly impaired.

In addition to the Hayes-Binet Scale, the verbal subtests of the Wechsler Intelligence Scale for Children were administered to the testable subjects. Average intraindividual performance on these various subscales was fairly even, except that the average score for comprehension was significantly lower than the averages for the other subtests. This held true for all the children, for those with IQs above as well as below 95. The unusually low comprehension scores were perhaps due to one or more of the following factors: a lack of social experience on the part of the subjects; reduced abstract ability; or inapplicability of the test items to the subjects. With regard to digit memory, the group with below average IQs had a significantly higher average score than the group with above average IQs. This superiority of the below average subjects was attributed to the extreme emphasis parents and teachers place on verbal recall when a child shows few other intellectual capacities. In general, the results of the foregoing measures agreed with ratings of school performance and appeared to reflect adequacy of personality functioning, as well as of intelligence.

In twenty-eight children with RLF, there was observed a high incidence of EEG abnormalities, indicating that neurological anomaly was a major determinant of behavioral retardation in these cases. Moreover, such abnormalities were not confined solely to the occipital lobes but were also frequently found in more anterior locations, suggesting the existence of relatively diffuse cortical damage.

The EEG findings—plus social and medical histories; general neurological and psychological data; and interview information obtained from parents—led to the tentative conclusion that a majority of the children with below normal intelligence (and consequently not making adequate adjustments) were handicapped by generalized physiological impairment. Only in a minority of cases could physical factors be ruled out, with the chief responsibility for developmental deficiency being safely ascribable to emotional problems. Likewise, when basic neurological structures were intact, the constitution of the child seemed to be the deciding factor in adjustmental outcome. Brain impairment often resulted in poor intellectual functioning and inadequate adjustment, even in families where emotional climate was optimally satisfactory. Also, there was no convincing evidence to indicate that prematurity, coupled with over-oxygenation and blindness, had resulted in more brain damage than might have arisen out of the same degree of prematurity, per se.

There was no evidence to show that the partially sighted were generally more maladjusted than the totally blind. However, partial sight, when eventually lost, did tend to be associated with severe behavioral regression.

Cohen concluded as follows: "We have seen children with gross multiple handicaps make good academic progress and develop apparently normal personalities without serious emotional problems. Others either lacked within themselves the motivation and ability or were too damaged by parental rejection and lack of opportunity for healthy growth. . . . If a child is able to compensate for his lack of sight by utilizing his other senses and has experienced healthy emotional relationships, he may achieve a normal adjustment and a normal or even high level of intellectual productivity, despite complicated handicaps."

Blindness in the Aged

There are today roughly half a million totally and administratively blind persons in the United States, "administrative" or "legal" blindness being defined by the Social Security Act of 1935 as: visual acuity for distance of 20:200 or less in the better eye after correction; or visual acuity of more than 20:200 if the widest diameter of the visual field subtends an angle no greater than 20 degrees (Bauman, 1969). Above fifty percent of this blind population is over fifty-five years of age. As the lifespan increases, blindness is becoming more characteristic of the aged and, because of improved preventive measures, less characteristic of the young (Saterbak, 1969). The problems usually associated with blindness (including prejudicial attitudes and discriminatory social practices) become greatly amplified with age.

Based on his observations of the elderly blind, Riffenburgh (1967) has pointed out that, for the old, the secondary gains connected with blindness may come to be even more rewarding than vision itself.

Consequently, it may be difficult to wean the aged from dependence on blindness, partly because of their loneliness and partly because of the natural diminution in somatic and sensory faculties, perhaps also because of the presence of other serious health problems in addition to blindness. The elderly have significantly less rehabilitation potential than do the young. Often they are unable to learn to read Braille, and physical inactivity in them is a more serious problem than it is for the young, as such inactivity frequently leads to a variety of added physical ailments, which is not the case in the young. The rehabilitation counselor should encourage all types of potentially meaningful activity, e.g., hobbies can be especially therapeutic. Rehabilitation potential is markedly reduced for blind persons who live alone or who are without any form of family assistance. This is even more true of the aging blind than it is of the younger blind.

The Adjustment of the Blind versus the Deaf

Results of research on this question are contradictory as to general or specific handicapping effects of blindness in comparison with deafness. Still, most investigators agree that blindness, by and large, is less socially and communicationally handicapping than is deafness, especially if the latter is present from birth or the early years of life. David Wright (1969), an authority on the educational history of the deaf, concurs in this judgment.

Personality Characteristics Associated with Physical Disabilities Other than Blindness

McDaniel (1969), in his review of research on the psychological aspects of physical disability, affirmed the continuing appropriateness of Wright's (1969) conclusions regarding the relation of disability to personality: "(1) there is no substantial indication that persons with an impaired physique differ as a group in their general or overall adjustment; (2) there is no clear evidence of an association between types of physical disability and particular personality characteristics; (3) although personality patterns have not been found consistently to distinguish disability groups as a whole, certain behaviors are very directly connected with the limitations." Wright, like Blank and Cholden, stressed the normality and therapeutic importance of mourning or depression in all individuals suffering sudden onset of any major disability; while denial of the handicap (the antithesis of mourning) interferes with rehabilitation. Similarly, Blank (1969) emphasized the role of mourning for patients handicapped with serious physical conditions other than blindness.

Conclusions

Now let us return to the question posed at the outset of this chapter: What is the nature of the handicapping effects of blindness? Those who regard blindness as a mere physical nuisance do not see it as a handicap at all—or, at worst, only a minor handicap. On the other hand, those taking the disaster view consider blindness a massive or total disability and, accordingly, stress numerous negative factors or limitations presumed to be intrinsic to the physical condition of blindness. However, from the preceding review of objective evidence regarding the adjustment of the blind, it is apparent that neither the nuisance nor the disaster view is appropriate, for neither view accurately represents the known facts concerning the relation of blindness to behavior. Blindness is neither a minor physical nuisance nor a generalized, overwhelmingly incapacitating disability; rather it is something between these two grossly oversimplified extremes. It is a serious handicap but, nonetheless, one which can be mastered, given favorable conditions of intelligence, motivation, education, and social and economic environment. As was pointed out in the foregoing pages, blindness as such has no direct effects on personal or social adjustment but is, nevertheless, associated with a number of indirect effects in these areas. As Lowenfeld indicated, the only direct effects of blindness upon behavior are to be found in the cognitive and mobility functioning of the individual.

In 1963, Lowenfeld said of research in this field: "Studies of the psychological implications of blindness are either of a primarily descriptive nature with no reports of statistical support or of a primarily statistical nature with little or no reference to actual behavior." In the latter category, investigators have relied on personality inventories, interview records, and attitude and behavior rating scales, the applicability of which depends, to a large extent, upon the accuracy of self-report or rater opinion. Lowenfeld cautioned that results obtained through such procedures must, therefore, be taken with a grain of salt, regardless of the degree of statistical refinement and objectivity on which such devices may be based. On the other hand, observations of overt behavior cannot reliably be related to blindness unless such quantitative validation supports the attempted connection. In addition, Lowenfeld pointed out that in many studies the distinctions between individuals who are totally or partially blind and between those who are congenitally or adventitiously blind have not received proper attention. According to Lowenfeld, blurring of such important distinctions as these is largely responsible for the ambiguous results produced by so many investigations, as well as for the flatly contradictory findings of numerous others. Research in this area "must overcome serious methodological problems and employ clearer theory if it is to have better results."

During the years that have elapsed since Lowenfeld offered the above assessment, the research picture for this field has remained essentially unchanged. For the period prior to 1963, there were, as previously indicated, some outstanding instances of both quantitative and clinical research (Bauman, 1954; Cowen et al., 1961; Blank, 1957), but unfortunately, these were exceptions. Similarly, the bulk of research since 1963 has continued to show relatively little in the way of methodological progress, although a few investigations, like that of Cohen (1966), have achieved a high degree of rigor. Certainly further work of this caliber is needed if we are ever to have a truly satisfactory understanding of the psychology of the blind.

References

Chapter 6/ Adjustment in the Visually Handicapped

Bauman, M. 1954. *Adjustment to blindness.* Commonwealth of Pennsylvania: Pennsylvania State Council for the Blind.

Bauman, M. 1969. Dimensions of blindness. In M. Goldberg & J. Swinton, eds. *Blindness research: The expanding frontier.* University Park, Pa.: Pennsylvania State University Press.

Bauman, M. & Yoder, N. 1966. *Adjustment to blindness reviewed.* Springfield, Il.: Charles C. Thomas.

Blank, H. 1958. Dreams of the blind. *Psychoanalytic Quarterly, 27:* 154-178.

Blank, H. 1957. Psychoanalysis and blindness. *Psychoanalytic Quarterly 26:* 1-24.

Blank, H. 1969. Reactions to loss of body parts or functions: Research priorities in rehabilitation. In M. Goldberg & J. Swinton, eds. *Blindness research: The expanding frontier.* University Park, Pa.: Pennsylvania State University Press.

Chevigny, H. & Braverman, S. 1950. *The adjustment of the blind.* New Haven: Yale University Press.

Cholden, L. 1958. *A psychiatrist works with blindness.* New York: American Foundation for the Blind.

Cholden, L. 1954. Some psychiatric problems in the rehabilitation of the blind. *Bulletin of the Menninger Clinic,* 18: 107-112.

Cohen, J. 1966. The effects of blindness on children's development. Children 13: 23-27.

Cowen, E., Underberg, R., Verillo, R. & Benham, F. 1961. *Adjustment to visual disability in adolescents.* New York: American Foundation for the Blind.

Cutsforth, T. 1933. *The blind in school and society.* New York: American Foundation for the Blind.

Cutsforth, T. 1951. *The blind in school and society.* Revised ed. New York: American Foundation for the Blind.

Cutsforth, T. 1950. Personality and social adjustment among the blind. In P. Zahl, ed. *Blindness: Modern approaches to the unseen environment.* Princeton: Princeton University Press.

Davis, C. 1964. Development of the self-concept. *New Outlook for the Blind* 58: 49-51.

Lowenfeld, B. 1963. Psychological problems of children with impaired vision. In W. Cruickshank, ed. *Psychology of exceptional children and youth.* 2nd ed. Englewood Cliffs, N.J.: Prentice-Hall.

McDaniel, J. 1969. *Physical disability and human behavior.* Elmsford, N.Y.: Pergamon Press.

Riffenburgh, R. 1967. The psychology of blindness. *Geriatrics* 22: 127-133.

Saterbak, M. 1969. Developments and research needs in work with the aged blind. In M. Goldberg & J. Swinton, eds. *Blindness research: The expanding frontier.* University Park, Pa.: Pennsylvania State University Press.

Wright, B. 1960. *Physical disability: A psychological approach.* New York: Harper.

Wright, D. 1969. *Deafness.* New York: Stein and Day.

7

Empirical Studies of Dreaming in the Blind

The relation of visual impairment to dreaming is a topic that has long interested psychologists, as well as curious laymen, both blind and sighted. For the most part, research here has focused upon the imaginal constituents of dreams, comparing various visually handicapped groups with one another, the seeing, and occasionally other disability groups. Notwithstanding the great value of dream analysis for the understanding of personality, relatively few studies have explored the nature of motivational or other characterological factors in the dreams of the sightless. Although some important investigations have thrown considerable light on certain developmental aspects of the subject, their emphasis has typically been upon cognitive rather than psychodynamic variables. Thus, much is known about the sensory structure of the blind's dream life but little regarding the bearing of their dreams upon individual attributes of personality or characteristic patterns of waking behavior.

The relevant empirical work has involved a wide range of methods: (1) introspective; (2) clinical; (3) experimental; (4) questionnaire; (5) interviewing; (6) qualitative content analysis; and (7) quantitative content analysis.

The vast majority of published reports rest upon introspective, questionnaire, and interviewing techniques, the latter two often occurring in

combination. Both clinical and experimental studies, though usually mor
informative, constitute only a handful of the total available publication
Among the former, the chief emphasis has been psychoanalytic, while in th
latter category, the most reliable findings have been those c
psychophysiological investigations, utilizing the EEG method. Th
qualitative content analysis of recorded dream reports, involving a
extensive series of dreams derived from one or more subjects, is a
approach rarely applied—though occasionally a short dream series
evaluated in this way.

A study that I recently conducted in collaboration with Calvin Hall (t
be described in the next chapter) is, so far as we know, the first in this fiel
to employ the method of quantitative content analysis. A second stud
employing this method, conducted with Kathy Cannistraci, will be describe
later in the chapter. This approach consists of tabulating the frequencies c
numerous kinds of manifest dream content (such as those involved i
aggressive, friendly, or sexual interactions) and, therefore, yields precis
numerical scores for each of the classifications in question. In this manne
one can assess the relative strength or weakness of various elements in th
dreams of the individual or group under study and also make exac
normative comparisons. Previous comparative research in this area ha
often been extremely ambiguous because of a chronic failure to use reliabl
quantified norms. Indeed, such statistical data (based on a genuinel
representative population of normal people) was not even available fc
dream researchers until the recent normative investigation of Hall and Va
de Castle (1966). In conjunction with the latter authors' broad conten
analysis system, this information should be of considerable value to futur
investigators, as it was to us, in clarifying certain critical issues regardin
the dream life of the blind.

In the present chapter I shall examine a comprehensive body of studie
concerned with the key empirical and theoretical questions in this field: (
characteristic dream imagery; (2) common dream themes and the
motivational implications; (3) dream mentation in blind children; and (4) th
nature of dreaming in the deaf-blind and individuals otherwis
handicapped.

Dream Imagery in the Visually Handicapped

The two earliest systematic studies of dream imagery in the blind—those of Heermann (1838) and Jastrow (1888)—are generally acknowledged as classics in the literature on this subject, for subsequent research has almost invariably reproduced their central findings. Before discussing the details of the Heermann and Jastrow investigations, I shall summarize their most important, empirical generalizations—for both, these were the same, as Jastrow's work, though independent, was largely a duplication of Heermann's original pioneering effort. (1) There are no visual images in the congenitally blind; (2) individuals blinded before the age of five experience no visual imagery; (3) those who become sightless between the ages of five and seven may or may not retain such images; (4) most persons losing their vision after the seventh year continue to experience optical imagery, though its initial photographic clarity tends to fade markedly with the passage of time. Over the intervening decades since Jastrow's study, these generalizations have received frequent corroboration from researchers employing a variety of methods and diverse blind populations. With at most only slight qualifications, they may be regarded as empirical cornerstones, equally applicable to the blind's visual imagery waking life, as well as dreams.

According to Jastrow, the years five to seven constitute a critical period for the retention of mental pictures, prior to which the visual cortex is receiving its "elementary education," and, therefore, requires an incessant input of external stimuli to maintain its integrity. Blindness prevents this stimulation and consequently leads to the degeneration of the sight center, with the result that all visual imagery is lost. By age seven, the occipital region is sufficiently mature to sustain appreciable visual activity in the absence of environmental input, so that blinding at this time does not eradicate the visualizing power.

In his study of fifty-three visually handicapped subjects, Heermann questioned fourteen totally blind persons, all of whom had lost their sight before the fifth year, and none reported dream vision. Four of his subjects had become completely blind between the fifth and seventh years. Of these, one claimed dream vision, while another said that he experienced only on rare occasions and then always dimly. The two remaining subjec were uncertain as to whether or not they experienced visual images i dreams. Of thirty-five individuals who had become totally blind after th seventh year, all reported dream vision.

Heermann's sample included many aged persons. From their report he concluded that individuals blinded in mature life retain the power dream vision longer than those blinded nearer the critical period. F recorded twelve cases in which dream vision continued after ten to fiftee years of sightlessness; four after fifteen to twenty years; and four othe after twenty to twenty-five years. One subject reported dream visic following thirty-five years of blindness; another after fifty-two years; s another said he had experienced it for fifty-four years, after which it fade out.

In addition, ten postmortem cases were examined. Heerman concluded that, allowing for considerable individual differences, the op nerve degenerates after about twenty years of blindness, often as far ba as the chiasma; therefore, the nerve is unnecessary to dream vision, th process being dependent on purely cerebral mechanisms. In this connectio Jastrow mentioned a case of visual hallucinations in a blind woma described by Esquirol. More recently, Rosenthal (1964) has discussed repo of such hallucinations in blind subjects under the influence of LSD, some whom had undergone bilateral enucleation. Such evidence clearly suppor Heermann's inference concerning the importance of cerebral structures.

Half a century later, Jastrow interrogated nearly 200 totally an partially blind persons of both sexes, from institutions for the visua handicapped in Philadelphia and Baltimore, and obtained results fu congruent with Heermann's findings. Fifty-eight of Jastrow's subjects we completely blind. Of these, thirty-two had become so before age five, an not one of them reported seeing in his dreams. Six subjects had lost sig between the ages of five and seven. Of these, four described dreams seeing, but two of the subjects stated that such dreams were vague an occurred infrequently. Two others claimed that they never dreamed seeing. Of the twenty persons who had become blind after the seven year, all reported dream vision. Jastrow concluded that, if blindness tak place between the fifth and seventh years, the preservation of the visualizing power depends upon the developmental status of the individual; yet if the capacity is retained, it is neither stable nor pronounced. On the other hand, if vision is lost following the seventh year, the sight center can, in spite of the deficit, maintain its function, and ". . . the dreams of such an individual are hardly distinguishable from those of the seeing person." However, Jastrow also found that the strength of dream vision was generally less in persons blinded nearer the critical period than in those blinded later in life. The former were, for instance, not as likely to retain color in their dreams.

Jastrow's findings for the partially blind were in accord with data from the totally blind. Of twenty-three subjects whose dream vision was similar in quality to their waking visual experience, all had been blinded no later than the fifth year. Of twenty-four subjects whose dream vision was markedly clearer than that of waking life, all had lost full sight no earlier than the sixth year. In general, those who knew color had more frequent and brighter dream vision than those who distinguished only light and dark.

Of 183 answers to the questionnaire item, "Do you dream?," percentages for the various alternatives were as follows: 25.7 percent "yes"; 1.1 percent "no"; 43.2 percent "seldom"; 22.4 percent "frequently"; 7.6 percent "every night." On the basis of these results, Jastrow concluded that ". . . the blind, on the whole, are not such good dreamers as the sighted . . . ," i.e., the sighted probably dream more frequently and more vividly than the blind. Nevertheless, blind females were better dreamers than blind males. On the above item, male percentages ran 54.5 "seldom," 19.2 "frequently," and 7.1 "every night"; whereas the corresponding female figures were 29.8, 26.2, and 8.3.

However, in the light of subsequent research, the foregoing generalization is untenable, especially insofar as it applies to the blind en masse, that is, both sexes considered together. The current literature contains numerous reports of frequent vivid dreaming in both the adventitiously and congenitally blind (McCartney, 1913; Wheeler, 1920; Deutsch, 1928; Blank, 1958; Von Schumann, 1959). Furthermore, the results of my own investigations with Hall and others have accorded well with those of the aforementioned researchers. In addition, contemporary EEG experiments, conducted under highly controlled laboratory conditions, have conclusively established that all people dream and do so for approximately twenty percent of the sleep period (Van de Castle, 1971).

Also, it is difficult to interpret Jastrow's percentages since none are given for comparable sighted groups. Moreover, the questionnaire method when applied to the study of dreams, is well known for its vulnerability to gaps in memory. The importance of trivial elements is easily exaggerated while other, more revealing contents are often forgotten or repressed. Any investigator who has attempted to collect more than an occasional dream report from normal seeing individuals knows that the task is highly frustrating unless his subjects have a strong prior interest in dreams. Many people are unwilling to report their dreams, owing to the very intimate nature of such material. Others simply claim they do not dream or do so only vaguely and infrequently. Among college populations, for example, is virtually impossible to obtain properly motivated subjects unless the researcher offers some appealing extrinsic reward, say, extra course credit or monetary remuneration. Considering these commonplace research problems, it is not surprising that many of Jastrow's "unrewarded" blind subjects reported little or no dreaming. One could, of course, not expect any more interest or cooperation from this kind of population than from a sighted one.

On the other hand, Jastrow's conclusion concerning the superiority of female over male dreamers has received at least partial support from later research. Females (whether blind or sighted) apparently do not dream more than males (blind or sighted); however, women in general appear to have better dream recall than men in general (McCartney, 1913; Van de Castle, 1971). As to vividness of dream imagery, Hall (1966) has found that adult females experience more color than do adult males, but this was the only respect in which the imagery of women was superior to that of men. Furthermore, the tendency to dream in color was not related to any particular feature of personality but appeared to be merely an aesthetic embellishment of the dreamer.

Jastrow found that when blindness occurs suddenly after the critical period, dream content is characterized by a preponderance of past experiences, which are more vivid than those of the present; but with the passing of time, recent impressions obtrude with increasing frequency until they constitute the major substance of dream life.

This finding seems to be of general validity, if we discount Jastrow's gratuitous tendency to regard vision as the only modality capable of producing vivid imagery. Later studies of dreaming in traumatically blinded individuals (e.g., Von Schumann, 1959) suggest that the ascendance of past impressions stems largely from the defense mechanism of undoing, that is, in dreams the blinded person magically abolishes his recent loss by returning to his sighted past. Jastrow assumed such regression to be based upon the mere vivacity of past visual experience in contrast with present blindness. Although this explanation is supported by reports of temporarily continued, normal dream vision following sudden blinding (Furness, 1921; Villey, 1932; Blank, 1958), it does not account for the great frequency of undoing dreams, which sometimes persist long after the initial photographic clarity of visualization has dimmed or disappeared entirely. In such cases, the wish to see or to undo the original trauma endures despite the growing scarcity of overpowering visual images from the past.

By way of illustration, one traumatically induced case informed us that for approximately the first eighteen months of the postblindness period, his dream vision had remained unaffected, with one recurring dream about his accident being particularly salient. In this dream all essential details of the accident were faithfully reproduced, save one—at the end of the dream, the subject actively prevented the event that had caused his blindness. Though this subject retained substantial visualizing power, the normal mental pictures originally present had eventually given way to a generally subdued imagery. However, for a year or so subsequent to this change, he continued to experience the said dream of undoing, but, of course, with significantly reduced visual intensity. In this connection, Von Schumann has described cases in which such dreams persevered for much longer periods.

Thus, dream regression of the type encountered by Jastrow probably involves potent psychodynamic factors peculiar to the individual, as well as the neural-phenomenological mechanics of visual imagery, per se.

Jastrow also asked those blinded in youth or later if they were wont to give imaginary faces to persons met after blindness, and some reported in the affirmative, additionally saying that they saw such faces in their dreams. Nonetheless, Jastrow concluded that this phenomenon occurs less extensively in the blind than in the seeing.

My observations incline me to be suspicious of the preceding conclusion. I have received reports from numerous individuals blinded after the critical period, testifying to a habitual ascription of imaginary faces to people not previously seen. The visual imagery involved often seemed vivid, yet even when dim, the tendency to impute such faces (both in dreams and waking life) still occurred regularly. Consequently, it seems likely that Jastrow's generalization covers a much narrower range of blind persons than he supposed. In other words, it is doubtful that the use of artificially constructed faces occurs more extensively among the sighted, but, when present, the visual imagery is probably more lifelike than that conjured up by the blind.

According to Jastrow, the blind are able to obtain color imagery through synesthesia, but the tendency is weak and occurs rarely. In this regard, he cited one case of a twenty-year-old man who saw color images on hearing certain sounds and words.

By contrast, Wheeler (1920) reported intense synesthesia in a twenty-seven-year-old man, accidentally blinded at the age of eleven. In both waking and dream life, this subject experienced very complicated synesthetic phenomena, e.g., schematic forms associated with persons, voices, and directions of the compass, while many other sounds and objects were identified by specific colors. Auditory imagery was deficient, but this was largely compensated by visual associations. Visual images outnumbered those from other modalities, both in dreams and waking experience, even though such imagery was vague in form at the time of the study, with images from the other senses providing details to fill the lapses in visual memory.

More recent investigators have found that synesthetic associations (referred to by some as "photisms") take place fairly often in individuals blinded after the critical period (see Chapter 6). Thus, on this point, Jastrow would simply appear to be in error (Lowenfeld, 1963).

As to the relative influence of the various senses on the overall imagery of the blind, Jastrow found audition to be the most critical in dreams, as well as in waking, with kinesthesis being second in importance.

interestingly enough, his subjects reported that they almost never dreamed of reading embossed writing with the fingers.

On this issue, other observers have tended to concur with Jastrow (Klein, 1819; McCartney, 1913; Deutsch, 1928; Fraser-Harris, 1928; Blank, 1958; Duran, 1969). At least with respect to individuals blinded prior to the critical period, there is general agreement that auditory images predominate, while tactile and/or kinesthetic elements are next in impact, and gustatory, olfactory, and thermal experiences are rare.

In regard to the above, Deutsch found that long coherent conversations and secondary revision of the dreamwork were more common in the dreams of the congenitally blind than in those blind who still possessed visual imagery.

Similarly, in a much earlier introspective study, Hitschmann (1894), blind since his third year, reported hearing entire lectures in his dreams. He also dreamed frequently in poetry and believed this tendency to be common among the sightless. Hitschmann indicated that his dream life was characterized primarily by abstract rather than sensuous elements.

As stated at the beginning of this chapter, the most scientifically reliable findings of both Heermann and Jastrow were those pertaining to visual imagery as such. With respect to this question, subsequent investigators have almost universally produced similar or identical results (McCartney, 1913; Deutsch, 1928; Bolli, 1932; Villey, 1932; Blank, 1958), while reviewers of the stature of William James (1918) have accepted the Heermann-Jastrow generalizations as valid. McCartney, however, also reported visual residues in several cases blinded before age three and qualified the Heermann-Jastrow critical period to allow for maturational precocity in the visual brain; whereas Bolli set the critical period at age four to six. Nevertheless, most researchers have agreed with the limits originally placed by Jastrow.

Several fairly recent EEG studies of the blind have also obtained findings in accord with the conclusions of Heermann and Jastrow.

Berger et al. (1962), in their subjects, found that characteristic frontal EEG waves significantly often preceded the rapid eye movements (REMs) associated with dreams. REMs were absent during the dream periods of three men with lifelong blindness and of two men with thirty and forty years of blindness, respectively. However, REMs were present in three men sightless three, ten, and fifteen years, respectively. These findings were considered confirmatory of Dement and Kleitman's (1957) hypothesis that attributes REMs to visual scanning activity during dreams.

Offenkrantz and Wolpert (1963), studying the EEG activity of a thirty-nine-year-old congenitally blind male, found dreams to be coincident with Stage 1 EEG but not with REMs. The subject reported no visual imagery in his dreams and followed nothing in his dreams with the eyes. The investigators concluded that Stage 1 is a physiological concomitant of dreaming, while REMs only reflect visual activity in dreams.

However, judging from the results of subsequent REM studies, the visual-scanning hypothesis no longer appears tenable (Hartmann, 1967; Dement, 1969). Though the biological function of REM sleep is not as yet adequately understood, a number of recent hypotheses (not necessarily mutually exclusive of one another) offer possible explanations for different aspects of the REM phenomenon (Hartmann, 1967). With respect to the findings of the Berger et al. and Offenkrantz-Wolpert investigations, just described, the current hypothesis of most direct relevance holds that REM sleep innervates the brain in the specific service of depth perception. No other popular hypothesis would seem to be capable of explaining the long-term persistence of apparently normal REM states in persons blinded after the critical period and the relative absence of such states in the congenitally blind or their lack of correlation with dreaming in the latter group. Since many congenitally blind persons possess ocular musculature as healthy (and frequently healthier) as that of the later blind, they would seem to have at least as much mechanical potential for normal REM states as the latter group, unless, of course, REMs do, in fact, bear some connection with past visual functioning (whether such functioning be related to depth perception or some other type of cerebral-visual phenomenon). That such, indeed, is the case is suggested by the above two EEG experiments; to this extent, their results, without being directly related to the critical-period hypothesis, are still compatible with it.

Regarding the complete loss of visual remnants in some individuals blinded after the critical period, Blank has hypothesized "sensory typing" as a crucial determinant, viz., the classification of people into sensory types based upon the predominance of one modality over the others in the person's ego functioning. In this connection, he cited the case of a thirty-year-old teacher, sightless since the age of eight, who could call forth only the vaguest visual memories and experienced no visual images in his dreams (which were, nonetheless, fairly frequent and quite vivid). Despite his negligible visualizing power, this man possessed an active intelligence, as well as superior memory for early childhood experience (including the events of his illness and subsequent blinding). He was a musician by avocation, and, during infancy, had demonstrated great musical ability, together with precocious speech development. He appeared to be an 'auditory type," which perhaps was the chief cause of the almost total disappearance of his visual memory.

In a further study of visual imagery, one of the most original and fascinating in the literature, Von Schumann (1955) analyzed the dreams of *The Iliad* and *The Odyssey,* and on the basis of the imagery therein, concluded that Homer had been blinded in early life. According to Von Schumann, the Homeric dreams differ phenomenologically from other dreams described in ancient Greek literature. They are characterized by fleeting materiality, by airy beings, and other uncertain forms. This investigator, in his work with the visually handicapped, found that the dreams of individuals blinded during childhood tend to possess the same visual quality, i.e., foggy shapes, pictures that appear suddenly, then quickly fade out or remain only on the border of the visual. Children blinded young, for example, often dream about spirits of which they can give only the vaguest descriptions. Although one might argue that Homer was simply trying to represent the ghostlike forms of Hades, this solution, in Von Schumann's view, does not explain why other dreams in Greek literature are so dissimilar. Likewise, the dreams of the Old Testament and of Virgil's *Aeneid* are visually clearer than those in Homer. In further support of his thesis, the author pointed out that of the dreams recorded in the Holy Tablets of Epidaurus, twenty-three are purely visual, six predominantly so, five partly visual and partly acoustic, while only six are mainly acoustic and only six purely acoustic. Similarly, in Classic dramas optical images greatly outnumber the auditory. In contrast, ninety percent of the sensory elements in the Homeric dreams are auditory, which is unusual for any long epic employing the present tense. In addition, strong feelings of isolation and aggression, which were typical of the dreams of

Von Schumann's blind analysands, are also pronounced in the Homeric dreams but, at the same time, are not characteristic of the dreams of ancient drama in general.

As to the above, we need not debate the legend of Homer's blindness or, for that matter, the possibility of one-man authorship of *The Iliad* and *The Odyssey*. Von Schumann's evidence is, if not conclusive, at least highly persuasive. Even if one man did not, in fact, write either of the works in question—and these were composed by a number of poets—it still seems likely that some members of this group were individuals blind from early life.

Common Themes and Psychodynamic Elements
in the Dreams of the Blind

While a number of observers have been interested in the narrative aspect of sightless persons' dreams (e.g., Jastrow, 1888; Furness, 1921), my search of the literature uncovered only four studies primarily concerned with the relation of such contents to actual personality functioning (those of McCartney, 1913; Cason, 1935; Blank, 1958; and Von Schumann, 1959). So far as I have been able to determine, the investigations of Blank and Von Schumann constitute the only serious clinical work in this area, whereas the studies of McCartney and Cason rest chiefly upon the questionnaire method. However, before reviewing these more pertinent researches, let us briefly consider the findings of Jastrow and Furness.

According to Jastrow, the dreams of the blind tend to be composed of realistic and commonplace ingredients, lacking the romantic or imaginative qualities so prominent in the dreams of the sighted. For example, his boy subjects tended to dream of playing, running, jumping and the like; the men of broom making, piano tuning, teaching, and other types of work; the females of sewing, fancywork, household activities, and so on. Although he noted that the incidence of fanciful elements decreases with age in the seeing as well as the blind—even to the point of rarity—he also went on to state: "What is most typical in dreams of the sighted is unusual in dreams of the blind." For example, "ghosts," "elves," "fairies," and "monsters" are much less frequent among the blind than among the sighted.

In this connection, Hall (1966), after studying over 50,000 written dream reports derived from a wide cross section of normal and abnormal subjects, concluded that the contents of most dreams are prosaic rather than fantastic. He also found that dreams typically mirror the concerns and activities of everyday life—including patently mundane behavior like that which Jastrow generalized to the dreams of the sightless. Moreover, Hall and I have found that some blind dreamers are extraordinarily imaginative, and one such case will be discussed at great length in the following chapter. Thus, the seeing do not appear to be any more inclined toward creative dreams than the unseeing—though the latter's dreams may, in fact, be less symbolic (a matter to be discussed later in this section). Jastrow's conclusion was apparently founded upon an inadequate knowledge of the typical contents of dreams in the general population. Since the Hall-Van de Castle (1966) system of content analysis permits the quantification of most types of empirical elements to be encountered in dreams, it makes possible accurate comparisons of dream reports from different populations. This scientifically more rigorous method was unfortunately not available to Jastrow.

Furness (1921) found dreams of flying to occur frequently among the sightless. One man informed him that sensations of floating took place in seventy percent of his dreams. According to Furness, such sensations are common to the blind, and in these cases all objects are usually visible.

Our own research has not revealed any marked tendencies of the above type in the blind as a group, though dreams of flying and floating with visualization were quite numerous in one male subject. At present, statistical data on thematic dream material procured from a large representative population of the blind are not available. Consequently, for the time being, generalizations, like those of Furness, are at best premature.

McCartney, in conjunction with a specially designed questionnaire, conducted interviews and analyzed two lengthy dream diaries (his own and that of a blind friend), and thus compared ninety-four subjects, who were either totally sightless or possessed only weak light reception, with nineteen seeing respondents. His major findings were as follows: (1) in both sighted and blind subjects, dream life tended to preserve the normal dimensions and attributes of objects; (2) the two groups did not seem to differ in the tendency to dream about thoughts uppermost in the mind during the preceding day; however, females (blind or sighted) dreamed more frequently of such material than did males (blind or sighted); (3) the blind and the sighted were alike with respect to general emotional content; but males in general were less emotional than females, with emotions akin to the sexual being most prominent in dreams; also, fearful objects and events were somewhat more common in the dreams of the blind, and more frequent in blind males than in blind females; (4) the blind and the sighted were similar in the extent to which they dreamed about death, with such dreams often being of a wish-fulfilling character; (5) pleasant events occurred with similar frequency in the dreams of both groups; likewise, they did not differ in the extent to which each group dreamed of things repulsive to them during waking life; (6) the blind were more affected by their dreams than were the sighted; (7) dreams of flying and falling had sexual significance for both groups; (8) the blind seldom read tactually in their dreams, but such reading was more common in those who had not previously read print; and (9) results were generally in keeping with Freudian dream theory.

It is apparent from the foregoing that McCartney's sightless population was generally similar to his seeing group in regard to both thematic and psychodynamic factors. Although the sightless subjects were more affected by their dreams, this tendency was not associated with an overall intensification of emotionality—with the one exception of fearful elements in dreams, and even on this variable the difference between the two groups was not great. Excluding all possible differences in sensory content, these findings suggest that the nature of dream life in normal blind individuals is essentially the same as that in normal seeing persons.

With respect to the contents of nightmares, Cason also found basic similarity between blind and sighted adults. For both subject groups the most frequent topics of recent nightmares were death and murder. In addition, he reported that his blind subjects tended to have few nightmares during the first hour of sleep, with more occurring after the fifth hour. The blind group reported the smallest number of recurring nightmares; mentally retarded subjects the largest; while normal adults and children fell in between. Thus, Cason's data indicate that sightless persons, on the whole, are no more (and perhaps even less) anxiety-prone in dream life than the general sighted population.

The discrepant findings of Cason and McCartney with respect to anxiety in the blind are not readily explainable, as both employed essentially the same methodology, and it is not clear which of the two subject groups was actually more representative of the total blind population. Consequently, it appears that resolution of this issue will have to await future research conducted on a broader cross section of sightless people.

In an important psychoanalytic investigation, Blank found audible verbalization, secondary revision of the dream work, transparent superego influences, and unsymbolized material to be more pronounced in the dreams of the sightless than in those of the seeing.

It will be recalled that Deutsch (1928) distinguished between the congenitally and adventitiously blind with respect to the first two of these factors. Blank's results were similar except that he found such tendencies also characterize adventitious cases in relation to the sighted.

Blank considered the prominence of the superego to stem chiefly from two sources: (1) guilt over the real or imaginary dependency incurred because of blindness; (2) increased needs for vigilance and persistent effort in solving the serious reality problems involved with blindness. Of the two determinants, the second was deemed to have the greatest impact. As an instance of this superego ascendancy, Blank cited dreams in which the blind person sees yet, at the same time, remains cognizant of his handicap. Here the dreamer seems to be interpreting the wish to see as a wasteful luxury, and remonstrates himself accordingly, for the energy invested therein might better be expended in the solution of his reality problems. In this connection, Blank found the dreams of the blind to be more problem centered and less given to disguise or distortion than the dreams of the visually normal. He regarded Freud's distinction between "dreams from below" and "dreams from above" as appropriate within the present context. The former are induced by potent, unconscious wishes that, typically in disguised (viz., symbolic) form, win admission to consciousness via the day residue; whereas the latter class arises from conscious thoughts or intentions of the previous day, with deeply repressed tendencies playing merely a supportive role. An overload of reality problems will produce a superabundance of dreams belonging to this type. In Blank's view, the superego dreams of the blind commonly are just such "dreams from above."

On the other hand, the dream reports of our visually handicapped subjects did not reveal, at least in their manifest content, any unusual weighting of superego over id processes. However, a qualitative inspection of their dreams did suggest generally less symbolic material than was present in the dreams of a comparable group of sighted persons. Even so, there is, to date, no satisfactory objective means for measuring overall symbolism in dreams; therefore, until such assessment can be made, the preceding finding should be accepted only tentatively. In any case, most of Blank's subjects were apparently suffering from serious adjustment problems; consequently, his results may not be replicable for the blind in general.

Interestingly enough, Blank's observations of sightless patients indicate a positive relationship between visual dreaming and psychological health. Wish-fulfilling dreams of seeing occurred much more often among those individuals who were learning to function despite blindness than in patients who were incapacitated by it. The latter group was wont to deny the handicap and could not even discuss it without experiencing considerable discomfort. Moreover, such persons recalled few dreams, and in these, displacements from the eyes were common. In this regard, Blank reported two cases of men who dreamed of blindness in conjunction with castration. Both were alike in that they felt their situation to be utterly hopeless; both were also repelled by other blind people. The dream of one of these men revealed that he viewed castration as a fate far less grievous than blindness. Of this type of displacement dream, Blank stated the following: "The dream of being castrated, as a reaction to the painful reality of blindness, is somehow reminiscent of an occasional occurrence in psychoanalysis, namely, the frank dream of incest, as a reaction to the emergence of dangerous transference feelings. While the two situations are not quite analogous, in both the remote intrapsychic danger is defensively substituted for the unbearable present reality." In addition, Blank found that displacements from the eyes in dreams tend to be associated with similar behavior during waking, viz., psychophysiologic symptoms and hypochondria.

As to healthier cases, he cited three blinded veterans who reported dream vision with concomitant knowledge and acceptance of blindness. He described these men as "active and productive with strong superegos." Furthermore, their war dreams were not of the classic anxiety type but, instead, were wish fulfilling.

Blank maintained that visual dreaming in the sightless is a favorable prognostic sign, attesting to the dreamer's efforts to cope constructively with reality. On improving, his patients tended to report more visual elements in their dreams, as well as more creative fantasy. By contrast, the more disturbed patients, like many seeing neurotics, scarcely ever reported dreams and manifested impoverished fantasy activity as well as strong resistance to free association. The visual dreams of the healthier individual proclaim his "equality and identity with the seeing" and his "attempts to communicate object relationships with them."

Although Blank found sex problems an important theme in the dreams of his blind patients (as they, likewise, are in the dreams of sighted patients), his observations also led him to conclude the following: "Where obstacles to freedom of movement and social contacts are removed, blind men have no problem getting sexual partners among blind or sighted women. There are greater difficulties for blind women whose choice and range are more limited."

These conclusions are largely in accord with my own observations of young blind people, especially college students. However, in this latter group I have not detected any greater sexual frustration among females than among males, though I have observed the tendency Blank described in middle-aged and older blind women.

Blank's findings did not indicate any basic, inevitable differences between the adjustment status of the adventitiously and congenitally blind. Also, he pointed out that, in general, the dreams of the latter are imaginally similar to the dreams of the seeing, except that there are, of course, no visual pictures. He regarded the absence of visual imagery in the congenitally blind as a clear refutation of Jung's hypothesis of the collective unconscious.

This criticism requires comment, as it is based on a misinterpretation of the archetype concept. Jung does not contend that man inherits specific states of consciousness but, instead, cognitive predispositions that give rise to a certain order of experience. In other words, much of man's experience follows patterns of ideation that have existed through countless generations of the species; the archetypally instigated experiences of diverse individuals, even when they relate to the same particular archetype, are not identical, for the identity in question is one of form, not content. Moreover, archetypes, as such, are not experienced directly, though they do engender certain raw experiences by which their existence can be inferred, i.e., universal symbols, images, and fantasy motifs. Insofar as they are unobservable, archetypes are hypothetical in nature, consisting of various unconscious genetic and neuropsychic events (as yet, not understood). Nevertheless, like the hidden planet that is known by way of its gravitational effects upon an observed planet, the archetypes are at least indirectly accessible to observation via their effects on consciousness and overt behavior. Furthermore, conscious phenomena pertaining to a given archetype can occur if, and only if, the individual possesses the prerequisite sensory and neural equipment. The congenitally blind are obviously deficient with respect to visual mechanisms. Even when the original defect lies in the receptors rather than the visual brain, the latter cannot function normally without the appropriate receptor stimulation and will, therefore, undergo a certain degree of deterioration. Whether or not an archetype yields experience, then, depends primarily upon the functional integrity of the relevant cerebral organs. Nor do archetypal thoughts take place in a sensory or environmental vacuum. Though the brain is more fundamental to such activities than either the sensory apparatus or the stimulating environment, no one maintains that neural organs function independently of the latter—i.e., archetypal ideas will not occur unless the necessary brain mechanisms can be reinforced by sensation. Thus, the hypothesis of the collective unconscious does not predict the presence of visual imagery in the congenitally blind. Only to the extent that the central visual apparatus is operative and receiving sufficient external input to remain so, would one expect any degree of archetypally engendered visual imagery.

Although a number of Blank's conclusions are questionable, owing to sample bias—most of his subjects appear to have been psychiatric cases—his study is, nonetheless, one of the most informative in this area. His knowledge of the psychological aspects of blindness is great, and he has been one of the few investigators to provide significant insights into the nature of psychodynamic influences on the dream life of the blind.

A further depth-psychological study, rich in empirical detail, is that of Von Schumann, another psychotherapist. His conclusions were based mainly, but not entirely, upon his clinical work with blind analysands. According to Von Schumann, the following types of dreams or dream elements are characteristic of the sightless: (1) undoing dreams in reaction to traumatic blinding; (2) blindness as a symbol of death and punishment for sin; (3) feelings of isolation and disturbances in interpersonal contact; (4) dynamic bodily movement, frequent falling, and profound reactive aggression; (5) marked anxiety and guilt; (6) heightened intellectual activity; (7) parapsychological phenomena; (8) increased spiritual sensitivity; (9) vicarious vision; and (10) personal prizing of the dream. I shall now summarize this investigator's observations and generalizations regarding these various points.

First, it was found that undoing dreams in reaction to blindness are common and tend to be quite vivid immediately after blinding but diminish in intensity and frequency as time passes. The later blindness occurs, the more likely one is to experience such dreams. Moreover, they do not take place in the congenitally blind. Individuals suddenly deprived of sight during war often dream repeatedly about the situation leading up to visual destruction. These repetitions eventually produce a reduction in the anxiety created by the physical trauma. Such undoing dreams continue for a number of years. They are more than merely reactive, insofar as frustrations in daily life subsequent to blinding can often reactivate them. Von Schumann, for example, referred to one soldier, blinded in World War I, who had recurrently experienced the same "reactive dream" over a period of thirty-five years.

Blank mentioned that blind people, in talking about their eyes, frequently refer to them as "dead." In this connection, Von Schumann hypothesized that the "death of the eyes" is unconsciously identified by at least most of mankind with the death of the body. This association occurs in dreams, just as it does in waking life. By way of illustration, Von Schumann cited the dreams of certain Soviet soldiers who were blinded during World War II and discovered that they manifested the attitude in question. Some dream reports described optical hallucinations of rabbits with the long beards of old men and humped backs, as well as other misshapen figures. Others saw both animal and human characters as moving, but lifeless, objects.

Von Schumann's patients frequently experienced blindness as a form of punishment, and this attitude was likewise manifested in their dreams.

In this regard, our most intensively studied subject, an adventitiously blind male, reported that he had experienced just such a dream within a few days following eye injury. In it he was looking at a naked girl who suddenly turned into a monster that leaped on him and attempted to claw out his eyes. The obvious erotic content of the dream suggests that, for this man, blindness was being interpreted as a chastisement for forbidden sexual wishes.

Also, Von Schumann found that the dreams of both the war and civilian blind are characterized by the theme of personal alienation and manifest problems in social interaction.

However, since most of this researcher's subjects were psychotherapeutic patients, his finding here may be typical only of the psychologically disturbed blind. In a sample of seven psychologically normal blind subjects, we did not observe the above deviations. On the other hand, another subject, with a previous history of neurosis, did show such trends in dreams immediately following blinding, as well as in a much later dream diary recorded during the neurotic period. After relatively successful psychotherapy, the estrangement motif became minimal in his dreams, though incidents of interpersonal conflict continued to be important.

According to Von Schumann, dreams involving highly energetic, physical behavior—viz., moving, falling, and aggression—are common among the blind.

He regarded movement dreams as a compensation for the restrictions upon motor behavior imposed by blindness during the waking state. In this connection, he reported that the blind often travel in their dreams.

However, with respect to movement, our subjects did not exceed comparable seeing individuals, and most of them were significantly lower than the sighted subjects. On the other hand, the blind were much higher than the seeing in references to highly circumscribed types of bodily movement, i.e., movement in small areas of space or with the body in a stationary position. Except for one subject who dreamed frequently of flying, we found little that could be considered compensatory movement. In our subjects, then, motor behavior during dreams was generally similar to that characteristic of waking life. Concerning references to travel, all but one of the blind group showed a considerably lower incidence than seeing subjects. Von Schumann's sample appears to have contained many newly blinded persons, a variable that could account for the marked, compensatory movement he observed. In each of our subjects, blindness was of long standing.

In addition, the aggression he found in his subjects' dreams tended to be massive, a trend that he imputed to the various frustrations associated with blindness. Because the visually handicapped experience continual patronizing and threats to their independence from the sighted, aggression accumulates and vents itself in dreams.

This finding also seems to have emanated from characteristics peculiar to Von Schumann's sample. The dreams of our subjects showed much less physical aggression than did those of the seeing, though when physical aggression occurred, there was a tendency for it to be extreme. Furthermore, the blind group greatly exceeded the seeing in incidence of covert or verbal aggression.

Von Schumann's sightless patients also reported falling dreams more often than did sighted patients. He interpreted falling as a compensation for feelings of isolation, i.e., falling in dreams usually stems from an inability to give of oneself and symbolically represents the wish to fall into the arms of the mother. According to Von Schumann, this meaning of falling is similarly typical of those seeing individuals who feel useless, e.g., children and the aged. He further related falling dreams to fear of failure and frustrated strivings for independence, self-actualization, and compensatory achievement.

By contrast, our blind subjects seldom dreamed of falling. The only major exception was the neurotically inclined individual, previously mentioned. His prepsychotherapy dream diary contained many falling dreams, though such dreams were not characteristic of his posttherapy diary.

Von Schumann concluded that the sightless have more anxiety in their dreams than do the seeing. In the unconscious of the former, fear of bodily injury is pronounced. Other stimuli to anxiety proceed from conflicting life and death urges, from the limitations inherent in blindness when these are not adequately compensated, and from the seemingly ubiquitous, unconscious linkage of blindness with impending death and old age. Among the sightless, in contrast with the visually normal, anxiety is more likely to be a personality-dominating feeling.

Anxiety, however, was not a central motif in the dreams of most of our subjects.

Von Schumann's observations also indicated that manifest guilt is greater in the dreams of the blind than in the dreams of the sighted. Often such guilt is massive, a condition peculiar to the sightless owing to their heightened awareness of self and stronger inclination toward introspection. Abnormal guilt feelings are especially characteristic of those who have lost vision unnecessarily, through their own or another person's fault. Such individuals experience great shame over being blind.

As stated earlier, manifest guilt was not characteristic of the dreams contributed by our sample.

According to Von Schumann, intellectual activity in dreams is more typical of the blind than the sighted. The former frequently show finer details in their dreams. The dreams of the sightless are more abstract than those of the seeing, with ideas often being embodied in words rather than in concrete sensory data.

The dreams of our own blind subjects were generally comparable to those of the seeing in terms of total number of descriptive elements. Problem-solving cognition was not pronounced in the blind, though they did greatly exceed the sighted with respect to verbal activity.

Von Schumann, who accepted the existence of extrasensory perception, claimed that parapsychological dreams occur more often among the blind than the sighted. The blind are more telepathic in their dreams. In addition, they dream more frequently about possible future events and are more adroit than the seeing in the use of subliminal cues from dreams to predict the future.

Our subjects, on the other hand, showed no evidence of parapsychological abilities.

Von Schumann further believed the blind to be spiritually more profound than the visually normal. The dreams of the former group manifest this proclivity through unusually frequent expressions of interest in aesthetic and moral values, metaphysical and religious questions, and the attainment of higher reality via the sublimation of instinctual drives. Their

eightened concern with God or the ultimate meaning of life is reflected
hrough an extraordinary number of references to sacred objects and
laces in their dreams, e.g., churchyards, cemeteries, cathedrals, shrines,
nd the Bible.

The above generalizations about extrasensory perception and
pirituality in the blind are, of course, basic ingredients of what I previously
esignated as the "Tiresian archetype." While Von Schumann's cases
ight, indeed, have shown such characteristics, it is also possible that his
bservations were clouded by a projection of this constituent from the
aditional, positive blindness stereotype. At any rate, our observations do
ot support the sweeping generality he credited to these traits. We have
nown many blind people who neither demonstrate nor claim any gifts of
SP or attraction to the "spiritual," as defined by Von Schumann. Regarding
ne latter topic, the dreams of our subjects revealed scarcely any references
f the type Von Schumann held to be characteristic of his patients.

Von Schumann found that a "vicarious sight," which is fed by
aterial the other senses have gathered during the waking state, is critical
o the dream life of the sightless, at least to those blinded after early life. It
 important for them to be able to build up pictures of the outside world. In
is connection, auditory elements are commonly transformed into visual or
ome other type of imagery. For example, while a blind boy was sleeping, a
recracker exploded outside his window, but in his dream, instead of
earing the sound, he saw the word *bang*.

According to Von Schumann, the blind person's dream is a substitute
or his lack of optical impressions, a compensation for the lacunae in
henomenal life during the day. Thus, the blind highly value their dreams,
nd, for this reason, they often look forward to sleep. On the other hand,
is investigator also found that the sleep of his blind patients, on the whole,
as not as deep as that of those who could see.

Our observations indicate that prizing of the dream is typical only of
traceptive blind persons, i.e., those who tend to place high value on
trapsychic states. The average blind person does not appear to have any
ore interest in his dreams than does the average seeing individual.

Notwithstanding its shortcomings, Von Schumann's investigation, like
lank's, is both probing and of considerable heuristic value. Judging from
ur experience with the blind, a number of his clinical conclusions are

sound and, hence, likely to be confirmed by future research o representative samples of the blind population.

Quantitative Content Analysis: A Fresh Approach to the Dreams of the Blind

The present study, carried out by Kirtley and Cannistraci (1973 addressed itself to the dream diaries of seven visually handicapped me and women, ranging in age from twenty to fifty-three and representing o major categories of empirically and/or governmentally recognized visuc impairment: total blindness or mere light reception versus partial sight wit distance acuity at or less than 20/200 in the better eye after correction—o also after correction, partial sight with the widest diameter of the visuc field subtending an angle no greater than twenty degrees; impairment from birth or prior to age five versus impairment with onset following age sever blindness of traumatic, rapid onset versus blindness with slow, gradue onset.

The Hall-Van de Castle System

In this study, subjects' dreams were scored by means of the Hall and Vo de Castle (1966) content analysis system, which permits the classi fication and tabulation of a broad range of manifest dream element To date, this is the most comprehensive approach of its kind, consisting c fifteen empirical and six theoretical scales. The former apply to suc contents as (1) physical surroundings (e.g., indoor versus outdoor setting familiar versus unfamiliar settings); (2) objects (e.g., body part architectural structures, and other external objects); (3) characters (e.g family members, animals, prominent persons, familiar versus unfamilic characters); (4) aggressive, friendly, and sexual interactions; (5) incidents c good fortune versus misfortune, of success versus failure; (6) variou sensory, motor, and psychological activities (e.g., movement, and visuo auditory, and verbal behavior); (7) emotions (e.g., happiness, sadnes apprehension); (8) references to time (e.g., past, present, future, time of da specific units of time); (9) negative words (e.g., *no, not, nor,* including word with negative prefixes); and (10) modifying terms designating certai bipolar physical, perceptual, and value dimensions of objects and person atural forces and mental activities, animal and other characters (e.g., hromatic versus achromatic color, high versus low velocity, high versus w intensity of stimulation or energy expenditure, positive versus negative oral and aesthetic evaluations). The theoretical scales are based upon sychoanalytic theory, viz., Freudian hypotheses concerning the meaning of articular types of dream symbols. These scales purport to measure ttributes central to the castration complex (i.e., castration anxiety, astration wish, and penis envy), as well as characteristic oral behavior nd tendencies toward repression. Another unique feature of Hall and Van e Castle's approach is its inclusion of extensive normative statistics based n the content analysis of 1000 written dream reports obtained from 200 ormal adult subjects: 500 dreams from 100 males and the same number om 100 females. These sighted norm groups provided the chief omparison standards used in the present investigation, to be discussed in is chapter.

In recent years, a large body of content analysis research has emonstrated the general validity and reliability of the Hall-Van de Castle ystem. It has been fruitfully employed with the dreams of literally ousands of culturally, physically, and psychologically diverse people: g., normal adults and psychiatric patients, children and the aged, istorical personages and nonliterate primitives (Hall, 1966; Hall and lordby, 1972; Bell and Hall, 1971; Bondshu, 1972; Van de Castle, 1971; mith and Hall, 1964; Hall and Domhoff, 1968; Hall and Lynd, 1970).

Dream diaries kept over a two to four month period were obtained om seven visually handicapped volunteers, five females and two males. iary instructions followed the Hall-Van de Castle format, except that llowance was made for tape or Braille reporting. Altogether, the subjects ontributed 128 written dream reports; 82 of these met the Hall-Van de astle criterion length of 50 to 300 words, and, consequently, were the only reams content-analyzed. The range of diary length ran from ten to thirty- ve dreams with a median length of eighteen.

Five of the subjects were adventitiously impaired from ages nine, velve, sixteen, eighteen, and thirty-three—four of whom were totally blind, xcept for one case of mere light perception, while the remaining sub- cts had some useful vision. Two subjects were congenitally impaired, one tally, the other partially. The ages of the female subjects were twenty, thirty-one, thirty-six, thirty-nine, and forty-seven; those of the males thirty-one and fifty-three. All subjects were Caucasian and of the middle class, with the completed level of formal education varying from high school to the Ph.D. One subject was a housewife, three were college students, and three were professional people, one of the latter being retired at the time of the study. Save for their visual handicap, these individuals appeared to constitute a psychologically normal sample.

Although the central thrust of the present study consists of a demonstration of the overriding importance of individual differences in determining dream content for our subjects, certain findings may, nonetheless, have stemmed more from visual handicap than from other variables. The results to which we refer are grouped below into five broad categories and concern the impact of visual deficit upon: (1) mobility; (2) aggressive behavior; (3) friendly interactions; (4) self-perception; and (5) perception of the physical environment. A number of additional findings— viz., those highlighting similarities between the blind and the sighted—are also of particular interest, in that they suggest a variety of content in the dreams of the blind comparable to that which has been found in the dreams of the seeing; that is, our subjects' dreams did not show the paucity of imagination which some researchers have thought characteristic of the dreams of the blind, especially individuals blind from early life. These latter results will be discussed toward the end of the section.

Factors Related to Restricted Mobility

Because blindness by its very nature profoundly limits freedom of movement, most blind people probably do not travel about the environment nearly so extensively as do the seeing. Such a fact would explain a number of our results. Compared with the sighted norms, our subjects' scores were, on the whole, lower with respect to total number of outdoor settings, geographical regions, objects associated with travel, thoroughfares of various types, and public places of entertainment. Likewise, they were relatively high in references to household articles and to numerous kinds of narrowly delimited physical movement, e.g., standing up, sitting down, combing the hair, brushing the teeth, pacing, walking across a small room, and the like. Thus, in dreams, as in waking life, the blind are restricted in their mobility and would appear to spend less time outdoors and more time within the home than do the sighted. Although some seemingly compensatory movement (e.g., flying, running, swimming, and so on) was reported by some dreamers, such instances tended to be exceptional, suggesting that previous investigators (Von Schumann, 1959), who have stressed such movement in the dreams of the blind, may have assigned it greater importance than it actually deserves. Moreover, it should be pointed out that dream mobility in our subjects was not strongly related to degree of vision, for those individuals with some functional sight differed only modestly here from the totally blind; and the one subject who showed the highest incidence of travel, even exceeding the norm, possessed only light reception. This man, a retired health professional, enjoyed traveling and had been overseas a number of times, all facts from his waking life that were clearly mirrored in the manifest content of his dreams.

The Effects of Visual Handicap upon the Discharge of Aggression

The dreams of our subjects were comparatively low in incidence of physical aggression, i.e., murder, assault, destruction of property, and so on. Yet when such aggression did occur, it tended to be unusually extreme, e.g., the dreamer dynamiting hated characters, beheading criminals, or observing other characters engaged in bloody combat, sometimes involving maiming and torture. In this connection, Von Schumann (1959) has reported that the dreams of the blind are characterized by much violent aggression, a finding he attributed to the immense frustrations experienced by the blind in everyday life, which arise partly from the limitations of blindness and partly from conditions extrinsic to it, namely, societal prejudice and discrimination. Our results, however, suggest that, for the blind at large, such massive aggression may be infrequent compared with its milder, nonphysical counterpart. Since Von Schumann's sample consisted primarily of patients undergoing psychotherapy (a number of whom were newly blinded), his emphasizing reactive dream aggression is not surprising, for one would expect such persons to experience the frustrations of blindness more acutely than do psychologically stable individuals whose blindness is of long standing (which, as previously indicated, were characteristics of our own sample). Thus, we suspect that the dreams of blind people, in general, are characterized by low, rather than high, physical aggression. Such a tendency would appear to issue from the obvious fact that visual handicap, in real life, does significantly reduce the ease with which effective physical aggression can be carried out; in other words, the general nature of dream aggression reflects the pattern of aggression characteristic of the individual during the waking state. On the other hand, the occasional episodes of dream violence do apparently serve a safety valve function of releasing reactive aggression cumulatively built up during the waking hours, for blindness, even in the healthiest individuals, invariably entails certain stresses that would be absent given normal vision. In our sample, extreme aggression was found in waking fantasy, though not in overt behavior. Thus, it appears that the cathartic role of dreams during sleep is taken over by fantasy during the waking hours.

In striking contrast to the scores for physical aggression, those for aggressive thoughts and verbalizations were much higher in the visually handicapped than in the norm groups. Indeed, with respect to verbal activities in general, our subjects greatly exceeded the sighted. Such findings, of course, follow naturally from the paramount part played by language (including covert symbolic processes) in the actual lives of sightless people. Visual loss deprives the individual of a major channel of communication and environmental representation, leaving, as it were, an experiential lacuna that can be bridged only by means of a highly augmented reliance on words and mental images. Earlier research (Blank, 1958; Von Schumann, 1959) has similarly stressed the special role of thought and language in the dreams of the blind, one comparable to that performed by these functions during waking. In regard to aggression, it may be concluded that language and fantasy readily assume priority in the blind person's hierarchy of outlets because the motor-locomotor modes of expression are less directly accessible to him. Related to this point are other findings from the present study that suggest that the blind may tend to displace or disguise their aggression much more extensively than do the seeing. Compared with the norms, our subjects' dreams revealed more negative moral and aesthetic evaluations, more witnessed aggression, and less good fortune to other characters. The fact that the visually handicapped were below the norm groups in references to strong external and internal stimuli perhaps also represents a symbolic extension of the tendency away from direct physical aggression. On the other hand, we cannot conclude that our subjects were "passive characters" in their dreams, since a great deal of their verbal aggression was straightforward and effective.

Two further results in the aggression category are of particular interest. The visually handicapped were much lower than the norms in mentions of the dreamer aggressing against himself or being victimized by other characters, suggesting relative freedom from masochistic and paranoid tendencies in the former group. As already stated, our subjects appeared well adjusted; perhaps such persons cannot afford traits like the above to the same extent that the sighted can, that is, successful adjustment under the stress of blindness may demand more energy for reality orientation and hence greater pressure to resolve merely intrapsychic problems that would be needed for the same level of adaptation, given the reality-testing advantages of sight.

Finally, neither quantity nor quality of aggressive dream behavior was related to amount of useful vision in our subjects, as the partially sighted manifested the same pattern as did the totally blind.

Characteristic Modes of Friendly Interaction

Our subjects' scores were higher in friendly speech and thoughts and lower in friendly acts involving long term relationships, gift giving, invitations, and physical contact (e.g., handshaking, caressing, and nonerotic kissing) than were the scores of the norms. Such findings are not surprising in view of the general importance of language and covert representational processes in the everyday life of the blind person. That the visually handicapped tended to be lower in the more demonstrative types of friendliness, while at the same time having friendly thoughts as their highest category, suggests that such persons may find it more difficult to act out their friendly impulses than do the seeing. The problem would seem to stem both from conditions inherent in blindness (e.g., restricted mobility and the unavailability of certain emotional cues communicated by vision, that is, gestures and facial expressions) and from irrational social rejection or misunderstanding of the blind. On the other hand, the dreams of some subjects showed considerable helping behavior toward other characters, and generally the scores for gift giving, inviting, and physical friendliness were not strikingly lower than those of the seeing. Similarly, the category for long term relationships involved the establishment of marriages, engagements, as well as lasting friendships; and most of our subjects, unlike the norms, were married and fairly well settled as to a circle of regular friends.

In regard to our subjects' high verbal friendliness, one further source would appear to be the great instrumental value of such behavior in meeting certain basic life needs that would tend to be heavily thwarted without it. Blind people may have a stronger inclination than the sighted to behave in a friendly manner toward others, since, to some extent, blindness realistically increases one's dependence on seeing persons for particular types of assistance, i.e., for guiding, reading, driving, information about the environment, and the like. If the blind person is to satisfy such needs adequately, his style of approach to those who can help him (especially when the latter are strangers) must at least be tactful and agreeable; otherwise he might easily induce an avoidance reaction or procure only insufficient assistance. In this connection, our subjects, compared with the norm groups, were somewhat lower in acts of befriending familiar characters (viz., family members and friends) and somewhat higher in the befriending of unfamiliar characters. Since needs for sighted aid from family and friends would seem to be relatively assured of satisfaction, the blind person might naturally have a greater inclination to befriend strangers, from whom the receipt of such help would, of course, be less predictable. Also interesting is the fact that, with respect to the character classes generally, the present subjects were more likely to befriend others than to be befriended by them, the reverse of what one would expect had the friendly interactions of these subjects been essentially passive.

The pattern of friendly interactions, described above, was similar for visually impaired and totally blind subjects.

The Effects of Visual Handicap on Self-perception

Blindness or extreme visual defect of the kind considered here appears to change the self-image in certain respects, mainly the body image. Compared with the norms, our subjects were much higher in reference to body parts. Blindness makes the body more immediate, more prominent in the perceptual field because of the absence of the superior distance reception afforded by vision. The incidence of body extremities was also somewhat higher in the visually handicapped group than in the seeing, perhaps because of the former's special concern for mobility and touch contact. Also, the male subjects were much higher than the male norms in mentions of the head or parts thereof, but this deviation may only have arisen from the fact that in both these cases blindness had been caused by traumatic injury to the head or neck region.

In their dreams, our subjects were generally below the norms in references to clothing, indicating that the appeal of clothing is primarily visual. However, female subjects tended to be more interested in clothes than were the blind males, and in this regard, the interest of the partially sighted was no greater than that of the totally blind. Nonetheless, wearing apparel, including jewelry, seems to play a less important role in the self-image of the visually handicapped than in that of the visually normal.

Although the present subjects differed widely in most pleasant and painful emotions, they did, nevertheless, consistently exceed the norms in instances of dreamer sadness. Such a finding, of course, is not surprising insofar as visual handicap, even in the best adjusted of persons, must, to some degree, add to the ordinary complications of daily living. However, we would not label any of our subjects as "depressive types." As pointed out above, self-aggression in their dreams was low, the opposite of what one would expect to find, were he to be dealing with pathological depression. In addition, a qualitative examination of the diaries did not reveal the general drabness of content that would tend to characterize the dreams of the depressively inclined. In any case, the difference between the visually handicapped and the seeing in the sadness category was not great.

The Impact of Visual Deficit on
General Perception of the Environment

Normal vision seems to be especially important in determining interest in certain features of the physical environment.

Our subjects' dreams were lower than those of the norm groups in references to building materials and various kinds of implements, including tools, weapons, and recreational articles—though the latter deviation was not marked. Similarly, the visually handicapped were either slightly or considerably lower in the use of modifying terms concerned with small or minute size, thinness, narrowness, shallowness, shortness, or lowness; fullness and emptiness, crowding and vacancy; fast and slow speed;

straightness and crookedness, or flatness and curvature. Of the preceding, those attributes that pertain to the size, density, and linearity of objects are often highly accessible to the sense of touch, while velocity can easily be perceived kinesthetically and, to some extent, even aurally. However, with respect to these particular dimensions, the present findings indicate that vision may generally produce greater phenomenal saliency than any of the other sensory modalities, even when the latter function cooperatively in some specific object perception. On the other hand, the visually handicapped did not differ from the sighted in the total number of modifiers used in dreams.

Other findings suggest that the visually handicapped have a stronger need than the sighted to identify environments in terms of their familiarity or unfamiliarity. Our subjects had fewer dream settings questionable as to this dimension than did the norms, for whom the latter is a high frequency category. Nevertheless, the visually handicapped were comparatively low in the incidence of familiar settings and high in that for unfamiliar settings, and, moreover, exceeded the norms in the number of settings ambiguous as to whether indoor or outdoor.

Any one of the following explanations could resolve this seeming contradiction. (1) In the recognition of physical surroundings, visual cues are far more important than those from the other senses; that is, the blind are more likely than the seeing, in dreams as in waking experience, to find themselves in unfamiliar ones. This alternative, however, strikes us as improbable, since the majority of blind people we have observed over the years appeared to spend most of their time in known environments (especially the home and place of employment). Furthermore, the blind man studied by Hall and Kirtley—whose diary, as previously mentioned, contained 307 dream reports—manifested a pattern opposite to that of the present subjects (i.e., many more familiar and many fewer unfamiliar settings than the male norm group, and relatively few settings unspecified with regard to their being in or out of doors). Which of these patterns is more typical of the blind is, of course, a question that only future content analysis research can answer, though we suspect the second type will be found more often, owing to a natural carry-over of known waking environments into dreams.

(2) The results for familiar versus unfamiliar and inside versus outside

settings suggest that the blind may tend to feel substantially alienated from the external environment. Yet we find this explanation even less plausible than the first. Our subjects' dreams did not show any trends toward isolation from physical objects or other people, and feelings of loneliness or depersonalization were infrequent, all of which should have been pronounced, had these individuals, in fact, felt environmentally estranged.

(3) In recording their dreams, the sighted norms may have been less careful than our subjects about reporting degree of setting familiarity, so that the results at hand artificially exaggerate the true differences for this dimension—assuming there are any. Since the sighted do not share the environmental orientation problem of the blind, they could easily be less inclined to label dream surroundings in terms of familiarity versus unfamiliarity, for this variable would be of much less consequence to the sighted than to the blind in affecting freedom of movement. Likewise, for the orientation of the blind, the latter type of identification would seem to be of much greater importance than that concerning indoor versus outdoor location, which elicited as little specific labeling from our subjects as did degree of familiarity from the norm groups. Once the blind person has established whether the dream situation is known or not, the further step of labeling its indoor or outdoor nature may seem somewhat trivial and hence tend to be ignored; that is, we suspect that the indoorness or outdoorness of settings is just as often discriminated by the blind as by the seeing, but the former, for reasons given above, are less interested (unconsciously less inclined) to report such characteristics. Of the three explanations here presented, we find this last the most cogent.

Other findings lend support to he hypothesis of the visually handicapped's heightened need for environmental clarification. Our subjects were lower than the norms in the number of dreams entirely lacking in physical setting, also lower in references to characters of uncertain identity.

Regarding characters in the "known" category, subjects' scores tended to be relatively low or else were similar to those of the norms. This finding, however, should not be interpreted to mean that the visually handicapped were often lower in all types of known characters, for the category only covers friends and acquaintances; it does not, for example, include immediate family members, distant relatives, or prominent persons.

Low scoring in the "known" category seems to have stemmed, at least in part, from a high incidence of family members in the dreams of several subjects. Also, it seems likely that visually handicapped people generally would tend to have fewer friends and acquaintances than do the sighted, owing to the importance of normal mobility in the widening of the individual's interpersonal contacts.

In conclusion, it appears that in proportion as visual handicap "shuts one off" from the environment, the normal human need for environmental knowledge concomitantly intensifies, not so much with respect to information about the physical dimensions of particular objects (e.g., their size, linearity, and density), but chiefly through pressures to identify other persons and certain broad aspects of the physical environment (i.e., one's position in space relative to surrounding objects and their positions in relation to one another). In other words, the dominant need is for environmental Gestalts or cognitive maps, which can facilitate mobility—the class of behavior, we believe, most seriously frustrated by visual loss. All things being equal, the need for environmental awareness would seem most fully realizable in individuals with some functional sight or at least visual memory.

The Relation of Visual Handicap to Originality and Variety of Dream Content

From their research on the dreams of blind children, Kimmins (1937) and Singer and Streiner (1966) have reported a lack of the originality and variety of content that is so common in the dreams of seeing children. They regarded early blindness, sui generis, as profoundly detrimental to the development of imaginative ability. On the other hand, four of our subjects had been blind or nearly so since childhood (two from birth, one from age nine, one from age twelve), and they, as well as the three subjects blinded later, were generally comparable to the sighted norms in variables such as: average number of settings per dream, total architectural structures, average number of characters per dream, total human characters, total single humans, total males, total unfamiliar characters, general references to time, and average number of descriptive elements per dream. For the above content categories, our findings clearly suggest that the dreams of these persons were not devoid of variety. Furthermore, a qualitative comparison of their dream reports with several hundred contributed by sighted college students did not reveal any greater novelty of content in the latter. Consequently, we strongly suspect that the above-mentioned studies, because of major methodological shortcomings, both substantially exaggerate the damaging effects of childhood blindness.

Theoretical Implications

In general, the present findings were congruent with Hall's (1966) continuity hypothesis: dream mentation is continuous with waking behavior in the sense that dream concerns and activities tend to be repeated during the waking state, either explicitly through action or implicitly by way of conscious thoughts, fantasies, attitudes, and preoccupations. The identity, however, is one of general behavioral form, not of specific behavioral content. Contrary to the compensation hypothesis, the continuity position holds that dreams do not typically embody total reversals of waking tendencies. Dreams are, of course, compensatory to some extent in that they frequently fulfill wishes that cannot adequately be gratified through waking action. Yet in most such cases, conscious daydreaming plays a similar compensatory role, and there is continuity in this respect. Thus, the same personality organization appears to underlie both dreams and waking behavior, and the visually handicapped cannot escape it any more than can the seeing.

The Dream Life of Blind Children

Research on the dreams of sightless children has been sparse, largely because of certain obvious and unavoidable methodological problems involved in the elicitation of reliable dream reports from children, especially the very young. Consequently, findings in this area are much less conclusive than those for blind adults.

In an early anecdotal inquiry, Kimmins (1937) compared the dreams of blind and deaf children and reported a number of content differences that he believed to be generally characteristic of these groups. According to Kimmins, "concerts, parties and domestic activities" are very important in the lives of blind children, but their experience lacks the variety characteristic of "the much fuller life" of deaf children. Thus, the latter have richer dreams. For example, "visits of the town child to the country" make up a major theme for the deaf, especially among older children; whereas in blind children there are scarcely any references to such experiences: "the railway journey, the change of scene and even the seaside have no message for blind children. On the whole, blind children dream less than deaf children up to the age of twelve years." Furthermore, "bravery and adventure" play no part in the dreams of the sightless child, and fairy stories are much less appealing to him than to the deaf child. Bravery and adventure form salient motifs in the dreams of deaf girls far more often than in the dreams of normal girls attending elementary or secondary schools. In this respect, deaf girls tend to be similar to normal elementary school boys of comparable age. Also, deaf girls dream more frequently about personal adornment, a theme that never occurs in the dreams of sightless girls. At the same time, dream descriptions of the attire worn by others are common in the deaf but rare among the blind. The fears of both blind and deaf children are somewhat more intense than those of normal children. The former groups are more afraid of animals than is the latter, and the deaf here are twice as anxious as the blind, though the blind are more troubled by anxiety dreams involving animal characters. Moreover, talking animals may appear in the dreams of the blind child, but the tendency is unusual; whereas among deaf children not one such instance was reported. Regarding the tendency to hear conversations in dreams, blind and normal children are approximately alike, while among deaf children such dreams are significantly more frequent. Family and friends appear in the dreams of blind and deaf children about as often as in the dreams of physically normal children.

Although some of Kimmins's findings possess at least intuitive cogency, many of his conclusions are untenable or highly dubious in the light of the overall research picture for this field.

For example, his contention concerning more frequent dreaming among deaf than blind children is insupportable, considering the results of the EEG dream research previously discussed.

In addition, the weight of the available evidence runs directly counter to his assertion regarding the greater importance of audible speech in the dreams of the deaf. For instance, both Deutsch and Blank found this element to be far more prominent in the dreams of blind children than in those of the seeing, while investigators generally, beginning with Heermann and Jastrow, have agreed as to the ascendancy of auditory imagery in the dreams of the sightless, whether young or old—barring perhaps a small percentage of persons blinded after the critical period, in whom dream vision remains more important than dream hearing. Furthermore, there is evidence indicating the existence of a critical period for the retention of auditory imagery among the deaf, comparable to that for visual memory in the blind. According to Walsh (1920), this critical period covers the years three to seven. Thus, if deafness occurs prior to age seven, the individual is unlikely to hear in his dreams. Kimmins's conclusions regarding dream conversation appear to have arisen out of biased observation or carelessness in data collection. Indeed, the general tenor of his report is somewhat hostile to the blind child, giving one the impression that the blind child is a vacuous, bland, ineffectual little creature at best. His tendency to de-emphasize the role of visual imagery in blind children, while simultaneously stressing the importance of auditory memory in the deaf, is a blatant instance of this lack of objectivity, one contradicting not only typical empirical findings but common sense as well.

Moreover, some investigators, like Von Schumann, have found talking animals to be fairly common in the dreams of the blind, while, for the dreams of blind children, Kimmins concluded just the reverse. In this connection, he cited one case of a blind girl who dreamed of a talking dog. The dream was attributed to a neurotic condition, though he offered no reasons for adjudging the girl or her dream neurotic. On the other hand, Von Schumann did not regard dreams of talking animals as indicative of neurosis; and certainly there is no prima facie connection between the two.

Also, regarding changing scenery, our own findings are inconsistent with those of Kimmins. Though about half our subjects had been blinded during childhood, they all tended to be similar to seeing individuals with respect to the average number of physical settings per dream. They were, however, like Kimmins's subjects, relatively low in references to travel and geography.

Unfortunately, Kimmins provided virtually no information concerning the exact constitution of his subject populations, i.e., their demographic and psychological characteristics. Similarly, no clear description of research procedures was given, though the latter seemingly consisted mainly or solely in face-to-face interviewing. Consequently, even his more plausible generalizations lack the credibility they might otherwise possess.

In a later, much more carefully conducted investigation of imaginative processes, Singer and Streiner (1966) contrasted the self-reported dreams, fantasies, and play characteristics of twenty pairs of blind and seeing children, matched for age, sex, IQ, and socioeconomic status. The children ranged in age from eight to twelve, and all were from the lower middle or upper lower class, having a mean IQ of 90. The sightless children all lacked functional vision, with impairment having occurred prior to age five. The subjects were individually interviewed about the nature of their play activities; also, questions were asked regarding the frequency of dreaming, and one dream and two fantasy reports were obtained from each child. The criteria for imaginativeness consisted in general behavioral flexibility, originality in content, variety of characters, and changes in space and time. The interviews and spontaneous accounts of play, fantasies, and dreams were recorded and subsequently rated for imagination by independent judges.

The investigators found visually normal children more imaginative on each of the above criteria, with sightless children, on the whole, manifesting constricted, concretistic imaginative content—barring the one exception of the latter's more frequent utilization of imaginary companions. It was concluded that children blinded during early life tend to be handicapped in the development of imagination, and the need for improved techniques of stimulating imaginative activity in such children was stressed as educationally critical.

Since the blind children in this study had all lost their sight before the advent of the critical period, one would expect a lack of visual imagination. However, the finding that such children were deficient in general imaginative ability, though perhaps valid for this small sample, does not, of course, necessarily hold for the majority of blind children. Indeed, that Singer and Streiner actually measured general imaginative ability is highly questionable, for their criteria seem most appropriate to visual or literary imagination, insofar as auditory and tactile-kinesthetic factors were largely ignored. In this connection, Blank did not find congenital blindness as such to be linked with intrinsic ego defect, though he did observe unusual concreteness in the dreams of blind children as well as adults. Similarly, Deutsch's finding of vivid, nonvisual dreaming in congenitally blind children would seem to indicate no inevitably massive impairment in general imagination. Also, as to variety of settings and characters in dreams, our own findings differed from those of Singer and Streiner. Although all our subjects were adults, several had lost vision prior to age five but, nonetheless, were similar to a sighted group with respect to the preceding variables.

On the other hand, even if children who were blinded early in life do tend to be weak in imagination, this fact would not erase the great relevance here of individual differences. Not every blind child in the Singer-Streiner investigation was rated low, but the nature of such individual differences was not discussed, nor apparently even examined. In this regard, the paramount question of the study was entirely ignored: viz., Is blindness, at any time or to any extent, inherently destructive of imaginative capacity? If only one blind subject had demonstrated above average ability, the researchers' answer would obviously have been either "no" or "only to a negligible degree." Although this condition was seemingly met in their study, they nevertheless appear to have regarded blindness, in itself, as seriously damaging—at least when it takes place during the first five years, perhaps even when it occurs in adulthood. And while they credited innovative education of imagination with the potential for mitigating such loss, they apparently did not believe that all the inimical consequences of sightlessness could be so overcome.

That early visual loss is associated with reduced likelihood of creative achievement was noted by Jastrow (1888) in his examination of the relation between age of blinding and mental development in the eminent blind. Out of a list of 114 such persons, provided by an institution for the blind, only eleven were deemed very distinguished, and ten of these had become blind during advanced youth, middle age, or still later—the single exception having been Nicholas Saunderson, the eighteenth-century English mathematician. The group next in eminence contained twenty-five individuals, most of whom had lost their sight during later childhood. In this group, those blinded earliest were generally musicians. According to Jastrow, the rest of the list was not characterized by genuinely notable achievement and probably had been included merely by reason of blindness. The average age of blinding for this group was seven, while that of the musician members (of whom there were fifteen) was three years.

Although Jastrow's list was by no means complete, his findings, nonetheless, indicate the immense importance of vision in childhood education. On the other hand, these data do not suggest a generally diminished creative capacity among the early blind, as certain talents (e.g. those for mathematics and music) were clearly left unhampered. Moreover, we could, of course, cite certain cases discussed in Chapter 5 as patent proof that scholarly, literary, commercial, technological, and other types of creativity may likewise function quite fully, despite early onset of blindness. Jastrow's results, while highlighting the advantages of sight from birth through the critical period, at the same time reveal the major developmental impact of individual differences involving intelligence, innate talents, personality, and environment. His work does not in any sense imply that blindness, ipso facto, impoverishes, in blanket fashion, the imaginative faculty. Instead, blindness may (and often does) significantly contribute to such a deficiency, but the ultimate deficit is always the product of some combination of determinants—i.e., blindness plus low intelligence, underprivileged socioeconomic status, individual or familial psychopathology, other physical disabilities, and so on—never of the one isolated determinant of early visual loss.

The Dreams of the Deaf-blind and Other Handicapped Groups

As one would expect, studies of the deaf-blind indicate that the sensory composition of their dreams is essentially identical with that of waking experience, with the critical periods for visual and auditory imagery being equally applicable.

In 1881, G. Stanley Hall described his observations of Laura Bridgman, a well-known deaf-blind woman who resided at the Perkins Institute for the Blind, then in Boston. The study was conducted in 1878, when Laura was forty-seven years of age. When twenty-six months old, she had undergone a siege of scarlet fever that left her completely sightless, deaf, and markedly deficient in both olfactory and gustatory sensitivity. In 1837, she was enrolled in the Perkins Institute, where Samuel Howe, the school's director, commenced her education.

According to Hall, Laura retained no memories of infancy. Visual auditory, smell, and taste imagery were all absent in her dreams. She reported that she dreamed frequently but experienced difficulty in recalling her dreams, which were regularly disturbing. While sleeping, she would often abruptly form a few letters or words with her fingers, in the touch language used during waking hours, but, because of their swift execution, the meanings of these expressions could not be detected. Every character who appeared in her dreams communicated with his fingers, as did Laura. Lip movements and alternations of facial expression were also noticeable during sleep. A typical dream was described by Laura simply as: "hard, heavy, and thick." Other dreams were described largely in terms of internal sensations, such as "blood rushing" and rapid heartbeat. Thus, the sensory core of her dreams consisted of tactile-motor and visceral images that mirrored the sensations uppermost during her diurnal existence. Laura's heavy reliance on such experiences was probably responsible for the suddenness, as well as anxiety, with which she so frequently would awaken from her dreams. In the words of Jastrow, who later reviewed Hall's study of Laura: "She is perchance dreaming of an animal which to us would first make itself seen or heard, but to her is present only when it touches and startles her. She lacks the anticipatory sense."

Jastrow subsequently interviewed a sightless deaf-mute whose dreams, as well as waking experience, differed sharply from Laura Bridgman's. This subject, a male aged twenty-three, was a self-supporting broom-sewer who took an active interest in world affairs and resented being regarded as abnormal. By the age of twelve, he had been rendered functionally blind, completely deaf, and almost mute, at which time he entered the Baltimore Institute for the Blind. When observed by Jastrow, this man's oral speech, though poor, was comprehensible to those who were used to it; in addition, he employed the tactile language. Jastrow described his subject's dreams as vivid with respect to visual and aural memories, though dreams about present life experiences tended to be couched in images from the remaining senses, particularly those of motion and touch. The persistence of seeing and hearing in the dreams of the young man was not surprising in view of the critical periods for retention of such imagery.

Jastrow (1900) also studied the dreams of Helen Keller, while the latter (1908) in her autobiography, *The World I Live In,* devoted two chapters to the description of her dreams, including some recalled from early childhood. Before discussing this material, let us note some important facts about this woman's life.

When nineteen months old, Helen was stricken with scarlet fever which resulted in the total loss of vision, hearing, olfaction, and speech. At age six, she began learning to read, write and communicate with the finger alphabet under the instruction of Anne M. Sullivan. At eleven, she started developing some capacity for articulation, but despite all her efforts toward mastery, she never became proficient at oral speech. Thus, in *vis-a-vis* communication she depended primarily on the finger-to-hand technique, though she was also adept at comprehending another's oral language through applying her fingers to the lips or throat of the speaker. In 1904 Helen graduated *Cum Laude* from Radcliffe College, being the first deaf-blind person in history to receive higher education. Furthermore, she was fluent in several languages. During her long life, she traveled widely, championed humanitarian causes and authored numerous successful books and articles. William James considered her bright, though not a genius; the product of superior intellectual endowment and an excellent education, coupled with great powers of motivation and perseverance (Ross, 1951).

In reading Helen's dreams, Jastrow detected occasional references to visual and auditory elements, especially the former. However, he regarded these descriptions as merely verbal—i.e., deriving from linguistic associations and fantasy rather than from actual imagery. Indeed, he found her dreams generally sparse in sensory ingredients but rich in affect and creative imagination. (Verbalistic references to odors also occur in her dreams; however, Jastrow did not mention these.) Helen's tendency toward verbalism, as well as certain other dream contents characteristic of the congenitally blind, can readily be identified in the following passages from *The World I Live In*:

"In my dreams I have sensations, odors, tastes and ideas which I do not remember to have had in reality. Perhaps they are the glimpses which my mind catches through the veil of sleep of my earliest babyhood. I have heard the trampling of many waters. Sometimes a wonderful light visits me in my sleep. Such a flash and glory as it is! I gaze and gaze until it vanishes.

"I see but not with my eyes. I hear but not with my ears. I speak and am spoken to without the sound of a voice. I am moved to pleasure by visions of ineffable beauty which I have never beheld in the physical world

Once in a dream I held in my hand a pearl. I have no memory vision of a real pearl. The only one I saw in my dreams must, therefore, have been a creation of my imagination. It was a smooth, exquisitely molded crystal. As I gazed into its shimmering deeps, my soul was flooded with an ecstasy of tenderness, and I was filled with wonder, as one who should for the first time look into the cool, sweet heart of a rose. My pearl was dew and fire, the velvety green of moss, the soft whiteness of lilies, and the distilled hues and sweetness of a thousand roses. It seemed to me the soul of beauty was dissolved in its crystal bosom."

In the above quotation, references to sight and hearing, in particular, are largely cloaked in literary allusion and metaphor, containing little in the way of concrete sensory detail, and those direct terms which are present (e.g., "light," "green," "whiteness") are so simple that they could, of course, have been much more easily acquired than the literary associations. Still, it is at least conceivable that in this case some imaginal remnants were retained from infancy; however, such a contingency is extremely improbable, considering the existing evidence. Investigators other than Jastrow (e.g., Blank) have also viewed the imagery here as pure verbalism, and the latter has, moreover, gone on to point out a relationship between this tendency and certain ego defects, involving a weakened capacity for reality testing. On the other hand, there appears to be no evidence to indicate such a deficiency in Helen Keller. Also, notwithstanding their sensory vacuity, her verbalisms seem to possess a degree of personal, emotional meaning and, therefore, were perhaps not merely a matter of unconscious distortion or premeditated fabrication.

Likewise, Helen's statements dealing with awareness in the absence of the appropriate sense—i.e., concerning seeing without the eyes, hearing without the ears, etc.—do not necessarily constitute verbalisms; rather, they appear to reflect an aspect of dream-consciousness that is common among the congenitally blind: the often reported, indefinable, intuitive knowing of setting, objects, characters, speeches and so on in the dream—apart from any specifiable type of imagery (Blank, 1958). Although such a tendency would, to some extent, seem to arise from a weak capacity for introspection (i.e., relative inability to differentiate and correctly label images of the various sensory systems), it may also be related to the alleged proclivity of the blind for abstract thinking in dreams (Hitschmann, 1894; Von Schumann,

1959). Hitschmann, who had been sightless from the age of three, maintained that the bulk of his dreams were of this class, being scanty in sensuous details. Insofar as such abstraction is, in fact, typical, it would appear to be more frequent among the congenitally or early blind than among those losing sight after the critical period.

In describing her dream experience, Helen further stated that much of it was comparable to her experience during waking life. However, the tactile modality, critical to her when awake, was less significant during dreams; for here she scarcely ever talked with her fingers, and it was still more unusual for others to spell into her hand. She also claimed that her mobility and independence were greater in dreams than in waking reality. In dreams, for example, she would seldom grope and could walk without a guide, even through crowded city streets.

Helen's increased physical freedom and self-sufficiency in dreams are obviously compensatory, since her bodily condition must greatly have frustrated such behavior during waking hours. As previously indicated, some investigators have found that compensatory dreams of this sort are frequent among both the congenitally and adventitiously blind. On the other hand, the reduced role of touch in Helen's dreams is surprising, in view of its great importance during everyday life. In this respect, she was quite different from Laura Bridgman, who dreamed so often in predominantly tactile imagery. Laura, however, lacked Helen's education and considerable store of verbal symbols, and thus in her dreams was largely confined to the concrete images of this sense. In Helen's dreams, experiences associated with bodily movement were far more common than tactile images, which is congruent with Jastrow's previously mentioned finding regarding the priority of kinesthesis over touch in the dream life of the sightless in general. Nonetheless, this priority has not as yet been empirically established, for some researchers in the field have found touch to be more important than kinesthesis.

Helen Keller's dreams, admittedly edited for publication, tell us little about her personality. They reflect an adherence to Victorian moral standards and humanitarian ideals; strivings for self-affirmation and fulfillment; and interests in foreign places, language, and literature—all major concerns of her daily life, according to biographical accounts of her actual habits and behavior (Ross, 1951).

In his research on the blind, Blank, as pointed out above, also considered the dreams of the deaf-blind. According to him, the disruptive emotional aftermath of nightmares and other unpleasant dreams, which occurs immediately upon awakening, tends to be more intense and longer lasting among the deaf-blind than the blind, with the latter, in turn, here exceeding the visually normal. This tendency, which is most pronounced during childhood, stems from the fact that the individual does not experience the instant "restorative influence of testing reality" that would be forthcoming through visual and/or auditory perception. In other words, recognition of the fact that one is only dreaming comes more slowly to the deaf-blind and the blind. In addition, Blank found that the deaf-blind experience significantly more anxiety dreams than do the blind, and many of these involve threatening or attacking animals. He hypothesized that this latter tendency results from "a projection of oral aggression." With increasing age, the frequency of such dreams diminishes markedly, and they are less characteristic, the later the onset of impairment. Interestingly enough, Blank regarded muteness in the deaf-blind as "a more serious internal frustration . . . than either blindness or deafness, as such."

Much that is true of the dreams of the blind and deaf-blind also holds for the dreams of other disability groups, i.e., cripples, amputees, and the deaf.

Heermann, for example, cited the case of a man born without the lower arms or legs, who, in his dreams, walked about on the stubs, as he did in waking reality. Jastrow (1888) found that individuals who had become crippled or undergone amputation in later childhood or adulthood continue to dream of themselves as physically normal for some time following the onset of disability, and mentioned one case in which such dreams lasted fifteen years. Kimmins (1937) also reported similar dreams among war amputees.

Regarding the deaf, Jastrow described the case of a man who had lost all sense of hearing at the age of thirty but, nonetheless, still experienced auditory images in his dreams. This subject reported that spoken language had persisted in his dreams for thirty years following the advent of deafness, toward the end of which time it became supplanted by pantomimic language. The dreams of this individual, as well as other deaf subjects studied by Jastrow, attested to the existence of a critical period for auditory memory, extending from age three to seven. In addition, these years appeared to be decisive with respect to speech retention, with deafness prior to age three usually resulting in muteness.

In a related study, Max (1935) experimentally demonstrated the great importance of motor activity in the dreams of deaf-mutes. He found that the occurrence of dreams in his sleeping subjects was almost invariably ascertainable through the onset of large action current responses in the peripheral musculature of the arm and fingers. When subjects were awakened during such periods, they regularly stated that they had just been dreaming, whereas awakenings at other times seldom elicited reports of dreaming. Later, Max artificially instigated dreams by exposing the sleeper to various external stimuli. Once more, dreaming was indicated by increasing action currents. The most persistent muscular response to accompany a dream continued for two-and-three-fourths minutes. Furthermore, hearing subjects did not manifest this pronounced pattern of motor currents in connection with dreaming. Max also hypnotized the deaf-mutes and suggested dreams, which produced the same type of action currents as did the nocturnal dreams. On the other hand, such behavior did not appear in association with the hypnotic dreams of normal subjects. Thus, Max's results indicate a greater tendency for motor experiences to enter the dreams of deaf-mutes than the dreams of normal persons.

As is readily apparent, the foregoing studies dealt primarily with imagery and offer little, if anything, in the way of psychodynamic insight. Such, indeed, is the typical emphasis of research on the dream life of the physically handicapped in general, as it has also been in the particular case of the sightless.

In conclusion, then, considerable knowledge is available concerning the influence of disability upon sensory processes in dreams, but regarding the part here played by personality characteristics (possibly associated with disability), there exists as yet only a modicum of reliable information. Indeed, the impact of the various types of disability upon personality (which might be studied through dreams) is a question seldom explored. On the other hand, this lack of interest in personality variables is justified to the extent that most adjustment research, employing techniques other than dream analysis, suggests that there is no general pattern of traits common to the handicapped at large or to any major grouping within this population (McDaniel, 1969). Nevertheless, personality studies based on dream data would still be of value if only for the light they could shed on individual traits, motivation, and development.

References

Chapter 7/Studies of Dreaming in the Blind

Bell, A. & Hall, C. 1971. *Personality of a child molester: A study of dreams.* Chicago: Aldine-Atherton.

Berger, R., Olley, P. & Oswald, I. 1962. The EEG eye movements and dreams of the blind. *Quarterly Journal of Experimental Psychology* 14: 183-186.

Blank, H. 1957. Psychoanalysis and blindness. *Psychoanalytic Quarterly* 26: 1-24.

Blank, H. 1958. Dreams of the blind. *Psychoanalytic Quarterly* 27: 158-174.

Bolli, L. 1932. Le reve et les aveugles. *Journal de Psychologie* 29: 20-73; 258-309.

Bondshu, E.1972. The personality of a female bisexual. Unpublished M.A. thesis, California State University, Fresno.

Cason, H. 1935. The nightmare dream. *Psychological Monographs* 46: 1-51.

Dement, W. 1969. The biological role of REM sleep. In A. Kales, ed. *Sleep: Physiology and Pathology.* Philadelphia: Lippincott.

Dement, W. & Kleitman, N. 1957. Cyclic variations in EEG during sleep and their relation to eye movements, body mobility and dreaming. *Electroencephalography and Clinical Neurophysiology* 9: 673-690.

Dement, W. & Kleitman, N. 1957. The relation of eye movements during sleep to dream activity: An objective method for the study of dreaming. *Journal of Experimental Psychology* 53: 339-346.

Deutsch, E. 1928. The dream imagery of the blind. *Psychoanalytic Review* 15: 288-293.

Duran, P. 1969. Imagery and blindness: A personal report. *Journal of Humanistic Psychology* 9: 155-166.

Fraser-Harris, D. 1928. Dreams. *Forum* 80: 575-582.

Furness, R. 1921. Dreams without sight. *Beacon* 5: 16.

Hall, C. 1966. *The meaning of dreams*. Revised ed. New York: McGraw-Hall.

Hall, C. & Domhoff, B. 1968. The dreams of Freud and Jung.

Hall, C. & Lynd, R. 1970. *Dreams, life and literature: A study of Franz Kafka*. Chapel Hill: University of North Carolina Press.

Hall, C. & Nordby, V. 1972. *The individual and his dreams*. New York: New American Library.

Hall, C. & Van de Castle, R. 1966. *The content analysis of dreams*. New York: Appleton-Century-Crofts.

Hall, G. 1881. *Aspects of German culture*. Boston: J.R. Osgood and Co.

Hartmann, E. 1967. *The biology of dreaming*. Springfield, Ill.: Charles C Thomas.

Heerman, G. 1838. Beobachtungen und Betrachtungen über die Träume der Blinden. *Monatschrift für Medizin, Augenheilkunde und Chirurgie* 1: 116-180.

Hitschmann, F. 1894. Über das Traumleben des Blinden. *Zeitschrift für Psychologie und Physiologie der Sinnesorgane* 7:387-394.

James, W. 1918. *The principles of psychology*. New York: H. Holt and Co.

Jastrow, J. 1888. The dreams of the blind. *New Princeton Review* 5: 19-34.

Jastrow, J. 1900. *Fact and fable in psychology*. Boston: Houghton Mifflin.

Keller, H. 1908. *The world I live in*. New York: Appleton-Century-Crofts.

Kimmins, C. 1937. *Children's dreams.* London: George Allen Unwin.

Kirtley, D. & Cannistraci, K. 1973. Dreaming and visual handicap. Paper read at annual convention of Western Psychological Assoc., Anaheim.

Kirtley, D. & Cannistraci, K. 1973. Dreams of the visually handicapped: Toward a normative approach. *Research Bulletin,* No. 27: 111-133. New York: American Foundation for the Blind.

Klein, J. 1819. *Lehrbuch zum Unterrichte der Blinden.* Vienna: Anton Strauss Co.

Lowenfeld, B. 1963. Psychological problems of children with impaired vision. In W. Cruickshank, ed. *Psychology of exceptional children and youth.* 2nd ed. Englewood Cliffs, N.J.: Prentice-Hall.

McCartney, F. 1913. A comparative study of dreams of the blind and the sighted with special reference to Freud's theory. Unpublished M.A. thesis, Indiana University.

McDaniel, J. 1969. *Physical disability and human behavior.* Elmsford, N.Y.: Pergamon.

Max, L. 1935. An experimental study of the motor theory of consciousness: Action-current response in deaf-mutes during sleep, sensory stimulation and dreams. *Journal of Comparative Psychology* 19: 469-486.

Offenkrantz, W. & Wolpert, E. 1963. The detection of dreaming in a congenitally blind subject. *Journal of Nervous and Mental Disorders* 136: 88-90.

Rosenthal, S. 1964. Persistent hallucinosis following repeated administration of hallucinogenic drugs. *American Journal of Psychiatry* 121: 238-244.

Ross, I. 1951. *Journey into light.* New York: Appleton-Century-Crofts.

Singer, G. & Streiner, B. 1966. Imaginative content in the dreams and fantasy play of blind and sighted children. *Perceptual and Motor Skills* 22: 475-482.

Van de Castle, R. 1971. *The psychology of dreaming.* New York: General Learning Press.

Villey, P. 1930. *The world of the blind: A psychological study.* New York: Macmillan.

Villey, P. 1932. The survival of visual pictures in the dreams of the war-blind. *And There Was Light* 1: 31-39.

Von Schumann, H. 1955. Phänomenologische und Psychoanalytische Untersuchung der Homerischen Träume. *Acta Psychotherapeutica, Psychosomatica et Orthopaedagogica* 3: 205-219.

Von Schumann, H. 1959. *Träume der Blinden.* Basel: S. Karger Co., pp. 1-59.

Walsh, W. 1920. *The psychology of dreams.* New York: Dodd Mead.

Wheeler, R. 1920. Visual phenomena in the dreams of a blind subject. *Psychological Review* 27: 315: 322.

8

Prospero: A Study of Personality through Dreams

The present chapter describes the results of a recent content analysis investigation (an intensive, individual case study) conducted by Kirtley and Hall and which centered upon a long dream series contributed by a thirty-one-year-old, adventitiously blinded man—a professional person—whom we shall call "Prospero" (a pseudonym chosen by the subject).

Though sample size in this, as well as the previously discussed Kirtley-Cannistraci study, precluded any firm generalizations, the findings of each were nonetheless highly suggestive and may be regarded as an initial step toward the eventual establishment of trustworthy, normative statistics on the dreams of the visually handicapped.

On the other hand, while these eight subjects provided us with sufficient data for assessing the impact of visual deficit upon dream content, as well as personality, the bulk of our results appear to have arisen from unique characteristics of the subjects rather than from their shared trait of blindness, whether total or partial. However, that the principle of individual differences should apply as much to the visually handicapped as to the visually normal is scarcely surprising, unless, of course, one insists on thinking in terms of the traditional blindness stereotypes.

Note: The study of Prospero was conducted in collaboration with Calvin S. Hall, Director, Institute of Dream Research, Santa Cruz, California.

There are a number of compelling reasons for the special emphasis given to the Prospero study: (1) to the best of our knowledge, the Prospero study was the first ever to apply quantitative content analysis to the dreams of a blind person—certainly the first to utilize a rigorous, comprehensive form of the method; (2) Prospero's dream series (307 written reports) is, by far, the longest yet to be described in either the scientific or lay literature on the dreams of the blind; (3) this wealth of data provided us with much deeper insight into the nature of blindness than it was possible to obtain from the far shorter dream diaries of the seven subjects subsequently studied by Kirtley and Cannistraci; (4) moreover, the latter investigation has already been described in detail elsewhere (Kirtley and Cannistraci, 1973). (Its central results, as well as population characteristics of its sample, were summarized briefly in Chapter 7.)

The Dreams and Personality of Prospero

Background

During his twelfth year, Prospero lost all sight in the left eye, owing to an accident in which an arrow, carelessly shot from the bow of a playmate, grazed the surface of the eye, producing what initially appeared to the ophthalmologist to be a relatively minor, remediable injury. However, within a few days after the emergency surgery, there resulted a massive, intraocular hemorrhage from which the eye never recovered. About two months later, a sympathetic ophthalmia developed in the right eye, to the ultimate effect that, by his thirteenth birthday, Prospero had become totally blind, save for light reception. Even this modicum of vision gradually faded out during the years that followed, so that at the time of the present study, he was experiencing only occasional, transitory sensations of light and no practically useful light perception whatsoever.

Prospero reported that normal visual dreams continued to occur for a period of approximately eighteen months following the onset of his sympathetic ophthalmia. At the same time, however, the quality of actual, waking vision was extremely erratic, ranging from near normal to functional blindness—owing to the waxing and waning force of the infection that was under continuous treatment throughout this entire period. During his fourteenth year, Prospero's dream vision began to weaken, fading over the next few years to the level at which it existed when he was the subject of the present investigation. Prospero has detected no appreciable changes in the clarity or intensity of his visual images during the last fifteen years. His dreams continue to possess visual properties, but such experiences are markedly subdued when compared with his previously photographic dream vision. He further stated that the nature of his imagery while dreaming is essentially the same as that of waking life. Only rarely now are dream pictures more vivid than waking visual images. Moreover, when having such a dream, Prospero always remains aware of the fact that he is blind, but this acknowledgment does not diminish his sense of seeing.

Our subject obtained high school education in a residential school for the blind. After graduating, he attended two state universities, eventually receiving a B.A. and two graduate degrees in his field of interest. At the time of this study, he was gainfully employed in his profession.

In addition to his professional interests, Prospero had long been intrigued by the psychology of dreaming, as evidenced by his fondness for recording his own dreams. Over a period of approximately ten years, he had at various times written down his dreams in diary fashion, altogether recording 307 dreams—206 between January and June of 1970; ten from October 1968 through August 1969; and 91 during the early 1960s, when Prospero was the psychotherapy patient of a clinical psychologist.

The two earliest series do not constitute dream diaries in the strict sense of the term, since during the period of their collection, no systematic attempt was made to record all remembered dreams; and the initial series (in addition to dreams then current) included many remembered from adolescence, as well as a few from childhood. Yet even if we omit from consideration all dream reports antedating January 1970 (owing to the probable biasing effects of selective recall), there still remain the 206 dreams of 1970, which were systematically recorded on a day-to-day basis. This last diary, alone, is of considerably greater length than any other dream series mentioned in the literature. Its nearest rival is the 177 dreams of McCartney (1913), the contents of which, though in part treated quantitatively, were by no means subjected to the rigors of the method here employed, for the classes of dream elements under study were not operationally defined in terms of concrete, delimiting content examples and specific scoring criteria. For the most part, McCartney's analysis of these dreams appears to have been merely impressionistic. Moreover, only a few of the dreams are actually quoted in the paper, so that the reader has no way of checking any of the investigator's conclusions regarding the series as a whole. Also, McCartney's diary may have contained a number of dreams selectively recalled from a relatively distant past, another point about which his paper is not sufficiently clear. On the other hand, Prospero's 1970 diary contains no dreams from the past.

It was through his interest in dreams (especially his interest in the 1970 diary) that Prospero came to participate in the present study. During the summer of 1970, he learned of Kirtley's work in this field through a mutual psychologist acquaintance—the previously mentioned psychotherapist from whom Prospero had formerly received treatment. The latter then promptly wrote Kirtley, to offer the above dream collection for objective analysis. By and large, Prospero's participation seems to have been motivated by a long standing curiosity concerning the meaning of his own dreams, as well as by the hope that their systematic study would contribute to scientific knowledge on the dreams of the blind. Certain other motives also appear to have played a part, but these will be discussed later.

Because the focal question of the present study concerned the relation of dreams to waking behavior, it was necessary to procure (along with the dream diaries) thorough case history information on the subject. All such material was gathered by Kirtley via correspondence and interviews with Prospero and his previous therapist—the former providing needed autobiographical data, plus his own subjective interpretation of the dream diaries; the latter, his general assessment of Prospero's personality at the time of therapy, as well as observations of current relevance.

The content analysis of the dreams, via the Hall-Van de Castle method (which involved not only a quantitative but also a qualitative thematic evaluation), was carried out by Hall with the assistance of Vernon Nordby. Working solely from Prospero's typewritten dream reports (primarily from the last 206), Hall gradually pieced together a personality blueprint, as it were, i.e., a succinct, yet comprehensive, inferential description of the subject's characteristic waking behavior—not only overt patterns (such as habitual work and recreational activities, interpersonal relations and physical hygiene) but also covert predispositions and reactions (including psychic preoccupations, typical fantasy themes, generalized attitudes, and particular values or preferences). The basic assumption underlying such "blind psychodiagnoses" is that the activities and tendencies manifested in nocturnal dreams generally gain some definite form of expression in actual diurnal behavior—either through publicly observable action or by way of the purely private sphere of the mental apparatus. This proposition, usually referred to as the "continuity hypothesis," is, moreover, well supported by a large body of contemporary dream research (e.g., Hall, 1966; Hall and Nordby, 1972).

Neither before nor after his analysis did Hall know anything substantial about Prospero, except that he was a college-educated, thirty-one-year-old blind male with a strong interest in dream psychology—all details communicated to Hall by Kirtley at the outset of the investigation. Indeed, for its duration, the latter was the only investigator ever to meet or correspond with Prospero. Thus, in Hall's personality evaluation, the possibility of confounding influence from knowledge external to the dream reports was reduced to a virtual minimum. In any case, appropriate normative comparisons could not have been made without prior apprisal of the subject's age and sex. Furthermore, the disclosure of blindness was apparently of no consequence to the analysis, since in his dreams, Prospero occasionally mentioned it, so that Hall, even had he been ignorant of this fact, would surely soon have uncovered it, simply by reading the dreams. Prospero's educational background was also obvious from the dreams, as in them he frequently referred to professional, as well as general intellectual, pursuits and concerns.

When the content analysis was concluded, Hall's inferences were checked against Kirtley's life history data, which comprised the therapist's report and the subject's oral and written autobiographies as well as his own written dream interpretations. In addition, Kirtley constructed a broad questionnaire, subsequently modified and supplemented by Prospero, dealing with the central features of the latter's waking behavior, whether past or present. This test, independently taken by both Hall and Nordby, contained fifty true-false and forty multiple-choice items, most of which concerned some specific trait, act, or event in the life of the subject, with the remainder constituting a dummy category viz., items whose alternatives were all irrelevant to Prospero's waking behavior. These trick questions were deliberately inserted to mislead the respondents wherever possible (that is, to gauge their level of credulity regarding the subject); for it was assumed that their dream-derived knowledge should by itself, if truly diagnostic, be sufficient to obviate the bulk of any such intended deceptions. On its completion, the questionnaire was scored by Kirtley with a key previously prepared by Prospero. In general, the results of the content analysis, together with the questionnaire answers of both Hall and Nordby, were highly congruent with the available case history information—including Prospero's written autobiography and subjective dream interpretations, especially where the latter materials entailed associations from recurring daytime fantasies.

In closing this section, it should also be pointed out that, with respect to the various content analysis categories, frequencies or, in most cases, proportions were computed for the 206 dreams recorded between January and June of 1970; whereupon these were divided into two sets (106 dreams for January, February, March, and part of April; and 100 dreams for the rest of April plus all of May and June) in order to determine the consistency of the series as a whole. No major differences were found, indicating a high degree of consistency in dream content over this six-month period. The 101 earlier dreams posed a serious methodological problem because of the likely operation of selective recall; hence they were not quantitatively analyzed. In many respects they differed from the 1970 dreams. However, the earlier dreams were thematically analyzed, and the results of this analysis will be described later. For the quantified dreams, proportions were compared with the Hall and Van de Castle norms for males.

Since the sections immediately to follow deal with the content analysis of Prospero's dreams, the findings and conclusions stated therein are Hall's. The occasional supplementary comments of Kirtley are specifically identified in parenthetical sentences and paragraphs.

The Quantitative Analysis of the 1970 Dreams

■ *Visual Imagery*—A careful examination of Prospero's dreams—that is, the written reports—reveals no significant differences between his visual imagery and that of the sighted male norm group. Were it not for a few specific mentions of blindness in the dreams, I would not have guessed him to be blind.

(Kirtley's note: thus, the generally dim or hazy quality of Prospero's actual dream vision is not apparent in his written dream reports. I would not, however, attribute this discrepancy to verbalism, for the subject's remaining visual memory could, in itself, be sufficient to account for such reports. Moreover, even in individuals blinded long after the critical period, it is extremely doubtful that completely normal dream vision could persist indefinitely. On the basis of my experience with persons deprived of sight at widely different age levels following the critical period, I would predict that substantial fading always occurs, the process tending to begin subsequent to the first few years of blindness and somewhat sooner in individuals blinded during late childhood or early adolescence. In any case, our findings in regard to Prospero's visual imagery [both from the standpoints of his self-description and the dream reports] are in basic accord with the result of Heermann and Jastrow, insofar as each found the fading process to be common but usually not so far-reaching as to eradicate all useful visual memory, including that involved in the production of visually normal dream reports.)

■*Characters*—Compared with the norm group, Prospero shows more familiar and more single characters, also more family members and relatives. The incidence of familiar females is particularly high, partly because of the frequent appearance of his wife and mother. (Kirtley's note: the subject is, in fact, married.) Since most of the norm group were not married, this difference is probably not surprising. Still, he dreams more about all members of his family than does the norm. From the dream reports, it is clear that he is married; also, it appears that he has one brother, no sisters, and both his mother and father are still alive. (Kirtley's note: all the foregoing conclusions are correct.) The results suggest that he is preoccupied with his relations to people he knows. A high incidence of strangers would suggest feelings of alienation, strangeness, and possibly aloneness. These he does not have.

The proportion of males to females does not differ importantly from the norm. Like the great majority of male dreamers, he has more male than female characters in his dreams. However, there is a slight imbalance in the ratio of males to females; he has a lower ratio because of the larger number of female family members and relatives. Nor does the proportion of animals differ from the norm. On the other hand, prominent persons in his dreams exceed the norm by three times. Yet the percentages for other character categories are much like those of the norm group.

CHARACTERS

		Prospero	Norms †
Total number of dreams	206		
Total number of characters	402		
Singles	307/402	.76	.65
Plurals	71/402	.18	.29
Animals	24/402	.06	.06
Males	202/332	.61	.67
Females	130/332	.39	.33
Familiar	230/378	.61	.45
Unfamiliar	148/378	.39	.55
Familiar males	116/378	.31	.25
Familiar females	107/378	.28	.16
Unfamiliar males	86/378	.23	.28
Unfamiliar females	23/378	.06	.10
Family and relatives	115/378	.31	.12
Prominent persons	23/378	.06	.02

*The denominators for males and females are the total number of characters that can be identified as to gender. The remaining denominators, 378, are the total number of human characters.

† The norms are for males in Hall and Van de Castle.

Table 1

■*Analysis of Roles of Family Members*—Toward family members there is a predominance of negative or ambivalent feeling. Friction exists in his marital relationship, there being little mutual cooperation or sharing, though in some dreams he and his wife have a good time together sexually. His brother appears to be an alcoholic, and it is clear that his mother is a drug addict. In the dreams, there is much tension and dissension between the mother and father.

(Kirtley's note: Though the above is largely accurate, certain important qualifications must be made. The case history, while indicating severe marital conflict, also suggests that the subject is appreciably more cooperative and sharing toward his wife than is she toward him. Prospero's parents have, indeed, spent most of their married life in strife, and his mother is a chronic drug addict. However, his brother is not alcoholic. On the other hand, Prospero is himself a fairly heavy drinker, but usually with reasonable control. Nonetheless, he has at times become apprehensive over the possibility of his eventually slipping into full-blown alcoholism. Thus, the dream in which Prospero's brother appears as an alcoholic is perhaps best interpreted as a projection of the subject's own drinking problem, an interpretation with which the latter concurs in his own written dream interpretations.)

■*Sexual Interactions, Orality, and the Castration Complex*—Prospero has many more sex dreams than the norm. In a large number of these, he is witnessing others, but the most significant deviation is the diversity of partners with whom he is involved. He appears to be polymorphous perverse in his sexual orientation, that is, not only heterosexuality but also exhibitionism, voyeurism, homosexuality, autoerotism, etc., figure prominently in his dreams. This, plus the high frequency of sex dreams, suggests that he is preoccupied with sex during waking hours as well as during dreams. However, his sexual tendencies are not acted out, just expressed in fantasy and thought; for their extremeness, by its very nature, would largely preclude their issuing into overt behavior.

He is also polymorphous with respect to body apertures, since fellatio, analingus, buggery, and the like occur frequently in his dreams. Moreover, some dreams are frankly Oedipal.

On the other hand, oral incorporation, castration anxiety, castration wish, and penis envy are all below the norm. Apparently, orality and the castration complex are not problems for him. Though some overt dreams of castration anxiety do occur, this still does not seem to be a problem for him to the extent that it is for the norm group.

SEXUAL INTERACTIONS, ORALITY, AND THE CASTRATION COMPLEX

Number of dreams	206	Prospero	Norms
Dreams with at least one sex act	39/206	.19	.12
Dreams with at least one oral incorporation	18/206	.09	.16
Dreams with at least one castration anxiety	26/206	.13	.20
Dreams with at least one castration wish	14/206	.07	.09
Dreams with at least one penis envy	4/206	.02	.05

Table 2

The nature of the sexual content in Prospero's dreams is well illustrated by the thirteen samples quoted below.

Dream 1: January 21, 1970

I am on a stairway fighting with someone, either my brother or my wife—I think my brother. He is trying to seize me by the testicles. Finally, he gets hold of one, partially crushing it. The pain and horror of this experience awaken me at once.

Dream 2: January 27, 1970

I'm teaching a class on sex. We seem to be meeting in the gym at the school for the blind which I attended in my teens. We're talking about the clitoris, and I say that I think everybody has one. Then a boy . . . stands up and shows the class his clitoris. It is attached to his leg, just above the knee, and doesn't resemble a real clitoris at all but is more like an earthworm with a long strand of hair hanging down from its end. Then I suggest that we all form two face-to-face lines and show each other our clitorises. I'm expecting the class to take this as a joke, but no one does, and I become embarrassed. I go back to my bench and sit down; and the class begins milling around the gym. I am now more or less withdrawn from them, just daydreaming. Then someone says, "Who is the leader of this class, anyway?" which again embarrasses me, as I am the professor and should be leading the class in discussion. So I say something to re-establish order, but this only helps a little. I have apparently lost most of my authority.

[Kirtley's note: The-school-for-the-blind setting in conjunction with loss of authority and the clitoris suggests that blindness is associated with impotence and femininity.]

Dream 3: February 26, 1970

A line of naked men, single-file, are marching up a steep, mountain path. Each is copulating anally with the man directly in front. Then a disembodied voice from the sky—God, I think—says something to the effect that the man at the rear is left out and feels bad on account of this. The man at the end of the line, who now all at once is possessed of a whip, begins beating the fellow just ahead. This is how the left-out man expresses his frustration over being at the rear. During the beating, he continues having anal intercourse with his victim. The latter becomes extremely agitated and tries to escape the lashes on his back but cannot. Nor do his entreaties for mercy have any effect on his attacker. Finally, this tortured man, also out of frustration, doubles his fist and starts striking the back of the man before him, which sets off a chain reaction, with each one in the line eventually hitting the man on whom he simultaneously performs anal coitus. There is a great deal of yelling and moaning along the chain and much violent swaying over one side of the path and then the other, but the chain still holds it formation and continues moving slowly up the path. I was aware of strong feelings of anger during this dream. Also, it impressed me as being quite funny, even while I was still asleep.

Dream 4: March 1, 1970

The scene is a room in a tall building somewhere in a big city. The room contains two beds, a large one near the window (which is open) and a smaller one close by the big bed.

Bishop S. is in the big bed, and a little black girl, about twelve, is in the small one. The building is some sort of religious headquarters. The black girl has at one time been affiliated with this religious organization but has since wandered away from religion and got herself involved with people of whom the bishop disapproves. She is generally very hostile and doesn't know if she wants to return to the Church just yet—or, for that matter, at any time. This bishop is lecturing her on her waywardness. Suddenly he becomes very emotional and tells her that the blacks, of all people, should most try to be Christians, because Christianity says all men are created equal; whereas no one else really believes this. Everyone else persecutes the blacks. His tone is rather vindictive, his voice maybe even a bit tearful. Then the girl begins to weep. She agrees with the bishop; she is coming back to the fold. The two embrace. A moment later they are together in the bishop's bed.

All the while, I have been observing the dream events, not as a spectator actually in the dream but as a moviegoer watching a film in which he has no part. The room is very high up, which makes the open window give me a feeling of anxiety. I'm afraid the bishop might fall out, as the bed's right side is against the wall alongside the window, with the mattress surface just a few inches beneath the sill.

Dream 5: April 19, 1970

It is night. I am in the town of X (where I lived during my later childhood and teens), driving a bus through a heavy, blackish fog.

V., a fat, middle-aged woman (whom I haven't seen for many years), is standing up front next to me. As I drive, V. begins to run her hand over the fly of my trousers, feeling my penis. Then on an impulse, she unzips my trousers, kneels down and begins sucking my penis, which I enjoy immensely. After a minute or so, she gets up and says: "Pull the bus over and stop so we can relax." I think this a good idea as I might also want to have coitus with her. I pull over and park the bus at the side of the road, and V. quickly pulls off her panties. Then we both notice an approaching police car. I put my penis back in my pants and tell V. to hide her panties, which she does, under one of the front seats, pushed up among some springs. She could have put the panties back on just as quickly, but I prefer to keep her private parts naked and instantly available.

Then the police car stops near the bus, and a policeman gets out. He walks up to the front of the bus and looks in with the aid of a bright light which he shines through the windshield. I feel reassured because I know he doesn't see anything amiss, and even should he decide to come in and look around, he still probably wouldn't find V.'s panties. Then I become worried that he might enter and ask V. to pull up her dress, to see if we've been up to anything; without her panties on, she could make him suspicious. But my worries are groundless, as he doesn't come in. Still outside, he tells me that I am illegally parked, and I reply very apologetically that I didn't know parking was illegal here and that I would gladly move on. This satisfies him and he leaves.

V. and I can't go to her house because she lives with several other women, all of whom would be home now—thus no privacy. So we head for my place, instead. The dream house very much resembles the one I live in now, in the city of Y.

We go into the living room and undress. Then I start feeling her up— breasts, buttocks, vagina, everything—whereupon she tells me this isn't done so much by real lovers. I inform her that since I can't see, I must rely more on the sense of touch to stimulate excitement. Her remark has irritated me, for I know sighted people use their hands as much in sex as do the blind, and I feel she is prejudiced against me on account of my blindness, equating me with the stereotype of the groping blind man, but I don't want to stir up an argument.

Then she gets on all fours, and I insert my penis and begin thrusting. My intention was to enter her vagina from this behind position, but something has gone wrong. I've missed both vagina and anus and am merely ramming a very resistant wall of flesh in the crotch area. Nonetheless, she is quite excited. She says I've hit a very sensitive region between the vagina and anus. However, unlike her, I don't enjoy this type of intercourse and prefer either the vagina or anus. For a moment I'm in conflict as to which to take; then I decide on the anus. I have to force my penis in as the passage is extremely tight. I make a number of quick thrusts, which she enjoys and I, too, though not as much as I'd anticipated. The idea of getting fecal matter on my penis causes me to become a little sick at my stomach. Also, an unpleasant odor is just beginning to rise up from her buttocks: a strong fecal, metallic smell. At that moment I realize that she is about to flatulate, so I immediately remove my penis and jump to one side. As I hit the floor, just out of her range, she gives off an explosive burst of flatus. After this, she says; "Boy, you were pumping me so hard shit suds were coming up into my mouth." Then she asks me what I want to do next, if I still want to have more sex. I yet have a good erection so I say I'll keep having sex, but first I want to wash off my penis and next time I'll use the vagina."

[Kirtley's note: The above reference to touch in lovemaking technique suggests that blindness is connected with sexual inadequacy.]

Dream 6: April 27, 1970

I am at the old home of my maternal grandparents (where I haven't actually been for over twenty years). I'm in the living room, talking with a young woman named Gladys (a complete product of imagination, as I know no such woman in reality). Though her husband is also somewhere in the house, Gladys and I are for the moment alone in the living room. Finally she says something—I can't remember what—that indicates she is open to sexual advances. I then suggest intercourse and she accepts. So I take her by the arm and lead her outside.

We go through the front yard and turn left at the left front corner of the house. I take her behind some bushes which stand just off the side of the front porch. There I undress her and press her to the ground. The ground is a little damp but still comfortable enough for sex.

As we begin having intercourse, she moans in pain, but there is also a large element of ectasy admixed with this pain. She acts as though my penis were tearing her apart, yet at the same time is enjoying the experience with complete abandonment. For a moment, my penis seems to become knifelike, and I think it is cutting her. I wish her to acknowledge this (but can't remember whether she said anything or not). Then my penis begins to feel more like a lead pipe, and I want Gladys to comment on the pleasure this wonderful lead-pipe penis is giving her, which she does before I can say a word. She says it is so big and hard that she can scarcely stand it. It is, in fact, so large that it barely fits her vagina. Then her writhing and moaning, her mixed pain and ecstasy, greatly intensify, quite to the point of frenzy, and she begins having one orgasm after another; she can't stop having them; she is in the midst of an orgasmic psychosis. I know that she will do anything I ask of her: fellatio, analingus, submission to beatings—anything. The power of my penis has made her my absolute slave. It has brought her to a peak of pleasure never before experienced by her a quality of pleasure which, even in her dreams, she has imagined only dimly, as one might imagine Heaven. My organ has become necessary to her happiness;from now on she won't be able to live without it. This is how I know she will be my slave. As she continues in the throes of this rapid-fire succession of superorgasms, I run my hands over her entire body and find that I can mold it to take any position I like. All of a sudden, I have an orgasm, one so deeply pleasurable that it sends sensations throughout my whole body, from head to toe. (This, however, was not actually a wet dream).

Now I begin wondering when Gladys's husband will start looking for her. For a moment, I think I hear him out on the front porch, but then I realize I am mistaken. Still, I somehow know he will be there very soon. Perhaps I would even like him to catch us, so he could see what I'm doing to his sweet little wife. Now I really do hear him; he's inside the house, calling her: "Where are you, hon? Where are you, hon?" (Or something of the sort) He's totally unaware of what is happening. He trusts her almost religiously. I smile over his naiveté. When I'm through with her, she'll go back to him, and he will receive and love her as always, as his own true love, as the innocent, devoted little wife she once really was. But tomorrow, perhaps while he's indulging himself in some tender, romantic reverie on his darling, little wife, she will again be at my service, performing analingus on me, and later anything else I might desire.

Dream 7: May 1, 1970

The scene is a room unfamiliar to me. M., G., and a few other fellows, all students . . . are in the room with me. However, only M. and G. do I clearly recognize.

G. is in bed, lying flat on his back, naked and uncovered by spread, sheet, or blanket. His legs are wide apart, knees up and drawn toward the torso, as if he's awaiting intercourse. At the moment I happen to be sexually aroused and feel I will have an involuntary orgasm if I don't do something fast. No girl is present, so I consider intercourse with G., despite the fact that this is repulsive to me—simply because there is nothing else around to put my penis into. G. is thick-set, almost obese, very hairy and usually not too well washed—there is absolutely nothing feminine about him. I think to myself that I would not at all mind having sex with a really feminine boy, someone soft, clean, and pliable. I wonder if G. has a vagina or if I will have to in via the anus. But I'm almost sure he has a vagina, which makes his hole at least clean, no matter how dirty the rest of him is.

Then M. and the other boys begin talking about some girl who always sings lullabies to her boyfriends, just before granting fellatio or intercourse. Oh, how I wish I could get to her, but I simply don't have time, because I'm going to have an orgasm right in my pants if I don't promptly do something.

[Kirtley's note: In his personal dream interpretations, all written, Prospero gave an interesting association to the above dream:

Lullaby and good-night
In the soft evening light,
Like a rose in its bed
Lie down your sweet head.
Oh, here's a blow-job—don't despair!
Now just pump me anywhere.]

Dream 8: June 2, 1970

I'm at home in bed, lying on my stomach masturbating. Then suddenly I find myself on my back. I notice that my penis has grown to a tremendous size. It is over-gorged with blood, with a diameter of about five inches. At that moment a great amount of blood rushes to the left side, producing a balloonlike protrusion which then explodes—violently squirting out blood, like water from a high-pressure hose. It seems I have strained my penis from too much masturbating.

Dream 9: June 6, 1973

I am visiting M.M., a college fraternity brother (whom I haven't actually seen for twelve years). He is showing me around his place of business. It is a funeral parlor but resembles the many-floored structures used by big-city hotels for stacked parking. The visual images are vague, so it isn't clear to me just what the nature of this building is. The various floors—or perhaps they are tiers rather than vertically arranged floors—are unusually close to one another—and the tiers very long and narrow; it seems there are both vertically stacked floors and tiered platforms on each floor. Each tier or floor is covered with a row of large stiff male bodies, which appear dead but may not be completely dead. Each man has very big feet, about which there is something vaguely unwholesome; these feet are clad in some sort of black material and are huge and boxlike, like the feet of the Frankenstein monster. Then M.M. tells me that each night he and some other fellows who work here have a lot of fun playing a game with these feet. At that moment I see M.M. suddenly jump onto one of the stiffs and begin wrestling with its feet. M.M. laughs and bounces up and down excitedly on the stiff's big feet, and while all this is happening, the stiff even laughs a little too. Then, all around me, men I don't recognize start jumping onto the other stiffs and playing the same game with the feet. There is loud laughter everywhere, from all over this floor and from those above and below. The whole affair strikes me as a bit gruesome, yet I almost feel like laughing myself. Also, I feel it is M.M.'s right to live his life in any way he pleases, even if that involves strange funeral parlor games.

Dream 10: June 10, 1970

The scene is a large, roofless, stone-walled boys' gym, which has been built in the shape of a trash can. The wooden floor is covered with plastic wrestling mats, pale blue or gray in color. A lot of adolescent boys are working out here. One of them is E. (a boy I knew during my teens, whom I alternately liked and detested).

I am also in this great trash-can structure, but near the top, flying about in a small, cigar-shaped, wooden plane. I am somehow the master or creator of this place and am in complete control—or almost complete control—of what takes place here.

I have a big metal pot inside the cockpit of my aircraft, and occasionally I defecate into this, then dive down and dump the contents on those below. I've now once again filled the pot and am hovering about fifteen feet over E. I drop my load on him, as though bombing him, and ascend rapidly to the top of the enclosure. I feel immensely elated and powerful. Below, E., utterly humiliated, rages impotently. He's naked, and his whole body is dripping with feces and urine.

Then a crowd of boys approach E., teasing him about his disgrace. When most of the filth has dripped away from E., one of the boys suggests that the group rape him anally. The thought of this anal gangbang horrifies E. and makes him feel reduced to an even worse level of degradation than before. He whimpers and begs for mercy, as the boys, now all naked, throw him to the floor and roll him over onto his stomach. In a quick, furious succession, the boys all bugger him, and at the same time teasingly threaten to cut off his penis or testicles. E. groans and squirms under the onslaught of the rapists, trying to escape, but all to no avail. The same boys bugger E. again and again. It seems his agony will go on forever.

Then I see a very large boy on top of E., one who strikes me as a bully. I want to save E. from this bully. I feel now like some avenging angel. I descend with another full pot which I dump on the head of this big bully. He jumps up and down, screaming and shaking his fists at me, as I ascend.

Then for a moment, I begin to worry about my motor. What would happen if I were to run out of gas and have to land down there, in the midst of that terrible butt-fucking orgy? I wouldn't stand a chance. Then I remember that I'm the controller of this place, that I have made it, and the plane too, and, therefore, there's no reason to worry. I can't run out of gas. I have a perpetually-running engine which needs no gas nor any other external source of power. All its power somehow comes from within. I'm not really aware of having made the engine in this manner, but since I am the controller here, I assume this to be the case—or at least I hope it to be the case.

Now the scene changes somewhat. I've somehow extended a long rope-ladder down the wall of the gym, its lower end hanging just above the reach of the boys below. The boys then begin stacking boxes one on top of the other, directly beneath the ladder-end, so that eventually the boy at the top of the stack will be able to reach it. However, while this is going on, I very slowly and imperceptibly draw up the ladder, so that the stack has to get higher and higher and always is just out of reach of the boy on top. Finally, when the stack is about 30 feet up the wall, I decide that it should get no higher, since I don't want it getting anywhere near the building's rim, which is maybe another 100 feet up. So I now begin pulling the ladder up very rapidly. But somehow one of the boys has got hold of it. He is being dragged against the stone wall, and the rough stone, plus friction, is skinning him alive. If he lets go, he'll fall to his death; if he hangs on, he'll be rubbed to death; or should he make it all the way to the rim, he'd probably fall to his death down the outer side of the wall. Regardless of what he does, he's doomed. All of a sudden I feel a bit sorry for him and wonder how I would feel or what I would do if I were in his position. I feel very glad over the fact that it's his problem and not mine.

Dream 11: June 20, 1970

An unfamiliar bedroom. A big bed is in the middle of the room. My mother and I are in the bed. My father is shaving in an adjacent bathroom. I'm lying on my back, naked; my mother is also naked. She wants to have intercourse with me, so climbs on top of me. My penis is only partially erect, so that to insert, I have to squeeze it at the base, which forces enough blood into the tip for penetration. However, I insert only the tip. My father is yelling in an angry manner from the bathroom. I'm afraid he will come out and catch me. Off and on, I don't seem to fear his seeing me like this with mother, but in the end my fear dominates and I get out of the bed. I go into the living room, just as my father is coming out of the bathroom. He sees a spot of vaginal secretion on the bed-sheet and knows that I have had intercourse with mother. The general feeling-tone of the dream is one of anxiety.

Dream 12: March 25, 1970

A dream fragment—generally vague. I seem to be outside, on the campus of X College, in the free-speech area—standing on some sort of stone platform. I talk to some fellow (whom I recognize in the dream but don't remember now). After he leaves, I reach down and notice that my penis is protruding from my pants. I have an erection; also, I have my pajamas on, neither of which facts were known to me during the immediately preceding conversation. I hope the person with whom I spoke also did not notice—nor anyone else, for that matter—but I don't see how such a thing could have been missed.

Dream 13: May 8, 1970

The scene is a barren rock mountain located far from civilization. I'm standing on one of its brownish yellow, rock-strewn slopes, looking at several cave-entrances above me. Legend has it that there is a treasure of old Spanish gold hidden somewhere deep in one of these caves. Also, I've heard that a sadistic old man, a hermit, lives in the treasure cave, where he keeps constant guard over the gold.

I enter one of the caves, crawling slowly forward on my stomach. Although the roof is high enough to allow walking, I crawl so that the hermit will be less likely to see me, should this particular cave be his.

Suddenly, off to my left, I see this very person, and he sees me too. He is old and haggard; with dry, yellowish skin, like faded parchment; long stringy white hair, a huge beak-like nose, a tall thin frame and dark evil eyes. He is an ancient creature who has always lived in this cave.

Now he laughs at me and begins telling me how he killed the last few intruders who tried to take his gold. His most recent victims were a man and his mistress, who entered the cave sometime during the 1800's: the hermit stabbed them to death. Just before that, during the 1700's, he caught a lone man in the cave. The hermit castrated this man, then ordered him to eat his testicles. When the man refused, his penis was also cut off—right at the root, so that a great spurt of blood shot forth, with the victim in a few seconds being not only castrated but dead.

Now this horrible old sadist announces that he is going to kill me. At that moment, I turn into Batman. However, even this doesn't entirely remove my fear. Then, without any prior warning, Robin suddenly crawls up behind me, saying he has just learned something important about the old man. (I don't recall the specific content of this information; perhaps it wasn't even clear to me in the dream.) Robin says he knows how to take care of the hermit, so I let him crawl ahead of me.

Soon Robin reaches the edge of a bottomless pit. He leaps into it, flapping his arms and cape. These quick, wing-like motions prevent him from falling more than a few feet down into the pit. Now his flapping elevates him to a position just above the mouth of the pit, where he hangs more or less suspended in midair, merely bobbing up and down.

The old hermit, now more furious than ever, wants to kill Robin, so he jumps for him. But having no flying ability, he goes out and down like a hand-thrown rock. He misses Robin, dropping just behind him, but in the descent, the hermit's big hooked nose becomes snagged in Robin's anus. Here he dangles helplessly, impotently trying to free himself or at least kill his enemy. With his long sharp claws, he keeps trying to rip open Robin's flesh, but each quick pass of the hand, though close, always misses its mark. The old sadist is simple doomed. His fate is to hang forever with his nose up Robin's ass.

I had this dream just after dozing off on the couch in my living room. The television was going, and the Batman program had come on just a minute or so before I fell asleep. Though I paid no conscious attention to the program, it apparently did have some effect on me, while sleeping, for I'm sure this was how Batman and Robin came to enter my dream.

Aggression—The most outstanding fact about Prospero's dreams is the extremely high frequency of aggressive interactions, there being much more witnessed and dreamer-involved aggression than in the norm group. However, the pattern of aggression with different character groups does not differ markedly from the norm. There is more aggression with males than with females, more with strangers than with known persons. This is also true of the norm group. But the intensity of his aggression is less than that of the norm—that is, he shows more verbal and covert aggression and less physical aggression, except for a few dreams involving massive physical aggression (the latter type being exemplified by Dreams 1, 3, 10, and 13 above). Also, he is more apt to be the aggressor than the victim, which differs from the norm. There is considerable aggression with known males and with female strangers and also much with the mother and father. In addition, he shows more self-aggression than the norm. It appears that Prospero lives in a world heavily endowed with hostility.

AGGRESSION

		Prospero	Norms
Total number of aggressions	221		
Total number of characters	402	.56	.34
Dreams with at least one aggression	109/206	.54	.47
Dreamer involved	150/221	.68	.80
Witnessed	71/221	.32	.20
Dreamer with males	80/202	.40	.28
Dreamer with females	31/130	.25	.17
Dreamer with familiar	78/230	.34	.19
Dreamer with unfamiliar	47/148	.32	.27
Dreamer aggressor	75/130	.58	.40
Dreamer victim	55/130	.42	.60
Physical aggression	76/221	.34	.50

Denominator for males, females, familiar, and unfamiliar is the number of dream characters in each of those classes.

Table 3

■*Friendliness*—Nor is Prospero's aggression counterbalanced by friendliness. There is very little friendliness in his dreams, much less than in the
norm group. There are 221 acts of aggression and just 42 of friendliness,
and these few friendly acts or feelings are spread thinly over all character
classes.

FRIENDLINESS

		Prospero	Norms
Total number of friendliness	42		.21
Total number of characters	402	.10	
Dreams with at least one friendliness	35/206	.17	.38
Dreamer involved	30/42	.71	.90
Witnessed	12/42	.29	.10
Dreamer with male characters	13/202	.06	.12
Dreamer with female characters	12/130	.09	.29
Dreamer with familiar characters	18/230	.08	.23
Dreamer with unfamiliar characters	10/48	.07	.16
Dreamer befriender	15/29	.52	.50
Dreamer befriended	14/29	.48	.50

Table 4

■*Good Fortune versus Misfortune*—Prospero shows a lower incidence of
misfortune than the norm, but more of this occurs to other characters than
to him, a finding that also contrasts with the norm pattern. This suggests the
presence of disguised hostility.

Good fortune is virtually nonexistent in Prospero's dreams.

MISFORTUNE AND GOOD FORTUNE

		Prospero	Norms
Dreams with at least one misfortune	49/206	.24	.36
Misfortune to dreamer	29/57	.51	.71
Misfortune to others	28/57	.49	.29
Dreams with at least one good fortune	2/206	.01	.06

Table 5

■*Objects*—Prospero is higher than the norm on architectural structures, communication devices and supplies, household articles, food, and body parts. He is lower on implements, streets and other types of thoroughfares, geographical regions, clothes, and objects pertaining to travel and nature. There is almost no mention of money in his dreams, which also distinguishes him from the norm. I assume from these results that he is more an indoor than an outdoor person. It is not clear whether this has to do with his blindness or is simply a matter of natural interests.

The largest difference, however, is in the category of body parts. He is preoccupied with the body, all parts but particularly the sexual organs and the bodily interior, including blood and various secretions. Considering the high number of sex dreams, this may not be surprising. There are a number of references to the anus and feces, which suggests an anal preoccupation. Moreover, the mouth, teeth, and hands are of dynamic significance in some dreams, and in one dream, feet play a symbolic role. Interestingly enough, there is no mention of the eyes in the first set of dreams (those recorded from January to mid-April of 1970). However, in the second set (those dreams recorded thereafter), there are six references to the eyes, and these suggest that the eyes, too, are of dynamic importance.

Examples of the preoccupation with genitals, blood, and body secretions appear in Dreams 1, 2, 5, 6, 7, 8, 10, 11, 12, and 13 above; while Dreams 3, 5, 6, 10, and 13 illustrate the anal preoccupation. The symbolic part played by feet is exemplified in Dream 9. Some instances of dreams in which the mouth, teeth, hands, and eyes constitute critical elements will now be presented.

OBJECTS

		Prospero	Norms
Total number of objects	750		
Total number of dreams	206		
Architectural	202	.296	.271
Household	94	.126	.082
Implements	23	.031	.066
Transportation	30	.040	.112
Streets	23	.031	.067

Regions	26	.035	.05
Nature	59	.079	.09
Body parts	173	.231	.10
Clothes	22	.029	.05
Communication	44	.059	.03
Money	2	.003	.01
Food	25	.033	.01
Miscellaneous	7	.009	.02

Table 6

Dream 14: January 28, 1970

A hand, which has no body attached to it, is in a barrel. A young woman reaches into the barrel, whereupon the hand grabs her by the arm or shoulder, growls, and shakes her to death. The hand then leaves the barrel and chases a policeman, finally catching and strangling him. then drives a car to some house in the country. The man who lives in the house is now on its upper floor. The hand has come to kill him. The dream ends as the car pulls into the driveway of this man's house.

Dream 15: February 12, 1970

I am standing at or near the North Pole. An old man, whom I don't know, who also is vague to me in the dream, is standing beside me. We are looking down upon a monstrous turtle—a giant which is much bigger than the largest of the sea turtles. Except for his head, neck and a sma portion of the upper shell, the turtle is submerged in a pool of water. This pool, which has been formed by a breaking of the ice, is barely big enough to contain the turtle. He is biting something at the edge of the pool—a piece of ice or a thick leather strap. He doesn't chew this object but simply holds it very tightly in his jaws, in a stubborn, clinging attitude. Though he is facing the old man and me, he apparently isn't looking at us, being too absorbed in his biting to notice any of his surroundings. His mouth is huge, the jaws extremely powerful; he is a prehistoric turtle.

The old man and I begin talking about this being the first period of biological evolution, during which real biting occurs. We seem to be in his prehistoric period, yet we are also in our own present time.

I wonder to myself how many other life-forms are now biting. I imagine that many different forms, all over the world, are just now beginning to bite. Then I think to myself, how can this be, if the turtle is really the first and the other, more advanced animals, for example mammals, haven't even come yet? Here the dream becomes increasingly confused, then fades out.

Dream 16: February 16, 1970

A tooth in the lower left front of my mouth is decayed. As I touch it with a fingertip, a loose piece falls off. I continue picking at the tooth. Finally, a large fragment, about half the tooth, breaks off. The whole tooth is rotten. Then I shake the big fragment, and innumerable tiny arrowheads fall out of it. These minute arrowheads now also roll out of the half of the tooth which remains in the gum. They are very hard, like large grains of sand.

[Kirtley's note: Since Prospero lost his sight through a bow-and-arrow accident, the symbolism of the present dream is transparent; the dream suggests that he associates his blinding with decay, with physical inadequacy, perhaps even castration.]

Dream 17: May 31, 1970

The scene is Vietnam, a battle zone somewhere out in the country. A group of American soldiers is looking for VC and NVA. They have just arrived at the foot of a hill, which is irregular in shape and is covered by dense foliage, except for a narrow path that leads straight up the slope in front of them. Now, in single file, the soldiers begin marching up this path. However, the men are still more or less separated from one another, since the intervals of space between them are fairly great—so much so that any given soldier can't always see the man in front of him or the one behind.

Suddenly, from the head of the line, screams are heard. They come from the lead man who has just been captured by the enemy. None of the Americans, however, has actually seen the capture, but all know what has happened from the terrible sound of the captive's voice. He is being tortured. He can be heard screaming: "No, I don't want to see what death looks like! No, no, no!" He has been reduced to the utmost depths of ignominy. His screams are both pathetic and disgusting, but mostly pathetic, since the torture is apparently quite extreme.

Then the enemy releases him and sends him running down the hill, back toward his outfit. As he comes down the path, he weaves from side to side, as though he has lost nearly all control of his body; he is moaning and bent over with great pain. An eighteen-inch long wooden spike has been run through his head, and its two protruding ends are plainly visible—one from the back of the head and the other from the front where a few inches of spike jut forth out of the corner of the left eye near the bridge of the nose. One GI becomes hysterical and begins weeping and cursing the Communists.

Finally, the wounded man is examined. Now, however, the front end of the spike is protuding from a different place—from between the eyes rather than from the corner of the left eye.

[Kirtley's note: Prospero's blindness resulted from injury to the left eye; consequently, the dream suggests that Prospero may be identifying with the tortured soldier in the above dream; if so, this would also mean that he tends to associate blindness with death, as the victimized solider said he did not want to see death—in other words, be blinded by having a spike driven through his eye.

This interpretation is supported by the subject's own dream associations, which, in addition, state that the said soldier may constitute a symbolic wish-fulfillment—viz., Prospero wishes to free himself from his blindness through the magical act of giving it to another. Thus, he identifies with the soldier in a purely negative way: like Prospero, the solider suffers the pain of traumatic blinding, and it is in this sense that the two are identified; yet at the same time, the soldier's blinding rids Prospero of his blindness, and at this level the identification ceases. Another possible interpretation, which Prospero mentions but considers less appropriate than the foregoing, rests upon the "misery loves company" idea—that is, he simply wishes other people, like the solider in the dream, to suffer as he has suffered. The ending of the dream makes Prospero doubt this last interpretation. Here the protruding spike-point moves from the corner of the left eye to the bone between the two eyes. Prospero believes that, at this stage of the dream, he at least unconsciously realized the utter absurdity of his wish to transfer blindness and that the movement of the spike served, to some degree, as a protection against shame over his stupidity in allowing himself to entertain so irrational a wish.]

■*Modifiers, Temporality, and Negativity*—In regard to descriptive elements—namely, terms designating size, linearity, intensity, color, temperature, density, velocity, age, and value,—the most significant deviation in Prospero's dreams is the large number of unfavorable or derogatory evaluations of objects, characters, and situations—over six times the figure for the norm. Words such as *bad, dirty, weak, dishonest, disgusting,* and *morbid* appear frequently in his dream reports. On the other hand, positive evaluations are the same as for the norm. Similarly, his use of negative words—such as *no, not,* and so on—does not differ significantly from the norm. Nor do temporal references deviate—that is, mentions of past, present, and future; seasons; the time of day, and so on.

DESCRIPTIVE ELEMENTS

		Prospero	Norms
Total number of modifiers	273		
Linearity +	5	.018	.004
Linearity −	3	.011	.012
Chromatic color	13	.047	.067
Achromatic color	9	.033	.039
Size +	58	.212	.180
Size −	22	.081	.095
Density +	18	.066	.016
Density −	5	.018	.008
Temperature +	2	.007	.005
Temperature −	5	.018	.007
Velocity +	1	.004	.036
Velocity −	1	.004	.007
Intensity +	39	.143	.295
Intensity −	0	.000	.051
Evaluations +	14	.051	.052
Evaluations −	62	.226	.035
Age +	11	.040	.040
Age −	5	.018	.051
Dreams with no negatives	70	.344	.282
Dreams with at least one negative	136	.656	.718
Dreams with no temporal reference	168	.83	.66
Dreams with at least one temporal ref.	38	.17	.34

Table 7

DEFINITIONS OF TABLE 7 DESCRIPTIVE ELEMENTS

Linearity + = Flat, straight, etc.

Linearity- = Curved, crooked, etc.

Chromatic colors = Pertaining to color or colors.

Achromatic colors = Black or white.

Size + = Large, tall, high, thick, broad, deep.

Size – = Small, thin, short, low, narrow, shallow.

Density + = Any reference to bounded area or container. Referred to as full, bulging, crowded.

Density – = Empty, etc.

Temperature + = Warm or hot.

Temperature – = Cool or cold.

Velocity + = Fast movement of people, objects, or mental activities.

Velocity – = Slow movement of people, objects, or mental activities.

Evaluations + = Any positive moral or aesthetic evaluative remark about people or objects, e.g. good, beautiful, etc.

Evaluations – = Any negative moral or aesthetic evaluative remark about people or objects, e.g. bad, ugly, etc.

Age + = Any reference to characters or objects as old.

Age – = Any reference to characters or objects as young or new.

Intensity + = Strong force or expenditure of energy towards any physical or mental activity.

Intensity – = Weak force or expenditure of energy towards any physical or mental activity.

■*Emotions*—In his dreams, Prospero is higher than the norm group in fear, apprehension, and anxiety and lower in the happy emotions. A few sample dreams manifesting both anxiety and unhappiness are given below.

EMOTIONS

		Prospero	Norms
Total number of emotional references	61		
Dreamer happy	4/61	.07	.18
Dreamer sad	5/61	.08	.13
Dreamer angry	5/61	.10	.09
Dreamer confused	3/61	.05	.20
Dreamer apprehensive	43/61	.70	.40

Table 8

Dream 18: February 23, 1970

A sadistic killer, who has just escaped from a hospital for the criminally insane, is tapping at my bedroom window. I am in bed, just below the window. I'm very frightened but try to tap back, thinking that the boldness of this act might scare him off. But I can't bring myself to tap the window, for I'm frozen with fear. Then I try to yell out, either for help or else simply to frighten him, but I only emit a feeble groan.

Dream 19: February 25, 1970

Another nightmare. It's night, and I'm in bed. Suddenly, I hear someone opening the kitchen door. The door strikes against the night-chain, and I'm afraid the intruder will soon work the chain loose and enter the house. He is a sadistic killer, a homicidal psychotic. I wake my wife and tell her a madman is trying to break in.

Dream 20: March 8, 1970

A nightmare. It's night, and I'm in bed. A strange man enters my bedroom. He walks toward my side of the bed. As soon as he reaches it, he turns into a gorilla. His head is large and fierce looking. He is about to attack but moves back a few steps when I strike at his face with my fists. Now I'm out of bed, hitting with all my strength to keep him off, and I'm afraid I won't hold out long enough to drive him from the room. He is determined to stay and wear me down. Though I continue to fight, I'm always just on the verge of being overcome.

Then I tell myself not to worry as this is only a dream; yet my fear, which is extreme, persists. In the dream itself I realize that the only way I can stop this fear is to wake myself up, and finally I succeed in doing this, but I have to struggle to become awake.

Dream 21: May 2, 1970

The scene is X School for the Blind, my last room in the dorm for older boys. I'm in my old bed where I awaken late at night. I wonder why it is that I'm still at the school for the blind, when I'm no longer a teenager. How could a thirty-one-year-old man still be a high-school senior, which is what I seem to be in the dream? Before tonight I thought I'd graduated a long time ago, when I was seventeen. Now it occurs to me that perhaps I did graduate but have since had to return to fulfill some overlooked requirement, a deficiency unnoticed at the time of graduation. I'm quite upset with myself. I'm far too old to be back in the school for the blind, still in high school. I wonder when I will finally get out.

[Kirtley's note: Prospero's dream associations and autobiographical account reveal that he is fully aware of the essentially adolescent character of his fantasy and dream life. He interprets the present dream as a symbolic expression of his guilt over this continuing immaturity—the school for the blind being a place for the ignorant and uninitiated. However, it should also be pointed out that guilt feelings are rare in his dreams, at least in their manifest content, and, as a rule, they show little unhappiness over immaturity but rather the contrary, for he usually seems to enjoy his adolescent preoccupations.]

Dream 22: June 7, 1970

I'm very close to the moon, just hovering above a flat, barren plain—though I'm not in any type of spaceship, but am simply there by myself, looking down at the moon. The surface below is a pale yellowish brown color, but the intense heat sometimes makes it look white. It is completely dried out, even worse than Z (the city where I now live). I think of how terrible it would be for one to get stranded here, and I'm glad that I'm not, though for a moment I fear this might happen.

[Kirtley's note: In this dream, Prospero clearly indicates that he is unhappy with the city in which he now resides. In his associations he suggests that the dream is telling him to make the best of his present environment, one in which he sometimes feels stranded because his job is there, and he has not, as yet, been able to find an acceptable job in a better environment; the dream shows him a place "even worse than Z" in order to console him and to warn him against backsliding in his present life situation, as the ultimate penalty for this could be a situation still less desirable than that which he already has.]

Thematic Analysis of the 1970 Dreams

Let us now examine the predominant themes in Prospero's dreams.

■ *Anality*—There are a large number of anal dreams, both anal erotic and anal sadistic. Particularly striking is the number of dreams in which anal intercourse and analingus appear, and even more so, the number of times fecal matter disgusts or nauseates the dreamer. Perhaps this is a superego reaction to his strong anal fixation.

■ *Castration Anxiety and the Oedipus Complex*—Though Prospero's castration anxiety is lower than that of the norm, he has it as does everyone. It appears in at least eighteen dreams, taking various forms, and is sometimes quite overt (see Dreams 1, 8, and 11, while Dream 2 provides a more symbolic example). Furthermore, forthright Oedipal dreams are present (e.g., Dream 11).

■ *Orality*—There is much biting in Prospero's dreams, suggesting oral sadism (e.g., Dream 15). On the other hand, there is little oral eroticism. It may be significant that in his oral dreams there are two mentions of soggy or bad-tasting cheese,. and in two other dreams a man is reluctant to provide food (one of these characters being the dreamer's father).

■ *Dependency*—Dependency appears in some dreams, but the tendency is not pronounced. This suggests that Prospero is not a dependent personality, unless, of course, everything else in his dreams constitutes a reaction formation against dependency, which I doubt.

■ *The Icarian Complex*—There is some confusion of genders in Prospero's dreams, e.g., a male with a clitoris (Dream 2) and another male with a vagina (Dream 7). Even so, the phallic component is far more salient.

Prospero is in many respects an Icarian character (Murray, 1955). He has delusions of grandeur, but, like Icarus, he gets punished for his desire to overcome his father. After the fashion of the Icarian, Prospero uses both sex and aggression to conquer (e.g., Dream 6—a spotlight dream, as it suggests the central motifs of the dreamer's waking fantasy life). I assume Prospero has grandiose fantasies accompanying masturbation, as most phallic characters are masturbators. The Icarian type is also predominantly phallic and given to frequent masturbation. Flying dreams are also characteristic of the Icarian syndrome, and Prospero has a number of these (see Dream 10, as an excellent example). Moreover, Icarian characters are afraid of falling and being killed. In Dream 10 Prospero worries about his plane engine running out of fuel or developing a malfunction. Also, he has a number of nightmares in which he is attacked by killers while in his bed (e.g., Dreams 18, 19, and 20).

■ *Symbolism*—Prospero's dreams are generally somewhat less symbolic than those of the norm group—barring some highly symbolic dreams involving biological evolution, prehistoric organisms, outer space, heavenly bodies, and the Incas of Peru—all of which are probably best interpreted by way of Jungian rather than Freudian theory. In three of these dreams, turtles play an important symbolic role (e.g., Dream 15).

■ *Minor Themes*—Lesser themes in Prospero's dreams are competition and bad feelings with fellow workers, unpleasant experiences with subordinates, and sibling rivalry.

■ *Conclusions*—Based on the foregoing, the overall characterization of Prospero is that of an anal-phallic, Oedipal, Icarian personality. For such a person, what could be better than anal intercourse with either sex, or defecating on one's enemies, or delusions of grandeur accompanying masturbation, or taking mother from father, the ultimate delusion for which one is castrated or killed?

Analysis of Dreams from the Same Night

Are the dreams of the same night related by a common theme or through wish and punishment? Some investigators have tried to show connections between such dreams but have not used a rigorous, quantitative method. In Prospero's 1970 dream series, there are some interesting examples in which, during a given night, sexual behavior appears in one dream and aggression or castration (the latter being either overt or symbolic) appears in another dream. Consequently, I examined all dreams of the same night, noting any common features or wish-punishment pairs. Then the problem arose as to whether there was an actual contingency between or among dreams of the same night or whether the association was a chance one. In order to test this, I selected the forty-two nights for which Prospero reported only two dreams and subjected these to a Chi-square analysis. Nights with more than two dreams were not considered since the statistics become almost impossible if one tries to work with a figure greater than two. Also, the analysis was restricted to sex dreams and dreams involving either aggression or castration, because these themes are frequent enough for statistical study. The results, however, failed to support the wish-punishment hypothesis, as the seeming association of sex with aggression-castration was statistically insignificant.

Thematic Analysis of Dreams Prior to 1970

■ *The 1968-1969 Series*—This group contains only ten dreams and reveals nothing basically different from the 1970 series. The sexual tendencies and disturbed interpersonal relations (especially with family members), which characterize the 1970 diary, also appear in the present one—though, of course, less markedly so, owing to the much smaller number of dreams.

Four of the dreams involve open family strife or conflict, while over half are primarily sexual in nature—three dreams being essentially exhibitionistic. In one of the latter the dreamer shows his sexual prowess by engaging in coitus with a woman in the presence of two male spectators. However, the most interesting sex dream is Oedipal, consisting of overt incest with the mother, followed by punishment—this time from the dreamer's mother, who attempts to stab him with a knife. In this sample there is only one strikingly symbolic dream, which perhaps expresses a return-to-the-womb motif.

Dream 23: January 5, 1969

I'm flying in a little silver-colored spaceship with a few other people (whose identities I don't now recall). We are approaching a tiny planet which is composed solely of ice, a planet even smaller than the moon. Its orbit is extremely irregular, almost chaotic, as it bounces and wobbles along in an aimless fashion; or perhaps it is completely out of orbit and simply wandering through space; but the sun or some star to which it may belong is dimly visible in the distance. Then we land but decide not to get out of the ship because outside it is very cold and dark—we've come down on a vast, desolate glacial plain, surely an environment hostile to life. There is nothing living in sight, only ice—

plains, mountains, hills, and valleys of it. The sun-star is so far away that its light is reduced to a slight phosphorescent glow along the horizon.

Now the scene abruptly changes. Somehow we get our ship into a huge cavern which descends very deep into the planet. Then we slide or crash into a pool of gray, icy water and begin sinking. This pool seems to be bottomless, just a bottomless pit of water. Water starts leaking through the openings of the ship, and for a while it looks as though we are all going to drown. But suddenly our ship is pulled out of the water. Some strange, primitive people living here under the ice have somehow found out about us and have sent a few of the tribe to rescue us.

We get out of the ship and with the cavern dwellers go even deeper into the planet. There are many passageways with lights along the walls. There is an entire culture here under ice, almost a civilization. These people even have music and dancing. I wonder to myself how they can stand to live in such a place—never being able to go out into the open air, never seeing the sun; yet they all seem to be reasonably happy.

■*Dreams from 1956 through 1965*—The seventy-two dreams in this series (none of which are exactly dated) occurred between the ages of seventeen and twenty-six. (Kirtley's note: It should be pointed out that during a substantial portion of this period, Prospero was suffering from an anxiety neurosis—with secondary symptoms of depression and intermittent erectile impotence—for which he sought psychotherapeutic assistance. Those dreams quoted below from this period will be identified by an asterisk at the beginning of each report.) Polymorphous perversity is again conspicuous, even more so than in the 1970 diary. Also, there is again much aggression, but this time it is often physical in nature and massively so. Here, too, there is virtually no friendliness.

The principal themes for this period are as follows: (1) sex—thirty-three dreams; (2) falling, flying, floating, or drifting in space—thirteen dreams; (3) being attacked by homicidal psychotics, animals, father, or other men—twelve dreams. All these themes appear more dramatically in this sample than in that of 1970. Moreover, although flying dreams (in which fear of falling is apparent) occur in the latter series, it still contains no falling dreams, as such; nor, for that matter, any dreams involving floating or drifting.

Freud suggests that falling dreams represent anxiety over separation from the mother, while dreams of being attacked symbolize castration from the father. Thus, one might conjecture that to Prospero being blinded meant separation from mother and castration by father or that castration resulted in separation from mother, since a castrated son cannot have intercourse with his mother. Consequently, many of Prospero's sex dreams, particularly those of an aggressive-phallic nature, may constitute an attempt to prove the opposite of castration; whereas the numerous unsymbolized Oedipal dreams could serve the added purpose of overcoming separation from mother. Indeed, there are dreams in which Prospero's being blinded is viewed as castration. (Kirtley's note: See Dreams 2, 5, 16, and 17 in the 1970 group, as symbolic instances.)

The following are examples of overt or symbolic castration dreams in the present series.

Dream 24 *

It's night and I'm in my bed. Suddenly I see an arrow, shooting through the air straight toward my face. The arrowhead flashes like copper in the sunlight. It becomes larger and larger. Then all at once it changes into the earth. The earth has a bluish, cold-looking haze about it and through the haze I can see only mountain ranges with tall, jutting peaks. I'm floating in cold black space, far away from the earth, but the earth is rapidly bearing down on me, to crush me.

I had this dream often. Sometimes the earth would change into the head of a rattlesnake or penis.

Dream 25 *

My university apartment at night. I'm in bed, and the big floor fan at the foot of my bed is going full blast. Suddenly the fan begins to rock back and forth, then topples forward onto my body, with its blades now hacking at me. I quickly push it back, but in doing so, my hands slip into the blades. They make loud thumping sounds as they strike my fingers. There is great pain, and I'm afraid that all fingers and even penis will be cut off, because one of the blades has struck my penis too.

The fan crashes backward onto the floor, and I at once get up and check my penis, to see if it's all right or irremediably damaged. It is bleeding at the tip, but I find the wound isn't serious. It's only a nick and will soon heal.

Dream 26 *

In my parents' bedroom, in their bed. I'm having coitus with my mother. Suddenly my father runs into the room. He's naked, and I know if I don't hurry up and get out of the way, he will mount me from behind. I don't want to be caught in the middle: with me on top of mother and my father on top of me, as this would be almost too degrading to bear. But I seem to be unable to move.

Dream 27 *

I'm drifting aimlessly in space between the earth and the moon. The earth and the moon are rushing toward one another, and I fear I will be caught in between them, smashed to a pulp when they collide.

[Kirtley's note: According to Prospero, this interesting dream occurred a day or so after Dream 26. Since in his associations to the present dream, Prospero identifies the moon with mother and the earth with father, the dream appears to be a symbolic version of the events in Dream 26, whose content is only slightly symbolic, if symbolic at all. Although earth, like moon, is usually a mother symbol, for Prospero it is clear that earth also may have masculine or father meaning. By way of illustration, see the "mountain ranges" with "tall jutting peaks," a phallic symbol, in Dream 24.]

Dream 28 *

I'm in a strange building with Dr. D. (my psychotherapist) and C. (a girl I once dated in the town of X, a girl I liked very much who promptly rejected me, partly because of my blindness and partly for other reasons). We go to a room somewhere in this building, and Dr. D. opens the door and asks me to go in first. On entering, I notice that the room is small, about twelve by twelve, and also quite dark. Then suddenly Dr. D. pushes me from behind, and I tumble forward into a big black pit. This pit is about ten feet deep and even darker than the room above.

Dr. D. then slams the door and locks it. I hear C. laughing. Now Dr. D. will have her all to himself. They are both together and free on the other side of the door, while I am alone and trapped in this awful room, in this pitch black pit. I shout at them with impotent rage and struggle to climb out of the pit; but all to no avail.

[Kirtley's note: In his own subjective interpretation of this dream,

Prospero equates the black pit both with blindness and with sexual impotence.]

Let us now return to the three main themes of the 1956-1965 dreams: polymorphous sexuality; falling, flying, floating, or drifting; and physical attack.

Among the more intense sex dreams, one finds the following kinds of behavior on the part of the dreamer: copulation with his seventy-year-old grandmother; with a female dog; with a knothole in the board of a fence; with various female high school teachers, some young and some middle-aged; and anally with both his father and his brother, as well as several other males—the dreamer always being the aggressor. In one wet dream he is doing nothing more than luxuriating in an ocean swim—the emission occurring as he takes a final dive into the warm salty waves. In another such dream, he is having intercourse with his mother while his father and brother watch, and in still another, his father encourages him to copulate with his (Prospero's) mother, which he does, despite feelings of anxiety. In several other dreams, he hears his parents engaging in coitus and becomes angry at his mother for allowing herself to be thus degraded. However, he has many dreams of mother-incest and is usually not disgusted by his own behavior. Furthermore, there are a number of dreams involving simultaneous cunnilingus and fellatio with peer females, as well as intercourse in the conventional manner. Also, his male sex partners are generally repulsive to him, which is not true in the case of female partners. In the dreams of this series, the penis is often symbolized as an attacking, biting, clubbing, stabbing weapon. Although a variety of homosexual interactions take place, the predominant mode of intercourse is anal. In this connection, fecal disgust also seems to operate in this set of dreams, just as it does in that for 1970. For instance, in one dream Prospero dislikes the mud at the bottom of the ocean, which he does not wish to touch while swimming deep under water (perhaps a symbolic expression of fecal disgust).

A few examples of sex dreams from this series will now be presented.

Dream 29

A hospital room. C., naked, is lying on her back on an operating table. I have a long white doctor's coat on and am standing beside the table, examining the interior of her vagina through a long telescope.

[Kirtley's note: C. here is the same girl who appears in Dream 28.]

Dream 30 *

I'm in bed with C., in my bed at home. We are both naked, but she has a black velvet boxlike mask over her face. There are no openings for eyes or mouth. I try to kiss her but can't because of the mask. She laughs at me in a mocking, hateful way. I feel extremely alone, humiliated and very cold—as though I've been walking through deep snow. I embrace her naked body, and she rolls about a little in my arms but makes no real attempt to escape; yet she continues to laugh at me—with contempt, with the utmost loathing and disgust.

[Kirtley's note: Again C. is the same girl as above.]

Dream 31 *

I'm in my parents' bedroom with my father. I am trying to jerk off his penis. I want to pull it out by the roots, but the harder I tug, the longer it gets. It is like a long dead snake or hose, very flaccid. I can't deprive him of it no matter how hard I try.

[Kirtley's note: While the above dream clearly expresses the dreamer's conflict over his wish to castrate the father, the term "jerk off," a common slang expression for masturbation, suggests a further wish, one that is homosexual in nature.]

Dream 32 *

I am in my parents' bedroom, having intercourse with my mother. Her vagina turns into an anus and I become impotent.

Dream 33 *

I am having anal intercourse with my father while simultaneously stabbing him in the back. In this dream he is quite thin—much more so than he is in reality. He yells and whines in a high-pitched voice, like a woman or an effeminate man.

Dream 34 *

My room at the school for the blind. Dr. D.—my therapist—and I are in bed together, sitting up hugging each other. I am telling him about all the girls I'm going to seduce. He slaps me on the back and says I have a big campaign ahead of me but he knows I can do it. We are laughing about all these girls who, as yet, have no idea what they are in for, no idea of the great joke Dr. D. and I are going to play on them.

[Kirtley's note: This dream occurred toward the middle of therapy, by which time Prospero's most severe symptoms—namely, his anxiety— had largely dissipated.]

Some characteristic dreams focusing on falling, flying, floating, or drifting will now be given.

Dream 35

I am falling head first down an unusually narrow elevator shaft, about four square feet in area. Outside the shaft there is nothing but an infinity of black space. Inside the shaft it is also pitch black, and there is no bottom. I am terrified because I think I will fall like this forever.

This dream occurred fairly often—though sometimes I would fall feet first, and at other times there would be no shaft at all, only black empty space with me falling straight down forever.

Dream 36

I am falling in space—an empty, silver gray space which is infinite. Then I stop the fall by flapping my arms, as though they were wings, and I find I can fly. I can fly anywhere; no longer do I have to worry about falling because I can always catch myself and come up again. But there is no place to land, and I am utterly alone.

Dream 37 *

I am standing on the North Pole. It is extremely cold. Though it is also dark, I can still see the whiteness of the snow and ice stretching out around me. I am at the geographical Pole and see the earth curving downward all around me. Suddenly I begin to slip and slide on the ice. I'm afraid I will not be able to keep my balance and will fall off the earth—straight down into space, into the cold darkness of infinite space, to fall forever.

[Kirtley's note: This dream took place at a time when Prospero actually feared for his sanity.]

Dream 38 *

I am floating aimlessly in space—a cold, pitch black, empty infinity of space. I tumble this way and that, unable to keep myself in one upright, steady position.

Dream 39 *

At home in my bedroom. There is no longer any up or down, right or left, no longer any law of gravity. I am being hurled from wall to wall, from ceiling to floor; breaking plaster, lamps, and furniture. I feel deep pain in my head, knees, and elbows as I crash into all these objects. I am trapped here. It's as though I want to escape the room but cannot get out.

[Kirtley's note: This dream also occurred during the period when Prospero was anxious over the possibility of impending psychosis. At the time he was living with his parents, a living situation which he experienced as almost intolerably frustrating.]

Below are some illustrative dreams of attack.

Dream 40 *

In my bed at home. Nighttime. A man is standing just outside my bedroom window, shining a bright flashlight into my eyes and cutting through my screen with a knife. He is a homicidal maniac and has come to kill me. I don't recognize him, but there is something vaguely familiar about his clothing.

I wake up yelling.

[Kirtley's note: In his associations, Prospero mentions that this clothing, perhaps a white T-shirt and khaki pants, was of the sort customarily worn by him when lounging about the house. The killer in the dream thus appears to represent a projection of the aggressive component in Prospero's personality—i.e., self-destructive tendencies or, more generally, fear of losing ego controls over presumably dangerous aggressive impulses.]

Dream 41 *

I am in bed, with a huge rattlesnake lying coiled on my chest. Its fecal brown color, speckled with black and gray, makes it even more loathsome and hideous than it would otherwise be. The snake now raises its head, hissing at me, then strikes for my face—for my mouth. It wants to get its head into my mouth to bite the inside of my throat till I am dead.

This was a recurring nightmare.

Dream 42 *

A nightmare. I am in my bed. Suddenly a ferocious bear jumps on my leg and begins tearing at it with his teeth.

Dream 43 *

Nightmare. In my room, in bed. An amorphous group of monsters suddenly materialize before me and, en masse, begin attacking me. I see vague shadow figures, the faces of apes, of Neanderthal men, of giant turtles and prehistoric lizards.

Dream 44 *

At night. My apartment on the campus of Z University. I am in bed. A group of Maoist agents, all men, have just entered my bedroom. They are all standing around my bed, talking about me in whispers and low voices. Each man is wearing an old pair of faded, whitish blue overalls, and they are all covered with gray rock-dust, as if they've very recently been working in a quarry. A few men also have on old straw hats. One of these is holding a pickaxe; another a shovel. Another has in his hand a long, thick rope with a noose at one end. The biggest man of the three, who stands in front of the other two, says I am a spy (or perhaps a traitor, I can't recall just which) and, therefore, must be executed. They plan to bury me in an abandoned stone quarry.

I feel I've somehow been betrayed. There is something hideously treacherous and evil about these men.

Dream 45 *

My parents' former home in the town of X. In the living room. My father and I are there; and my mother, brother, and a couple of other people may also be present. My father has just hit me over the head with a big club. I'm sitting on the floor—addled, with my head badly bleeding.

Dream 46

Night. In bed with my wife. Our last apartment in the city of Y. A small, wispy, ghostlike creature, whitish in color but vague in outline, has just come to my side of the bed. It makes an awful, little moaning sound, an evil sound. In each hand it holds a bunch of long, razor-sharp tin slivers, or else these slivers, by themselves, are its hands. Now, with these tin-sliver hands, it attacks me. With my fists, I fight the creature back, but the more I fight, the more it cuts into me, especially my hands. Finally, I succeed in ripping loose a long piece of the tin, with which I immediately decapitate the monster. I then run out into the hall adjoining the bedroom. I am still afraid and also feel very nauseous, for the recent act of beheading greatly sickened me.

Now my wife suddenly appears in the bedroom doorway. By its hair, she holds high the bleeding head and says: "Look what you did! Look what you did to your mother!" I feel stunned and incredulous; yet I know the crime is mine—I can't deny it, and the horror of it is almost unbearable.

In the present series, there exists one dream that is clearly suicidal in its manifest content. In that dream, Prospero leaps to his death from the upper floor of an apartment building. However, this is the only such dream in the entire collection of 307, though in the 1970 diary there appears a dream that centers on a suicidal attempt. The dreamer starts to kill himself, then decides he wishes to live after all, and so checks the self-destructive act in the nick of time. All in all, this suggests that suicidal tendencies are not a problem for him, although he has occasionally thought about doing away with himself. (Kirtley's note: Since Prospero's successful completion of psychotherapy, such has apparently been the case. On the other hand, he frequently indulged in suicidal fantasies during adolescence and the early twenties, i.e., for a period of about ten years following his blinding.)

■ *Dreams of Childhood and Early Adolescence* —These dreams (nineteen in all) antedate 1956, spanning the ages five through sixteen. Many of the themes appearing in this set also occur in the later dreams. They are fairly typical for the age range in question, this being especially true of the six earliest dreams. (Kirtley's note: These six dreams were recalled from the period prior to the eye accident.)

The first six dreams took place between the ages of five and eleven. They involve such themes as: being chased by monsters; fighting with Japanese soldiers; finding big piles of coins scattered over a lush, green meadow; being unclothed at school; and galloping a horse up a steep, winding mountain road but going over the cliff edge before reaching the peak (an Icarian dream).

Three dreams in this series appear to date back to the time of blinding (Dreams 47, 48, and 49 below). Dream 47 is the first to mention the eyes and suggests that blindness was viewed as a punishment for sexual wishes, while Dream 49 is a classical undoing dream. Dream 48, though not referring to the eyes or blindness, is dated between Dreams 47 and 49; this dream may be connected with those discussed previously in regard to fecal disgust, as it involves disgust over falling into a muddy ditch—a theme comparable to that of the dream about the mud at the bottom of the ocean, from the 1956-1965 series.

The remaining ten dreams occurred between the ages of thirteen and sixteen. Four dreams in this group are sexual. One entails gender confusion, as Prospero has intercourse with a boy possessing a vagina. In another, Prospero experiences an emission while riding a large fish across the surface of a lake. Two dreams are heterosexual, involving older women (perhaps mother figures). The theme of falling through space is also found in this group of dreams. One dream of the present ten consists of a negative reaction to dependency—a middle-aged man offers the dreamer help in getting about, but the dreamer refuses the offer, saying he can find his way by himself. However, the most interesting dreams from this period deal with Prospero's view of the universe and his hostility toward his father (Dreams 50, 51, and 52 below).

The following are some sample dreams from childhood and early adolescence.

Dream 47

G., the twelve-year-old girl who lives next door, is standing naked beside my bed. As I look at her, her body takes on an unusual clarity, a steadily increasing brightness of the skin. Her breasts are particularly prominent. The nipples look like little doorknobs.

Then, all at once, she changes into a four-legged monster, a hideous little thing with the body of a snake, the legs and tail of a dog and the head and wings of a bird of prey. The creature is about a foot tall from shoulder to paw, about two feet long from shoulder to rump, with a tail just as long. Its wings are big and white, like those of an eagle, but the head is less clear—sometimes it looks like that of an eagle, sometimes like a vulture's head. This monster immediately pounces on me and begins moving up and down the length of my body in a furious, frenzied fashion. The paws have sharp talons which the monster digs into the flesh of my legs, arms and chest, as it moves over me. It makes a dreadful lateral shaking motion, while running or jumping up and down my body; there is something almost obscene in this motion. Finally, the monster, with its terrible talons, goes for my face—for my eyes; and I awake in a panic.

[Kirtley's note: This extremely vivid nightmare took place a few days after the bow-and-arrow accident, when Prospero was already blind in the left eye but still normally sighted in the right.]

Dream 48

I'm tumbling into a ditch. The ditch is full of mud and dessicating leaves. I try to get out of the ditch but cannot. I can't even bring myself to stand. All I'm able to do is roll about helplessly in the mud and leaves, which are now beginning to stick to my body—a most disgusting experience.

[Kirtley's note: This dream occurred a few months after the onset of sympathetic ophthalmia—when Prospero was totally blind in the left eye and had little useful vision in the right. At the time of his accident, he was standing on a bank of the above ditch. The symbolism of the dream suggests that he equated his blinding with degradation and helplessness.]

Dream 49

I am once more at the scene of my eye accident, and everything is as it was at the time of the accident. I'm in a vacant lot, one side of which adjoins a big irrigation ditch. I'm with three friends, boys from my class at J. School, each of us with a bow and quiver of arrows, shooting at sparrows in several trees on the other side of the ditch. Then I run to the nearer ditch bank, from the top of which I can get a much closer, easier shot. But just as I reach the top of the bank, B., one of my friends, lets loose an arrow, hoping to hit a lone sparrow that has just alighted on the opposite bank, not far from me—and the shot is a bad one, for the arrow goes too high. Now I see B.'s arrow speeding toward my face, toward my eyes. I raise my arm to shield my eyes and am just in the nick of time—the arrow strikes my arm instead of the left eye.

[Kirtley's note: During the real accident, Prospero did not see the arrow flying toward his eyes, for at the time he was not directly facing B. Nor was he able to place an arm over his eyes to protect them. This dream of undoing was repeatedly experienced for several years following the accident.]

[Kirtley's note: The last dreams to be quoted—50, 51, and 52— occurred when our subject was fifteen years of age and attending a state school for the blind. All three belong to the same period, one of profound depression and near-schizoid withdrawal which lasted approximately a month. Such symptoms occurred intermittently during the first ten or so years subsequent to the onset of blindness, but at the time in question they were particularly intense. Owing to blindness, Prospero, at this time, saw his life situation as virtually hopeless.]

Dream 50

First there is nothing—only the dark void of infinite space. Then I see the head of God emerging out of the void. The head is tremendous, as big as a building. For a moment I see the face. It is like the face of some prehistoric idol god or Neanderthal man. The mouth is wide and partly open, showing huge sharp teeth, and the hair resembles that of my father. The face looks at me with eyes full of hatred.

Dream 51

I see the whole universe. It is dead and flattened out like a paper relief map. The planets, including the earth, are all dull, flattened out, brownish gray rocks. The sun and stars barely shine. They have a dull, brassy glow. But mostly there is just space, very dark and full of rock dust.

Dream 52

I am lying flat on my back in a compressed, coffinlike universe. It has an upper barrier or ceiling and a lower barrier or floor. A space of about eighteen inches separates the ceiling and floor. On all sides of me, there is only empty space, an infinity of it. I am aware that nothing lies beyond the two barriers, though I am not conscious of their having any particular thickness; they are simply barriers or force fields, as it were. Everywhere it is pitch black, and I am deeply depressed.

[Kirtley's note: In his written dream interpretations, Prospero associates the compressed, coffinlike universe with his blindness.]

Personality Evaluation

I have already described Prospero as an anal-phallic, Oedipal, Icarian character. However, such designations are highly abstract and do not provide a full picture of the concrete individual under study. Consequently, I will now try to be more specific. Given his dreams, what sort of person is Prospero in his waking life? The inferences thus derived will then be checked against the life history data gathered by Kirtley.

Dream-derived Inferences

■*The Family*—Prospero's conflicts and complexes, his preoccupations and concerns, are mainly with members of his immediate family (wife, mother, father, and brother), not so much with work associates. He is still tied to his family. It makes him angry, but he has not found a satisfactory way of breaking the ties. Moreover, it is easier to express aggression toward his family without fear of so much retaliation than it would be if he expressed aggression toward outsiders. The family also helps him to control his impulses while permitting some degree of expression of them. The outside world would not be as permissive. Relations with his family have both a positive and negative side. There is something adolescent about this involvement with the family. It may be due to his blindness, for it would seem to be difficult for a blind person to have as many relations with the outside world as the sighted person can have. Realistically speaking, the blind person is more dependent upon his family.

Life History Data

■ *The Family*—The clinical information, including Prospero's subjective report, supports the idea of a conscious preoccupation with family members, particularly the wife. Prospero states that he seldom has conscious thoughts of his parents or brother except in a fleeting way, although such thoughts do occur fairly often. Also, he lives some distance away from them, and they rarely visit one another. He agrees that his attitudes toward all members of his immediate family have always been mixed. Most of his emotion-laden interactions with people occur with family members. Moreover, he has a relatively narrow range of acquaintances, none of whom are close friends of long standing.

He attributes his preoccupation with family to his blindness and to certain personality traits antedating it. During much of his sighted childhood, he experienced comparatively little personal interaction with other children. His parents tended to be seclusive and hostile toward people in general. They seldom invited people to their house and had few real friends. In addition, they discouraged Prospero from forming friendships among his peers. Playmates who visited his home were regarded by his parents, especially his mother, as an unnecessary nuisance. Prospero never had a birthday party; nor was he ever allowed to ask a friend over for the night. As a result, he became quite introverted and spent a great deal of time alone, playing as often by himself as with other children. Following his blinding, the number of outside relationships decreased still further, as he was then realistically more home-bound than he had been while sighted. He was unhappy with this extreme social isolation but was unable to do much about it, largely owing to the neurotic attitudes of his parents.

Prospero says he has known a few people, blind from childhood or adolescence, whose social development was essentially normal, and he has always envied them. He believes that blindness in itself makes it more difficult to establish relationships outside the home but further maintains that it by no means absolutely precludes enriching variety in the individual's social life, as some blind people do in fact experience this. My own observations of the blind give me no reason to doubt Prospero's assessment on this point. Thus, it appears that blindness did not create Prospero's preoccupation with family, though it did help greatly to intensify a preexisting tendency in this direction.

Is our subject's preoccupation with family members in any way related to the relative safeness of the family as a target for his aggressive feelings? Case history data indicate that intense aggression rarely breaks into overt behavior, and when it does, Prospero has usually been drinking a great deal. At such times, his aggression, typically just verbal, is directed most often against family members—in the past, primarily his mother and father; more recently, his wife. On the other hand, it also appears that Prospero's family (particularly his father and wife) have been much more inclined to vent aggression on him than he on them. Moreover, Prospero's parents were apparently never permissive in regard to aggressive behavior on the part of our subject or his brother. In any event, the family preoccupation would seem to stem chiefly from introversion plus blindness, and only secondarily from the family's role as an easy target of aggression.

Dream-derived Inferences

■*Impulse Control: Characteristic Ego Defenses*—In exception to the preponderance of family characters in Prospero's dreams are the many strangers who enter his house and threaten him. Male strangers in dreams ordinarily represent the father, but they may also represent the estranged part of the dreamer—which in Prospero's case would be his impulses. He is threatened by his id (Jung's shadow) and feels that it will destroy him. His concern with locks (which is evident in a number of dreams) is to lock out the stranger—that is, the stranger father and the stranger id—so that they can do him no harm. He has probably achieved some degree of security in waking life by leading a fairly orderly, work-oriented existence and keeping his impulses under control, but at the expense of some anxiety and possibly some psychosomatic disorders. His associates may even regard him as being somewhat bland in his behavior. His impulses may come out in the way he dresses, but this probably happens only rarely. For the most part, he dresses in fairly conventional ways and tries to appear neat. He would like to let himself go but does not very often because he fears the consequences.

Given all the raw sex and aggression in his dreams, Prospero has had to find ways to control such impulses. With one exception (to be discussed below), it seems doubtful that he would make customary use of reaction formation, that is, he does not seem to be a moralistic person. He may do some projecting, but he is too knowledgeable to do it very much. For the same reason, repression is not an option for him. In the main, it seems likely that he just renounces—and this makes him both sad and angry; and certainly he also intellectualizes and sublimates, but with a pretty good idea of what he is intellectualizing or sublimating. He may get depressed from time to time, but he does not appear to be a depressive character. Nor is he self-punitive or masochistic.

In Prospero's dreams as a whole, there is so much raw aggression that I would expect reaction formations against it in waking life. He tries to be nice to people and to help them, and people probably think he is a friendly person. Underneath this person, however, is a great deal of hostility. It may break through from time to time. Surely it does with his wife and probably also with his mother, and it surprises people when expressed. He probably has a lot of aggressive fantasies. He may verbalize his hostility in the form of negative evaluations of people, although not to them directly. He may find it difficult to work closely with other people and would rather work by himself. He thinks people exploit him and take advantage of the consideration (reaction formation) he shows them. He probably does not have many or any good friends of long standing. In his private thoughts, he is critical of people and thinks how much better he is than they. He may sometimes make biting remarks about people that he later regrets making. Any expression of hostility or antagonism tends to make him feel guilty. He abhors any kind of violence or injustice (reaction formation) and has fairly strong aesthetic feelings (sublimation). The dreams in which he mentions his professional work show this most plainly. At the same time, he is also quite fond of pornography, more so than the average person.

Life History Data

■*Impulse Control: Characteristic Ego Defenses*—The clinical findings confirm the hypothesis that the threatening male strangers in Prospero's dreams represent both fear of id and fear of father—in recent years, more the former; earlier, more the latter. During his early twenties, Prospero underwent two years of intensive psychotherapy. A report from the therapist states that one of Prospero's major problems at the time was extreme passivity. He expressed little overt aggression, save verbally—and this was usually intellectualized through philosophical or psychological concepts. Sexual inhibitions were also very strong, tor Prospero almost never actively sought out sex partners, and when sexual opportunities chanced to come his way, he seldom took advantage of them. The therapist describes Prospero as having been an "over-controller," which, indeed, he still appears to be. Prospero's anxiety in relation to his father is described as having been immense during the early phase of therapy. This anxiety apparently dates to early childhood. Prospero characterizes his father as having been more or less consistently tyrannical and overpunitive. Throughout the subject's childhood, beatings were frequent and sometimes quite severe. The father seems to have been sadistically inclined, as his preferred instrument of punishment was a heavy, knotted rope, several feet in length; and, with his fists, he would sometimes strike Prospero, as well as his brother, directly in the face or on the neck and shoulders. Later, when our subject was a teen-ager, the punishments came to take the form of verbal insults—i.e., depreciations of Prospero's masculinity, his intelligence, his capacity for courage, his physical appearance, or, more generally, his character. The normal aggressive responses of the child and adolescent toward parents were not tolerated by either mother or father. Consequently, Prospero's anger was ordinarily expressed indirectly, through such behavior as pouting, failure to carry out household chores, fantasy, and wisecracking. Prospero says that he no longer has any conscious fear of his father, though he does occasionally feel concern over the intensity of his sexual and aggressive impulses, as manifested in his waking fantasies as well as in his dreams. However, except for a brief period prior to his therapy, he has seldom felt consciously threatened by these impulses, since he is confident in his ability to keep them harnessed. He almost never takes his fantasies seriously, regardless of their extremity, and considers them simply a convenient way of blowing off the inevitable steam of more or less chronically frustrated drives. He is highly introspective and is almost always aware of his impulses. He refers to himself as a "Walter Mitty type," a label applied with both philosophic humor and some regret, as he would prefer being more the doer and less the daydreamer than he actually is.

Prospero's chief defenses appear to be intellectualization and sublimation, while reaction formation, though apparently present, would seem somewhat less important. Prospero's therapist stresses the role of intellectualization, but the comparable influence of sublimation is evident in Prospero's creative professional work, as well as in his love of music, sculpture, and theater, and to a lesser extent, in his interests in philosophy, psychology, and anthropology. In one way or another, most of his creative work deals fairly extensively with the topics of sex and/or aggression. Even so, there typically remains a large residue of crude feeling, which is habitually discharged through daytime fantasy.

At the present time, Prospero is not given to projection or paranoid behavior in general. His former therapist reports, furthermore, that such traits were never characteristic of him during the period of his therapy. Quite to the contrary, Prospero speaks realistically about personal problems, as well as those more specifically related to blindness. He ascribes his own emotional difficulties, both past and present, primarily to irrational self-attitudes and disturbed familial environment, secondarily to social prejudice and discrimination, for he regards forces of the latter type as being relatively remote from the individual, compared with his family and his inner world.

Nor is Prospero at all moralistic. The contents of his dreams and fantasies have taught him to be tolerant of the sexual behavior and idiosyncrasies of others. For example, he believes that the diagnosis of sexual perversion is, for the most part, more a matter of clinical value judgment than of actual psychopathology. Similarly, though he strongly disapproves of any form of physical violence, he does not moralize about it but, instead, tries to understand the problem in philosophical or scientific terms. Prospero's therapist described him, at the time of therapy, as having been a liberal Democrat and ''the antithesis of an authoritarian personality.'' At present, Prospero calls himself a ''democratic Marxist,'' and, to all appearances, he continues to be relatively disinclined toward rigidity of thought or dogmatizing of any kind.

As indicated above, there is evidence of reaction formations to aggressive and sadistic impulses. Prospero believes that most people regard him as ''kind,'' ''helpful,'' ''friendly'' and ''easygoing''—and according to the therapist, these characteristics Prospero does in fact possess to a substantial degree. My own view is that if such traits are reaction formations (and neither Prospero nor his therapist wholly denies that they are), these qualities are nonetheless so deeply ingrained in our subject's personality that, for all practical purposes, they are as fundamental a part of him as the hostility they counteract. Certainly, Prospero, in person, does not give one the impression of being ungenuine, hypocritical, or effusive in his socially more positive behavior—all of which characteristics are typical clues to the operation of reaction formation.

As previously stated, Prospero admits to having frequent aggressive fantasies, e.g., shooting or blowing up hated people; sometimes torturing them by elaborate means involving blinding, castration, whipping, etc., following which the victims may be thrown into a pool of sharks, crocodiles, or sulphuric acid. However, one fantasy that began in sighted childhood and recurred in blind adolescence is of particular interest, as it highlights the anal-sadistic theme that is so salient in the dreams. This fantasy, quoted below, is taken from Prospero's written dream associations.

> This fantasy started when I was either seven or eight and came to me fairly often till I was about fifteen, at which time it just stopped. I usually would have it only while sitting on the toilet, defecating, and always I would be holding a cap-pistol or else some purely imaginary gun.
>
> "I imagine that I am some very powerful person, one who is both the supreme judge and chief executioner for the whole world. Before me passes a long procession of defendants, all of whom are acquaintances, friends, or relatives. Each must stop in front of me and my imaginary throne to plead his case and beg for mercy, as my verdict will mean life or death. Some people I allow to pass; others I shoot. Often I reverse a verdict and call back someone just exonerated, whereupon he, too, is shot; or else an executed victim is magically restored to life, then freed; but some individuals I kill over and over.

Though Prospero has much physical violence in his fantasies, he abhors all violent behavior in reality, whether in himself or others. He says he is glad to be aware of his own aggressive potential, as this makes it easier for him to prevent its overt release. He believes the world would be a far better place if people in general had similar self-insight and capacity for control. He thinks that man is irrationally aggressive by nature, a fact that most people deny because it is unflattering to human vanity.

The present evidence indicates that Prospero's overt aggression is ordinarily merely verbal. He states that he has always been a "chronic bitcher" and that from his sighted childhood on, people close to him have often chided him for being overcritical of others, as well as of life in general. Also, such negative evaluations, when they involve other people, are frequently indirect, a fact of which Prospero sometimes is ashamed, as it makes him feel a bit cowardly. He does occasionally make cutting remarks about people that he subsequently wishes he could retract, owing to their pettiness or injustice—but he feels this way only when the target of aggression has been someone who has done him no real harm or, at least, not meant to do him any. He feels little or no guilt over expressions of mild to moderate aggressive feeling but is very likely to feel conscience-stricken when the feelings expressed are strong. As already pointed out, Prospero scarcely ever shows his anger in a physical way. Years ago, at a cocktail party (when he had been drinking heavily), he got into a fight with another man who was also intoxicated. Everyone present was shocked at Prospero's behavior, as it was so unlike his accustomed manner of quiet reserve. This incident was exceptional. However, even today people are sometimes surprised at the intensity of anger he may express when under the influence of alcohol. He is sure that most of the people he knows believe him to be almost completely devoid of hostility. They would never suspect the aggressiveness of his fantasy life, not to mention his rather extravagant sexual preoccupation.

Prospero's daily life is orderly, though not compulsively so. However, there is one important exception to this need for order. Prospero suffers from insomnia and has an irregular sleep pattern, a problem that has beset him since his teens. At present, his dress is generally conventional, though during adolescence he occasionally wore unconventional clothing, e.g., scarlet or gold-colored trousers, purple or pink shirts, and so on. But these deviations from custom tended to produce feelings of embarrassment and, consequently, seldom persisted for more than a day or two at a time. Prospero wishes he could be more expressive of his affects, for he frequently feels emotionally flat, and from time to time someone is critical of him on account of this. Even so, the kind or intensity of feeling he would like to express is usually perceived as inappropriate to the social situation at hand. He appears to be much more fearful of his impulses than he need be.

Though for years now Prospero has experienced relatively little conscious anxiety, this was, largely because of his overcontrolling, a serious problem for him during his early twenties and was the chief reason he entered psychotherapy. The condition at the time was diagnosed as an anxiety neurosis. At present, a few psychosomatic symptoms occur fairly often (generalized muscular tension and neurodermatosis), but psychosomatic complaints were much more common and varied during adolescence.

Though Prospero would not describe himself as a depressive character, he says he suffers frequently from boredom or mild depression. Throughout his teens and into his early twenties, he experienced profound depressions quite often and thought of suicide almost constantly. According to his therapist,

Prospero's depressions were of secondary importance compared with his anxiety but nonetheless constituted a severe problem. After marriage, our subject was much less prone to deep depression, which suggests that the symptom was in large part connected with sexual frustration. None of the clinical information indicates self-punitive or masochistic tendencies at the present time, though these may have existed to some extent during adolescence; for, as just mentioned, suicidal ideas were abundant then, as well as intense feelings of shame over blindness. However, Prospero never actually made an attempt on his life, his suicidal inclinations having been expressed solely through fantasy. At any rate, such thoughts rarely enter his head now. Nor is he any longer troubled by feelings of humiliation or inferiority over his blindness. On the other hand, he also believes that his attitude toward blindness remains neurotic, yet much less so than it used to be.

As to pornography, Prospero confesses to having a liking for it but regards his interest here as being no greater than that of the average person. In addition, he says: "With dreams and fantasies like mine, who would need pornography?"

Dream-derived Inferences

■Sex—The high incidence of sex dreams and their polymorphous character, both in choice of sex partner and in body aperture used, suggest that Prospero is preoccupied with sex during waking life but that he has few, if any, outlets aside from his wife and that prior to marriage he had few outlets except for masturbation. He was probably a rather heavy masturbator, and masturbation was probably accompanied by rich fantasies. Masturbation may still be his favorite outlet because of the fantasy life he can enjoy while doing it. He is annoyed with his wife because she does not permit him all the liberties he wants. She will not let him act out his fantasies. Probably few, if any, women would. One reason is that he has a pretty sadistic conception of sex. It is lust rather than love. It is a way of gaining power over another person, of getting her or him in his power, so that he can do anything he wants with the person. His homosexual dreams are motivated by a lust for power over males rather than for satisfying, sensual relationship. He is literally and figuratively "fucking" them. There is no tenderness or lovemaking in his sex dreams. Also, the anal zone (the dirty zone) is his favorite erogenous region. Sex is dirty. What better outlet for the anal-phallic character than sticking his penis up another person's anus?

Life History Data

■*Sex*—During waking hours, Prospero has many sexual fantasies. The polymorphous orientation, previously mentioned, is evident here but less strikingly so than in the dreams. The main discrepancy is that there are more heterosexual interactions in fantasy than in dreams. Prospero considers himself basically heterosexual but not in the rigid, conventional sense. He reports having had only one homosexual experience, and that occurred when he was five, with a small group of boys his own age. He does not regard homosexuality in itself as abnormal and says he might easily have experimented with it during his teens, except that, being blind, he did not wish to risk bringing upon himself more problems than he already had. His present attitude remains the same, although he no longer has any conscious inclination toward homosexual exploration. In any case, he doubts that he could ever have become exclusively homosexual.

The eroticism of Prospero's sex fantasies is usually admixed with aggression. Below are some examples of sex fantasies taken from his written report.

A Recurring Fantasy of Sighted Childhood

I am Mr. Hyde, and I have just abducted a beautiful young woman, whom I have stripped of all her clothing. It is night, very foggy, and we are both inside a hansom, racing through the streets of London, with the police in hot pursuit. I force my captive to lie across my lap, whereupon I very vigorously spank her naked buttocks.

A Frequent Fantasy of Adolescence and Early Adulthood

I am having coitus *a tergo* with a young woman whose head and hands are pilloried. At the same time, I beat her naked buttocks with a quirt.

A Recurring Fantasy of Early Adulthood

B. (an ultraconservative radio commentator whom I detest) is on the air, delivering a political speech against the mental health movement, higher education, artists, and socialism. He is in especially good form. Suddenly, however, he is attacked anally by a flying penis—an invisible winged penis with no body attached to it, a purely magic penis which has just descended from the heavens like an avenging angel. Its furious thrusting causes great pain and reactivates all B.'s repressed homosexual fears. He begins to experience anxiety attacks, and his speech degenerates into an idiotic blubbering. He rushes out of the studio and runs frantically through the streets of the city. He is confused, utterly broken, and degraded. The magic penis has driven him insane. Finally, in total exhaustion, he collapses into a gutter and dies.

A Recurring Fantasy of Early Adulthood

I am masked, raping a naked woman who is on her back, bound in spreadeagle fashion to a huge sacrificial stone altar.

A Recent Fantasy

X (a man whom I dislike intensely) is stripped naked and placed in a specially constructed pillory which holds the legs as well as the hands and head. It permits him only one position, that of standing with the torso bent maximally forward and down, the neck and wrists being locked in just above the ankles, so that the face almost touches the floor. The legs are locked in at the knee as well as the ankle and are thus kept completely straight at all times. The buttocks are, therefore, maximally elevated.

X is then mounted from behind by a man-sized robot whose enormous metal penis emits scalding hot steam instead of semen. The indefatigable robot copulates ceaselessly—for hours, days, and weeks on end. The victim is in the utmost agony, moral as well as physical, for numerous male spectators are gathered round the pillory, laughingly ridiculing X for his ignominious status. X, by turns, screams with rage, then terror; first indignantly demanding his release, then obsequiously begging for mercy—but all to no avail. This amoral, butt-fucking robot simply will not relent.

A Recent Fantasy

I am standing at the top of a long flight of stairs. On each step a naked woman is lying on her back. I, too, am naked. I lie down and then begin to roll over and over down this wonderfully soft and sweetly scented stairway of hot, throbbing young flesh, inserting my penis into each woman as I roll over her.

Prospero reports that he did not begin masturbating until the age of twenty, owing to strong guilt feelings stemming from the belief that masturbation was a perversion practiced only by weak males. During adolescence his only outlets were fantasy, one experience with a prostitute, and nocturnal emissions which were frequent and usually associated with undisguised sex dreams. During the years just prior to marriage, his major outlets were masturbation and fantasy. During this period, he had intercourse with only three women: a number of times with a call girl, a few times with a middle-aged divorcee, and once with a young married woman. Since its adoption, masturbation has been habitual and frequent. During the act, Prospero almost always fantasizes, and these fantasies, in content, generally resemble the heterosexual ones previously quoted, but they tend to be briefer, less imaginative, and more conventional than the latter or, for that matter, the dreams. Though the motives of power and aggression are apparent in the masturbatory fantasies, they are here not as well elaborated as in the nonmasturbatory fantasies. Prospero states that, while he enjoys masturbating, he still takes less pleasure in his masturbatory fantasies than in those he conjures up when not masturbating. At present, his only sexual outlets (aside from sublimation through work) are his wife, fantasy, and masturbation.

He denies preferring masturbation to normal coitus but maintains he is compelled to use it as a substitute because his wife is frigid, usually being receptive no more than once a week and, during certain periods, no more than once a month. Prospero says he is sometimes irritated at his wife for her not allowing him to introduce more variety into their sex life, but he does not consider this a serious problem. At various times in the past, her sexual restrictions were an almost constant source of annoyance, but at present he feels so sexually frustrated that he would gladly give up the request for variety if only he could at least have the normal frequency of conventional intercourse. He states that, during the early years of their marriage, his wife was more receptive than she now is, but still not normally so. He has occasionally considered having affairs with other women but has never taken any action in this direction for fear that his wife might learn of his behavior, become angry and make his life even more frustrating than it already is.

Prospero attributes the absence of tender feeling in his dreams and fantasies largely to the sexual frustrations of his waking life. In his day-to-day behavior, he perceives himself as being at least normally affectionate toward his wife and those few persons with whom he is on intimate terms. Likewise, he believes the sadism of the dreams and fantasies is greatly augmented by this same area of frustration, though other frustrated needs (to be discussed later) also contribute substantially here.

Prospero agrees that his conception of sex is sado-masochistic. The therapist, in his report, ascribes this orientation to unhealthy sex models during childhood and adolescence. The subject's parents fought almost continuously, physically as well as verbally, and frequently would threaten each other with divorce, only to make up shortly thereafter. As indicated earlier, the mother was a chronic drug addict and, according to the therapist's report, was also anxiety-ridden and masochistically submissive to Prospero's father, whom the therapist regarded as a paranoid personality. In the view of the said therapist, Prospero's paucity of sexual outlets at the time of his treatment arose as much from internal inhibitions as from restrictions imposed by blindness, and the former were primarily the product of an extremely confusing and stressful home environment.

Our subject describes his general attitude toward sex as dual. Emotionally, he tends to feel that sex is "dirty," a feeling he regrets having, as he considers it not only irrational but self-damaging. At the intellectual level, his evaluation is exactly the opposite—sex is just another biological function, like eating or breathing, something simple, necessary, and wholesome, neither sadistic nor masochistic.

Although the anal zone appears frequently in Prospero's fantasies, he reports that he has never experienced any form of anal intercourse. However, he says he would like to try it with a woman (that is, mounting her from behind) at least once, perhaps even a few times, just to find out what it is like. But he doubts that he could ever come to prefer this to the vagina.

Our subject's sexual preoccupation obviously began some years prior to his eye accident, but the frustrations accompanying blindness in his particular environment greatly magnified this preoccupation, to the point of turning it into a pathological obsession, which was especially serious during adolescence and the early twenties.

Dream-derived Inferences

■ *The Oedipus Complex*—There is no need to comment extensively on Prospero's Oedipus complex, as we are all Oedipal animals. One striking quality of his Oedipal dreams, however, is their forthrightness. There is nothing symbolic about them. Moreover, he has both a normal and an inverted Oedipus complex—that is, he sexually desires his father as well as his mother. Perhaps one should call this an undifferentiated Oedipus complex, which results in polymorphous perversity and gender confusion. It seems likely that his sadistic conception of sex dates from a primal scene experience.

Life History Data

■ *The Oedipus Complex*—Prospero began to have undisguised dreams of mother incest about two years after puberty. Initially, they caused him considerable guilt during waking hours. He felt "loathsome and depraved, like some kind of pervert." Such dreams, however, continued to occur, and with increasing frequency—despite all his efforts to blot them from memory. It soon became clear that either he would have to go on feeling guilty or else somehow bring himself to accept the dreams as just one more unpleasant fact of his existence. He chose to try the latter, and eventually his guilt did diminish markedly. The high incidence of Oedipal dreams did not start to decrease until some time following his entrance into psychotherapy. Since the close of therapy, he has experienced them from time to time but not often. He did not indulge in conscious incest fantasies, except for a brief period before commencing therapy, and these fantasies were one important source of the anxiety that led him to seek treatment.

The present evidence indicates that Prospero was never able to identify wholeheartedly with either parent, owing to the hostility he felt toward both. The end result appears to have been a somewhat precarious, partial identification with each parent. Prospero's polymorphous sexual orientation appears to have arisen out of mixed (and rather confused) parental identifications, which also are the basis of his undifferentiated Oedipus complex.

As to the role of a primal scene experience in producing the subject's sadistic view of sex, Prospero reports that he does not remember ever having seen his parents engaged in coitus, though he frequently saw them naked in bed, playing with each other's genitals. Such memories date back to age three or four, and the experiences in question apparently stimulated considerable sexual excitement, together with feelings of perplexity, inferiority, and rejection. He remembers having been angrily ordered from his parents' bedroom on one occasion and then locked out. His parents, however, did not usually object to being observed by Prospero or his brother, for both often went about the house nude and talked openly about sex before the boys. The father was especially crude in this respect, as he habitually employed obscene language and gestures in relation to Prospero's mother. Often when the family was traveling by car (with the parents in the front seat and Prospero and his brother in the back), the father would reach under the mother's dress and fondle her thighs and genitals in clear view of the boys. One of Prospero's dreams repeats an actual incident from early childhood: the father is laughing contemptuously and pointing to the mother's vagina; he says her vagina is ugly and dirty. Such experiences, coupled with the sado-masochistic emotional relationship between the parents, might easily have led to a sexual orientation like Prospero's, even in the absence of a classical primal scene experience.

As stated earlier, the most striking aspect of Prospero's Oedipal dreams is their blunt concreteness. Sighted subjects seldom report such dreams. In this connection, Cutsforth (1950), a pioneer clinical researcher in the field of blindness, found conflicts over incestuous wishes to be common among blind children, a tendency that he attributed to excessive emotional intimacy in the blind child's relationship to his parents. While the latter condition existed in Prospero's family throughout his sighted childhood and might well have produced an incest conflict even had blindness never occurred, it appears nonetheless that visual loss was here a major contributor to the extreme intensity of the conflict. Following his blinding, Prospero's mother, who was already overprotective, became increasingly so, while his always ambivalent father grew still more rejecting as well as paternalistic. Our subject, already an introverted daydreamer, withdrew even further from extradomestic contacts and for a number of years was virtually schizoid in his behavior. Negative social reactions (especially from peers) and Prospero's own self-rejection, stemming from long-standing misconceptions about blindness, greatly facilitated this process of withdrawal. The real and unavoidable stress of blindness did not in itself cause Prospero's maladjustment, but blindness—summated with unhealthy personal, parental, and social attitudes—appears to have acted as a powerful catalyst toward engendering such maladjustment. What in Prospero had previously been a relatively minor psychological disorder

became—largely through the accidental (or indirect) effects of blindness—
a serious depressive neurosis. The profound reactive depression, which
normally follows traumatic blinding in late childhood or thereafter, was not
adequately worked through in Prospero's case, in that severe depressive
episodes over blindness persisted for at least ten years after visual loss.
During his early twenties, when the depressive symptoms were no longer
adequate to control the subject's underlying anxiety, that anxiety burst forth
in the form of a full-blown anxiety neurosis, with virtually all the classical
symptoms, the most severe of which were sporadic panic states.

At this point, it might be hypothesized that the blatant quality of
Prospero's Oedipal dreams, together with their unusually high frequency,
emanates primarily from four sources: (1) his blindness, in combination with
(2) his age and maturational status during blindness onset (our subject
reached pubescence a month or so before his thirteenth birthday, by which
time he was also nearly totally blind; it seems likely that blindness,
occurring at this critical period of development, would strongly tend to
produce serious sexual disturbance); (3) his relative inability to employ
repression as an ego defense; and (4) heightened parental sheltering (which
in the case of Prospero's parents was essentially a reaction formation
against their inability to accept his blindness).

As mentioned above, seeing subjects rarely report raw Oedipal
dreams. The same, however, may be said of blind subjects, as no such
dreams were related by the seven individuals whose diaries were studied by
Kirtley and Cannistraci (see Chapter 7). Nor, to the best of my knowledge,
does the literature on the dreams of the blind anywhere mention
unsymbolized incest dreams in connection with sightless persons. In this
sense, then, Prospero appears to deviate not only from the sighted but also
from other blind persons. On the other hand, I am convinced that he is both
more candid and less given to repression or censorship in the reporting of
his dreams than is the average subject in this type of research, whether that
subject be sighted or blind. Other sightless subjects or seeing subjects, for
that matter, may experience more undisguised incest dreams than they
actually report. Nevertheless, even given more accurate statistics on this
question, it seems probable that Prospero's frequency would still
significantly exceed those of the general blind or sighted populations,
simply because of the rather peculiar diversity of forces that suddenly came
to be allied against him at the time of his blinding.

Dream-derived Inferences

■*Orality*—The incidence of oral dreams is low. There are few breast symbols and dependency is not striking. There are no signs of Prospero's being an oral character in his dreams. His favorite erogenous zone is the anus, not the mouth.

Life History Data

■*Orality*—In the oral sphere, one finds the most salient discrepancy between dream activity and waking behavior. In waking life, Prospero experiences a great deal of oral gratification, as he enjoys smoking, drinking, and eating—all of which he often does to excess. Perhaps the extremely low incidence of orality in his dreams results from his more than ample satisfaction of such needs in everyday reality. On the other hand, as Hall points out, Prospero's dreams give no indications of his being an oral character, as the only oral trait of apparent dynamic significance in the dreams is oral sadism, and this is not nearly so prominent a component as the anal-phallic one. Also, on examining the extensive fantasy material in our subject's written report (nearly a hundred fantasies dating from early childhood to the present are here recorded as associations to various dreams or as autobiographical details), one encounters basically the same central themes which appear in the dreams—excluding the overt Oedipal theme. In Prospero's fantasies, as in his dreams, there is scarcely any oral eroticism or need for succorance or nurturance from other characters. In terms of social motivation, the fantasies do reveal a strong need for recognition or approval, but this is typically coupled with pronounced ambitiousness and, therefore, would seem to be chiefly motivated by exhibitionism or power strivings rather than the dependency of the oral character. (Some examples of these recognition-approval fantasies will be given in a later section.) On the other hand, since the subject's oral drives are apparently fully gratified during waking, it is perhaps not surprising that there are so few oral elements in his fantasies. Also, if Prospero were a dependent type, it could be that this need, too, is sufficiently met in reality to render any compensation through dreams or fantasies superfluous.

Yet the present evidence in regard to Prospero's waking behavior does not indicate anything that could reasonably be adjudged as a dependent mode of adaptation. His former therapist describes him as: "bright," "resourceful," "independent," and "responsible" . . . "even when living under the pressure of his most disruptive neurotic symptoms.'' Judging from my own experience, Prospero is, for a blind person, better than average in mobility. He seems to be no more dependent on his sighted wife than she is on him, and perhaps she is somewhat more dependent on him, as he works and she does not. He has always ridden a bus to and from work and hires various persons to do his reading and other secretarial chores. He says he has never asked his employer for special treatment on account of blindness; nor would he ever accept it, if offered. It appears that he has always competed with the seeing on their own terms. Moreover, he says that a blind person has no right to expect acceptance by the sighted unless he is capable of doing this.

Thus, the overall evidence, whether from dreams, fantasies, or waking behavior, clearly indicates that Prospero is not an oral character. His oral habits during waking are, therefore, probably just a substitute outlet for other (that is, nonoral) impulses that have to be kept in check. At least he can indulge his oral impulses without others seeking retaliation. All they can lead to is self-destruction, but this is a by-product and not a motive. The motive is to get whatever sensual pleasure he can, and since the anal-phallic outlets are more or less closed to him, he has to resort to oral pleasure.

Dream-derived Inferences

■*Body Narcissism*—Prospero is preoccupied with his own body, and there is a good deal of body narcissism. He takes good care of his body, and it disturbs him when anything is wrong with it. He is exhibitionistic, but probably there is a reaction formation against this in waking life, so that he is inclined to be modest and even self-effacing. He may also not like physical contact with people because it is too threatening. He keeps himself clean and is preoccupied with personal hygiene. He may have some doubts about his virility, specifically the size of his penis, and this may have caused him some distress, especially when he was younger. He is not athletically inclined—that is, he does not like body contact sports or competitive games. Swimming is probably his favorite pastime. He may use calisthenics to keep himself in trim. He is not an outdoorsman but is an indoor type.

Life History Data

■*Body Narcissism*—Prospero considers himself about average in his concern for cleanliness and personal hygiene, though he occasionally has fleeting hypochondriacal ideas, e.g., that he will someday die of rectal cancer, that he will die of a heart attack during his forties, and so on. He agrees that he is preoccupied with his own body and attributes this largely to the persistence of a childhood obsession with physical inferiority. As a child, he was below average in height, rather slight of build, and generally poor at sports, though he has always been fond of swimming and fishing. Throughout childhood and most of adolescence, he worried almost incessantly about his lack of physical prowess and was often teased about it by other larger, more athletically endowed boys. During adolescence, he came to dislike both indoor and outdoor sports generally, with the only two exceptions, besides fishing and swimming, being horse racing and boxing, the latter having always been his favorite spectator sport. He disagrees that he also dislikes competitive games. He likes a number of them, such as chess, checkers, and various card games, but not games of an athletic nature. When sighted, he also took great pleasure in pool and croquet. He rarely practices calisthenics—on the average probably no more than a week or two in any given year, as he quickly becomes bored with any kind of strenuous exercise other than swimming. On the other hand, during his early twenties, he did regularly lift weights for a period of about six months. He spends most of his time indoors and is not especially interested in nature, save for the ocean, for, as previously mentioned, he does enjoy swimming and fishing. During childhood and adolescence, he spent much more time outdoors than he does now. He attributes his indoor orientation mainly to his introverted, bookish interests, only in a minor degree to his blindness.

Our subject is fully cognizant of his strong exhibitionistic tendencies and regrets not having more outlets for them. His only important outlets at present are fantasy, a writing hobby, and what he considers to be a good sense of humor. With respect to Prospero's writing it is clear that his dream diaries served an exhibitionistic motive, as well as the other motives mentioned at the beginning of this chapter. Writing out his dreams was also a convenient vehicle for the displacement of his variegated sexual and aggressive impulses, a more satisfying outlet than mere fantasy and one more direct and less arduous than sublimation via professional work or artistic writing. Exhibitionism is, of course, a central characteristic of the Icarian personality. Prospero agrees that he tends to be over modest in most social interactions, a trait for which he regularly upbraids himself as it makes him feel almost obsequious. He seldom expresses strong exhibitionistic urges in public, save through occasional obscene jokes, but, for the most part, his sense of humor seems philosophical or satirical and not as scatological or generally primitive as one might think, if one were to judge from the written fantasies or dream diaries alone. In occasional social situations, he tends to be anxious about the possibility of going too far with his exhibitionism, yet he is not always conscious of any particular exhibitionistic urge at the time.

Our subject is frequently made uncomfortable by physical contact with people other than his wife, perhaps because this tends to stir up potentially dangerous sexual or aggressive fantasies, though he usually is not immediately aware of any specific fantasy in such encounters.

Prospero says he sometimes has doubts about his virility, but these are not serious at present. However, they were quite serious during his early twenties, as he was then periodically subject to erectile impotence, which did not disappear until he was well into his therapy. On the other hand, he has never entertained any serious doubts about the size of his penis, which he considers to be somewhat larger than average, though he does confess to an occasional wish for a still larger organ—one not too big for intercourse, yet big enough to be impressive to women; his own organ, he says, is so close to the average that it is not usually impressive to women. Even so, he claims he does not feel inferior over this.

On the basis of my experience with other blind people, I would conclude that Prospero's body preoccupation does not stem entirely from narcissism. Blindness, by itself, would seem to be equally or even more important than body narcissism in determining this preoccupation. In the Kirtley-Cannistraci dream study, described in Chapter 7, all the blind subjects were much higher than the sighted male and female norm groups in references to body parts. Certainly blindness significantly reduces distance awareness, for vision is obviously the most important distance sense. Thus, in any given perceptual field, the immediate body image or sensation complex should be far more prominent to the blind person than to the seeing perceiver, since, in any particular moment, the latter not only experiences his immediate body and the distance cues of audition but also the superior distance reception afforded by vision. Finally, while the foregoing consideration does not explain Prospero's preoccupation with sexual body parts (most of the blind subjects in the Kirtley-Cannistraci study did not show such a preoccupation), it does, at least, help to account for his heightened attention to body parts in general.

Dream-derived Inferences

■*Achievement Orientation*—Prospero is achievement motivated because this is an acceptable outlet for anal-phallic impulses. It is not a case of making something of himself for reasons of self-pride, but much more a competition with others, a need to conquer or best them. Of course, there are even dangers to this kind of competition, so that he may be reluctant to indulge it, or if he does indulge it, not to be very successful or to be just successful enough to best mediocre opponents. His many dreams about prominent people indicate that he identifies with them, but he is unwilling to challenge them (fears of father). He needs to transform competition into achievement. There are two sides to the superego: the bad-father side that results in the development of the punitive superego and the good-father side that results in the development of a prideful ego ideal—conscience versus ego ideal, beating others versus self-pride and self-esteem. Prospero has quite a bit of anxiety over achievement and is afraid he will not be as successful as he wants to be or should be, given his abilities. This stems from a fear of father. He tends to take refuge in grandiose daydreams.

Life History Data

■*Achievement Orientation*—On this matter, dream and case history material are nearly in perfect agreement. Prospero does have a strong need for achievement. He was the valedictorian of his high school class and an honor student in college. However, since leaving college, he has not been quite as successful as he had originally hoped he would be. He would like to be known in his field and sometimes feels like a failure because he is not. He considers his professional accomplishments to date as mediocre or, at best, only slightly above the average. He feels that up to now he has been wasting his professional life by devoting virtually all of his energy to hack projects. Even so, his professional competitiveness occurs mostly at the fantasy level. He seems as disinclined to express his competitive tendencies openly as he is to express his aggression. The main reason for this appears to be his fear of humiliation. If he only aims for mediocre goals, he may always feel unfulfilled, but this may be better than attempting a higher goal and failing, as the latter would not only be a powerful blow to the ego but also might greatly lower him in the eyes of his colleagues. At present, he keeps up with them and occasionally does a bit better and, by so doing, feels less threatened both from within and from without. Nevertheless, he is not happy with this accommodation to mediocrity and, on account of it, frequently suffers from feelings of torpor and mental stagnation. With respect to the prominent characters in his dreams, he agrees that he is too much inclined to adhere rigidly to what certain famous people (his heroes) in his field have said about that field, and not inclined enough to experiment with his own original ideas. On the other hand, he has just recently begun work on a novel, which he feels is by far the most meaningful (perhaps the only meaningful) literary project he has yet undertaken. He says he feels good about it, even should the finished book never see the light of publication, as its subject is very close to him and one truly worth writing about. Yet in the past, his typical way of coping with feelings of stultification, mediocrity, or failure has been simply to escape through megalomanic fantasy.

During the teens, certain recurring fantasies featured Prospero as a world-famous concert pianist, a supervirile Don Juan, a military leader of Napoleonic stature, a great writer, a master criminal or a great criminal lawyer (for Prospero the two were interchangeable), an Oriental wise man (a supersage or mystic) with a tremendous cadre of followers, or a world-traveling, world-exploring millionaire playboy-poet who owns his own luxury liner, jet passenger plane, and other similar possessions. A few examples from Prospero's written report appear below.

A Fantasy of Early Adolescence

I am a great concert pianist playing a magnificent concerto of my own composition. Suddenly all the women in the concert-hall become overpowered by the beauty of my music and excitedly begin stripping off all their clothing. Naked, they rush to the stage where I am performing and surround me and my piano. Then they turn their backs to me, and each gets down on all fours, spreading her legs as wide apart as she can, in the hope that I will honor her by a few strokes from my penis, before leaving the stage.

A Fantasy of Late Adolescence

I have an eternal erection and my penis is ten inches long. I can copulate for hours, even days, on end. Nothing slows me down except my needs for food, sleep, and elimination. Women from all over the world flock to me in order to partake in the pleasures of this wonderful organ.

A Fantasy of Late Adolescence

I am God—a tremendous giant—just sauntering through the vast stretches of infinite space. Suddenly the earth looms up before me. It is about the size of a volleyball in relation to me. I look down at it and see that man with all his corrupt and petty doings has befouled my creation. He engulfs the entire globe, like a swarm of bacteria, putrefying everything he touches. I decide the earth has lasted long enough. With man on it, even the things that are good can't survive. His soul is a cesspool of egoism and hate. He is just a germ with a big brain, and the planet reeks irremediably with the stench of him. So I take my godly penis in hand, like some giant redwood from Heaven, and with one mighty swing of it, slap the earth out of orbit—to send it tumbling off into the dark void, never to be heard from again.

The themes of Prospero's fantasy life have apparently changed relatively little since adolescence. Perhaps one recent example of the extravagant and grandiose type will suffice.

A Recent Fantasy

I am a sultan with a harem full of nymphomaniacs, and my palace is composed entirely of foam rubber—very, very thick walls, ceilings, floors, stairs, balconies, even the banqueting table and other furniture. This foam rubber is so thick and marvelously resilient that, with the slightest effort, one can bounce from floor to ceiling (even up to the highest inner balconies), from stair-top to stair-bottom or from one end of the banqueting table to the other—all in one easy motion—without any danger of injury. Every night my harem girls and I hold a night long orgy inside this fantastic foam rubber palace, just bouncing around all over the place.

It appears that inferiority feelings centering about blindness have played a part in shaping Prospero's needs for power and acclaim, but the same tendency toward megalomania is also apparent in many fantasies remembered from his sighted period: e.g., he is a world-famous jungle explorer who captures all sorts of ferocious animals and thereby wins the admiration of all the girls in his class; he is an ace pilot who shoots down thousands of Japanese or German aircraft, which also results in female approval; or he is the Shadow (his favorite childhood detective), walking unseen among ordinary people, learning all their secrets, through which he gains control over them. Thus, it seems that blindness did not create the proclivity for grandiose fantasizing, though it did considerably amplify a prior childhood tendency toward such fantasizing.

Dream-derived Inferences

■*Introversion*—Prospero prefers to spend quite a bit of time by himself. He is not particularly sociable and can do without people. He does a lot more daydreaming than the average person. Some of this is grandiose. People may think he is shy, but it is more disdain for people and not shyness. Basically, he does not like people, but he tries to pretend that he does. He has contempt for most people. People are no damn good.

Life History Data

■*Introversion*—Until the age of six, Prospero had few contacts with other children, as his parents traveled extensively and were never in one place very long. Moreover, as stated before, they did not especially like his having company in the home. During these earliest years, he usually played alone and was much given to fantasy, spending hours at a stretch dreaming up imaginary battles for his toy soldiers, cowboys, and Indians.

After starting school, our subject became more sociable, owing to the constant daily exposure to peers in the classroom and on the playground, as well as a few children in the immediate neighborhood; by this time his parents had purchased a house and settled down. However, he retained a strong need for solitary play and fantasy. He was generally regarded as shy and even strange by those who happened to find out about his frequent daydreaming and companionless play activities. Prospero says that during his first year or so at school, he really was shy (even painfully so), but he soon outgrew this, while yet remaining rather reserved in his general manner. From six to nine, he never had more than one or two fairly steady playmates (excluding his younger brother, who, during this period, became old enough also to serve as a playmate); and from nine to twelve, there were usually no more than three or four regular playmates. Prospero does not remember having been contemptuous of people during these years, though occasionally someone, adult or peer, would reprove him for being overcritical of people. But he admits that he was probably more negatively disposed toward others, more suspicious and fault finding, than were most of the children he knew at the time (simply because of his family background), but he also doubts that he was then ever truly extreme in this kind of behavior.

For two years following his eye accident, the subject had virtually no social contacts with peers, except for a neighbor girl who occasionally paid brief visits and, of course, his younger brother. His friends, he says, all rather suddenly and mysteriously deserted him after he went blind—in all probability because they were now afraid of him—that is, afraid to be around a blind person. Strong feelings of hatred rose up in Prospero at this time, and these were soon to be strongly reinforced by many additional encounters with social prejudice.

Prospero agrees that some might call his present attitude toward his fellow man contemptuous, as he does, in fact, dislike most of the people he comes to know, some very intensely, though most probably only mildly. He has little faith in the improvability of man as a whole. He states that most people see him as a pessimist, but he thinks of himself simply as a realist. The problem is that reality is much worse than people are ordinarily willing to admit; and when they do admit it, their insight is usually only intermittent and fleeting—they forget or repress it too soon to be able to do anything constructive about it. Consequently, persons like himself (those who cannot forget and so have to go on seeing reality pretty much for what it is) are labeled pessimists by most people. In Prospero's view, mankind has always been: "selfish and irrationally aggressive, petty and shortsighted, too vain and pompous for his own good." There is "far more hatred in the world than love, far more exploitation of people by people than cooperation among them, far more greed than generosity, far more prejudice and discrimination than realistic perception of people, far more moralizing than true morality, far more self-delusion than self-knowledge, far more empty rhetoric about human nobility than truly noble human deeds. Were reality otherwise, the history of the world would have been very different from what it actually has been, and the present situation in which man threatens himself with annihilation through nuclear war, environmental pollution, overpopulation, etc., would not exist anywhere near the extent it does now. If man is what the optimists say—good by nature, creative, loving, rational, cooperative, animated with a spark of the divine—then why is the world so bad? It isn't bad because of nature, for man is not half as threatened by nature as he is by the very environment he himself has created. How can one feel anything but contempt for such a race of weaklings and failures?" At the same time, our subject confesses that the emotional intensity of these opinions arises, in large part, from a fairly substantial reservoir of free-floating hostility within himself. Yet he also says that, even were he comparatively devoid of hostility, his thoughts about mankind would still be the same, since his own personal feelings or, for that matter, neurotic inclinations cannot worsen the already bad history or present of human reality; he would merely express his ideas with equanimity instead of hostility, perhaps even with a measure of compassion, for he further thinks that most human beings are too ignorant ever to realize the self-destructive tragedy of their ways. He denies considering himself any better than people generally, believing that all human beings have essentially the same psychological and biological imperfectibility, and, still more vanity deflating, he knows he is just as powerless to raise the quality of human life as any other single individual—excluding perhaps some political leaders and persons of great wealth. In one sense, however, Prospero does adjudge himself better than the majority of people. He believes he is more honest about himself and life than is the average person. In his words: "Truth is often painful; therefore, most people will not face it and choose, instead, to live in a world of make-believe optimism." He prides himself on having what he regards as a strong urge for truth and an equal capacity for facing it, no matter how unpleasant that truth may be.

Our subject's thoughts concerning human nature, at least as given above, are perhaps best seen as intellectualizations for his hostility toward people at large. Nonetheless, there are, of course, many reasonable and relatively nonhostile persons who would at bottom agree with the philosophical core of his statements.

As to Prospero's social behavior and attitudes in everyday life, there is again general agreement between Hall's inferences and the case history. Our subject seldom enjoys working with other people and is at his best when working alone. Also, he does feel that people often exploit him, but he goes on to say that this is largely the result of his own passivity and, consequently, more his fault than that of others. He does not agree that his consideration for others is entirely a matter of reaction formation, though he thinks an appreciable part of it probably is. At present, he has only a few real friends, and none of these relationships are of long standing. Although he sometimes wishes he had a fuller social life, he states that, since marrying, he has seldom felt lonely. Prior to marriage, he suffered frequently from feelings of loneliness. His social needs seem comparatively simple; he needs someone about the house, a person toward whom he can feel some emotional closeness, a woman since he would be unhappy if he could not at least occasionally have coitus. Socially, he needs other people to a degree but apparently not to the extent that the average person does.

Finally, as to the source of Prospero's introversion, it is clear that the trait did not begin with his blindness, for, as pointed out in this and other sections, he had been this way for many years prior to the onset of blindness. Blindness, however, obviously did act to intensify the trait by making social outlets beyond the immediate family more difficult than these previously had been.

Dream-derived Inferences

■*Ego Strength*—Prospero may have self-doubts, but he has a lot of self-confidence in old-fashioned terms (strength of character). He has to have this strength in order to contain his impulses. Other people probably see him in this light, too, and look to him for advice. He is probably well-liked for this reason, but he does not get involved with those who seek him out—he remains fairly aloof but not in an unfriendly way. He has much autonomy, and he does not put much trust in people generally.

Life History Data

■ *Ego Strength*—The therapist's report confirms Hall's inference of high ego strength. The report adds that, throughout his emotional crisis, Prospero's academic functioning continued to be commendable, though his interpersonal relations and his sex life left much to be desired. Still, he was not seen as having psychotic potential. He had never been hospitalized for mental disorder; nor did his history give any indication of latent psychotic trends. This therapist imputes our subject's psychological disorder (the condition for which he sought treatment) to strong neurotic predispositions that dated from early childhood and were later activated into a full-blown neurosis by blindness within the context of an unusually unfavorable family environment. The report goes on to state that Prospero's history suggested that his initial neurotic symptoms were mainly those of depression, which persisted intermittently for a period of approximately ten years; whereas at the time he entered therapy, the primary symptoms were such as to warrant the diagnosis of an anxiety neurosis. The therapist assesses Prospero's treatment as having been successful but not optimally so; i.e., by the close of therapy, all major symptoms (anxiety attacks, panic states, severe depressions, and impotence) had been removed, yet there remained "a certain level of adolescent immaturity that further treatment might have resolved, but I also thought that, in his case, this quite possibly could be a problem that only time and wider life experience would be able to cure." Nevertheless, the therapist says that Prospero demonstrated "exceptional stress tolerance," for "the stress of his home environment, coupled with blindness, would have been enough to drive many a person psychotic."

The remainder of the case history material also supports the hypothesis of high ego strength. He is economically independent, reasonably productive in his work, and more contented than discontented with his lot in life. A great many people (not all of whom are blind) are much less fortunate than he. Though he still thinks of himself as neurotically inclined (and the contents of his dreams and fantasies certainly suggest that this is the case), he nonetheless has long since ceased to suffer from crippling or severely disruptive symptoms, and, for all practical purposes, his overt functioning in everyday life appears normal, for his behavior generally seems to be adequate to his basic needs.

Prospero believes that he is fairly well liked. He thinks that most people see him as being affable, flexible, conscientious, and good-humored. People often seek him out for advice, information, or just casual conversation, but he typically finds encounters of this sort uncomfortably boring, except when the person at hand seems intelligent or has something particularly likable about his personality. (Prospero does not find most people either likable or intelligent.) Still, he almost always tries to be courteous to everyone. As to aloofness, he does not see himself in this light, but he says a number of people obviously do. For instance, a fellow worker once said to him, half in jest and half in earnest: "You have the nicest way of brushing people off. I've never seen anything like it."

While none of this subject's personality traits would seem to have arisen directly as a result of blindness (whether maladaptive, adaptive, or neutral), at least one important positive characteristic appears to be indirectly connected with his handicap—his intellectual interests and his love of books. When sighted, Prospero read very little beyond what his school required him to read. Not long after the time of his blinding, he began to read more or less constantly, so that reading was soon to become a fixed habit. He reports that he had to read, since there was virtually nothing else for him to do; consequently, he tried to make the best of his situation by reading all the educational books he could get his hands on, whether in Braille or recorded form.

The Relation of Blindness to Dreams and Personality

Blindness, as such, appears to have relatively little to do with what we have found in Prospero's dreams. The dreams do, of course, tell us much about his personal reactions to blindness, but these are by no means universal, for many blind people interpret the handicap far less negatively than does Prospero in his dreams. One certainly cannot generalize his polymorphous perversity, his unresolved Oedipus complex, his sadistic conception of sex, his anal-phallic fixation, or his Icarian megalomania to blind people at large. These, we conclude, are simply Prospero—nothing more. On the other hand, there are at least a few trends in his dreams that might plausibly pertain to the blind in general: the preoccupation with family members, in contrast to people outside the family; the heightened awareness of the body; the relatively low interest in physical nature, geographical regions, tools and other implements, streets, transportation vehicles, and other items associated with travel; also the small concern for clothing; the preponderance of familiar over unfamiliar settings; the high incidence of communication objects; and perhaps even the preference for indoor over outdoor settings.

The life history information, however, does indicate quite clearly that blindness was an important factor in Prospero's personality development. Yet even here blindness, sui generis, seems to account for very little that we would now call Prospero. In other words, its effects, while important, were nevertheless essentially indirect. Blindness did not alter Prospero's basic personality structure, but it did tend to amplify or suppress a variety of traits, all of which probably originated from early childhood experiences in combination with certain innate temperamental tendencies. Some of the traits affected by blindness were constructive and adaptive (intellectual curiosity), and others were maladaptive and destructive (various neurotic tendencies). Yet, in the last analysis, the inimical impact of blindness on Prospero's life apparently arose chiefly through its association with an extremely unhealthy family environment. In closing, we must say that it is our conviction that Prospero, as a personality, would still be pretty much as he now is, even had blindness never entered the picture.

References

Chapter 8/Personality through Dreams

Bell, A. & Hall, C. 1971. *The personality of a child molester: A study of dreams.* Chicago: Aldine-Atherton.

Blank, H. 1958. Dreams of the blind. *Psychoanalytic Quarterly* 27: 158-174.

Bondshu, E. 1972. The personality of a female bisexual. Unpublished master's thesis, California State University, Fresno.

Cutsforth, T. 1950. Personality and social adjustment among the blind. In P. Zahl, ed., *Blindness: Modern approaches to the unseen environment.* Princeton: Princeton University Press.

Hall, C. 1966. *The meaning of dreams.* Revised ed. New York: McGraw-Hill.

Hall, C. & Domhoff, B. June, 1968. The dreams of Freud and Jung. *Psychology Today,* pp. 42-45.

Hall, C. & Lynd, R. 1970. *Dreams, life and literature: A study of Franz Kafka.* Chapel Hill: University of North Carolina Press.

Hall, C. & Nordby, V. 1972. *The individual and his dreams.* New York: New American Library.

Hall, C. & Van de Castle, R. 1966. *The content analysis of dreams.* New York: Appleton-Century-Crofts.

Kimmins, C. 1937. *Children's dreams.* London: Unwin.

Kirtley, D. & Cannistraci, K. 1973. Dreaming and visual handicap. Paper read at annual convention of Western Psychological Association, Anaheim.

Kirtley, D. & Cannistraci, K. 1974. Dreams of the visually handicapped: Toward a normative approach. *Research Bulletin,* No. 27: 111-133. New York: American Foundation for the Blind.

McCartney, F. 1913. A comparative study of dreams of the blind and of the sighted, with special reference to Freud's theory. Unpublished master's thesis, Indiana University.

Murray, H. 1955. American Icarus. *Clinical Studies in Personality* 2: 615-641.

Smith, M. & Hall, C. 1964. An investigation of regression in a long dream series. *Journal of Gerontology* 19: 66-71.

Epilogue

At this point, it might be helpful to summarize the central conclusions of the text.

In Part I we examined attitudes toward blindness from a variety of vantage points: social reactions to the blind down through history; references to the word *blind* and cognate terms in common linguistic usage; observations pertaining to vision and visual dysfunction on the part of clinical psychopathologists; representations of the blind in literature, mythology, legend, folklore, music, and the graphic arts; and finally the results of contemporary social attitude research, largely based on the questionnaire method. All of these informational sources tended to reveal the same picture.

We learned that, aside from rational, constructive acceptance of the handicap, there exists a wide range of irrational, destructive attitudes toward blindness. For the sake of conceptual convenience, the latter were grouped into two broad categories: unrealistically positive and unrealistically negative attitudes. The attitudes in each of these clusters, as well as the two clusters themselves, appear to be intimately interrelated, since they are likely to occur side by side within one and the same individual. At any given time, several such attitudes may be simultaneously conscious; however, when one species of attitude is in awareness, its opposite type tends to be unconscious, i.e., both positive and negative attitudes are usually not consciously present at the same time. Moreover, it appears that in the average individual positive attitudes are more likely to receive conscious recognition than are attitudes of an unfavorable nature, for the latter will more often tend to provoke feelings of guilt or uneasiness. These irrational (or nonrational) attitudes toward blindness appear to be universal and relatively timeless in that they apparently occur in large numbers of people in all cultures and have roots tracing to remotest antiquity, if not prehistory. Such attitudes constitute stereotypes insofar as they consist of rigid overgeneralizations regarding the condition of blindness and blind persons as social stimulus objects. Like other types of prejudice, they are highly resistant to correction or eradication, regardless of the quality of the contradicting evidence. Since the late eighteenth century (and especially since World War I), various organizations and individuals in work for the blind have fairly consistently and systematically attempted to educate the public with respect to the true nature of blindness, and, of course, there have always been instances of patent life success in individual sightless persons. Even so, the old stereotypes remain with us, perhaps just as intense and pervasive in their influence as ever. While it is true that social rejection is much less a problem today for blind people than it was during antiquity or the Middle Ages, it still is the case that irrational rejection, particularly in the form of discriminatory employment practices, continues to be a critical source of frustration for the bulk of the blind population, not only in the United States but in all other countries of the world as well. The favorable and unfavorable stereotypes of the blind are customarily explained as the result of: (1) simple ignorance concerning the actual effects of blindness; (2) socially conditioned prejudice, which is comparable to that felt toward members of most minority groups, particularly racial and ethnic minorities; (3) castration (or generalized sexual) anxiety on the part of the prejudiced person; and (4) other internal psychological weaknesses, e.g., neurotic tendencies, inferiority feelings, authoritarian personality, inadequate body image or self-concept, and so on. To one degree or another, all of these hypotheses attribute the origin of the blindness stereotypes to the learning process; however, notwithstanding the merits of such explanations and the obviously important role of learning in the formation of any kind of attitude, the perennial and ubiquitous character of certain major components of the blindness stereotypes strongly suggests the operation of at least one further determinant—namely, innate psychic predispositions or fantasy modes (or archetypes in the sense of the universal thought forms of Jung's collective unconscious). Thus it is here contended that both the positive and the negative stereotypes contain an inherited core of ideational tendencies. In Chapter 3 I designated these as the Tiresian and Oedipal archetypes respectively.

The Tiresian mode embodies unrealistic fantasies imputing superior or supernormal mental, artistic, spiritual, or moral powers to the blind, merely by virtue of blindness. We might more generally refer to it as the "prophet archetype." While this fantasy complex has gone largely unchanged throughout most of history, it is, in its present form, less involved with the occult faculty and more concerned with religious, ethical, artistic, and intellectual capacities, including powers of extrasensory perception and psychokinesis. The prophet constellation appears to consist largely of two important archetypes long ago identified by Jung: those of the "self" and the "wise old man." The former is the archetype of personal equilibrium and oneness with nature. It represents man's recurrent proclivity to imagine and symbolize along the lines of self-fulfilment and mystical or aesthetic union with all being. The self archetype represents man's need to achieve such goals and provides the motive force for progressive development in their direction; although, as Jung points out, this growth process is not inevitable, being frequently thwarted by diverse conflicting tendencies within the individual—some arising from other archetypes and some from the life experience of the person. On the other hand, the archetype of the wise old man embodies man's perennial strivings for wisdom, for true understanding of self and world. These two thought forms presumably exist to some degree within all human beings and are not exclusively linked to either the visual world or blindness. In the case of the prophet archetype, however, the two patterns are combined and applied to blindness in particular.

In Chapter 3, it was hypothesized that the prophet archetype originally developed in response to two antecedent conditions: (1) primitive man's spontaneous fantasizing on the supernatural significance of dreams, in conjunction with the assumption that the blind, being relatively restricted in their experience of the external world, automatically tend to be unusually open to the internal psychic world—namely, dreams—and hence are more likely than the seeing to possess the supernatural power accruing from this source; and (2) spontaneous fantasies ascribing positive characteristics to the darkness of night, the state of blindness being equated with such darkness. Some examples of such positive characteristics are the following: female fecundity, i.e., the darkness of the life-creating womb, symbolically linked with the darkness of night; aesthetic experience in the face of the natural beauty and grandeur of the night sky; contemplative awe before the inexplicable mystery of infinite space—an experience that is perhaps more compelling during night than during day, owing to the night sky's sharper contrasting of visual elements, of being with nonbeing, viz., of the heavenly bodies brightly luminous against the black void of illimitable space; the sleep of night with its power to rejuvenate the fatigued body and mind; and so on. In mythology, folklore, legend, and artistic productions generally—not to mention the everyday fantasizing of ordinary mortals—associations to the night are often just of this sort. Indeed, such associations appear to be just as typical of modern man as they were of his ancient forebears.

In Chapter 3, it was also pointed out that the prophet archetype could simply be the product of reaction formation against aversive, guilt-provoking attitudes to blindness, in which case a nativistic explanation of its development would seem inappropriate and an account based on the principles of learning would have to be invoked. However, it still appears doubtful that every constituent of this fantasy mode was merely acquired.

The Oedipal archetype, on the other hand, connects blindness with images of sexual aberration, mental and physical incompetence, deliberate or unwitting evildoing, punishment for sin and ultimate personal degradation. This pattern might be referred to more broadly as the "pariah archetype." Throughout history, including the contemporary period, it has apparently exerted much greater influence on man's thinking about blindness than has its Tiresian counterpart. Indeed, there exists both historical and anthropological evidence indicating temporal priority for the pariah motif, suggesting a comparatively more important role for cultural conditioning in the genesis of the prophet fantasies.

The pariah fantasies appear to emanate in part from Jung's shadow archetype, insofar as the latter embodies man's primitive animal urges, especially those of sex and aggression, and is intimately linked with the idea of evil. The symbol of Satan, images of demons, and evil spirits in general, and the idea of sin are all associated with the shadow archetype, deriving their significance from its insatiable instinctual promptings and incessant fantasies of antisocial behavior. Accordingly, the elements of the pariah archetype that deal with moral devaluation would seem to be largely reducible to the shadow.

In Chapter 3, it was hypothesized that the Oedipal or pariah archetype initially emerged from three sources: (1) the darkness of night as a recurrent stimulus to fantasies of threat, mutilation, and death, which in turn gives rise to a fear of the unknown—with the condition of blindness being symbolically associated with this ominous darkness; indeed, though both artistic and popular fantasy have always been inclined to link the darkness of night with certain positive characteristics, the more common tendency historically has been to do just the reverse; (2) the interpretation of death as the absence of all sensation—with visual defect rather than other sensory handicaps becoming the ascendant death symbol, owing to the ease with which the seeing person may almost completely terminate all external visual stimuli by the closing of the eyes, in contrast to the greater difficulties involved in the voluntary shutting off of hearing, touch, and kinesthetic awareness; (3) the very real disadvantages inherent in blindness, the severity of which most sighted people easily tend to exaggerate because of insufficient knowledge of the actual effects of the condition—an ignorance, in turn, perpetuated by irrational fear of concrete blind persons and the concomitant tendency to avoid all or most meaningful types of social contact with such persons, a situation which, of course, merely acts to reinforce ignorance regarding blindness.

Before the dawn of civilization, blindness was, no doubt, a fate tantamount to death, as it curtailed the individual's capacity to hunt and forage and rendered him unusually vulnerable to physical accidents and successful attack from predatory animals and human enemies. With the advent of social organization, law, agriculture, and practical arts and crafts, blindness increasingly ceased to be so dire a calamity. The blind person of antiquity could at least survive by being a beggar, and even at this unenlightened time, some of the blind accomplished far more than mere survival. During the medieval period, the average blind person was probably no better off than the blind individual of early civilization, as he, too, merely survived, usually by begging. With the modern period, there gradually but steadily appeared a new objective understanding of the human condition, based on the revolutionary advances of natural science and empirical philosophy during the seventeenth and eighteenth centuries. This growing understanding included a more emotionally impartial approach to human deviations of all kinds, whether psychological, physical, or social. Moreover, the new objectivity developed hand in hand with an increasing humanitarian concern for the plight of all such unfortunates. The blind, like the mentally ill, the intellectually retarded, criminals, and other deviant groups, benefited from this era of rationality and empathy. The real disadvantages of blindness were still further mitigated by the mushrooming technological advances of the nineteenth and twentieth centuries—first the appearance of the Braille system and then the invention of electronic recording and the typewriter—so that today the actual limitations imposed by blindness are much less serious than they were during previous historical periods.

However, even during antiquity and the Middle Ages (without the advantages of modern technology, science, and humanitarianism), there was apparently a sufficient number of blind persons of average mental ability who were not beggars but were, instead, economically independent and productive and socially at home in the sighted world (e.g., bards, shepherds, jugglers, buffoons, fortune-tellers, and so on) to let their seeing fellows know, had they been willing to look, that blindness, in and of itself, was not the overwhelmingly incapacitating disability it was generally credited to be.

Finally, in regard to the positive and negative stereotypes of blindness, it should be pointed out that essentially similar attitudinal patterns exist for other major physical handicaps as well.

In Part II, we examined the relation of blindness to personality, the central question having been: What effects, if any, does blindness, sui generis, have on the basic personality makeup of the individual, whether of a major long-term or minor short-term nature?

In Chapter 5, we briefly reviewed the life histories of a number of blind persons who, over the centuries, had gained distinction, primarily owing to their contributions to the sciences, arts, humanities, and government. The chief concern here was with the impact of blindness upon general intelligence and creative capacity. The impressive achievements of the many individuals in question clearly demonstrated that sightlessness by itself had produced no inimical effects on intellectual or creative development, regardless of whether its onset dated from birth or thereafter. All of these persons were seemingly of innately superior intelligence and talent and probably would have been successful, whether blind or sighted. On the other hand, the vast majority came from the more socially favored, more economically affluent strata of their societies and hence possessed obvious, perhaps even critical, advantages that were entirely lacking to the blind of the lower classes. Indeed, up to the present century, significant achievement among the blind seems, in general, to have stemmed as much from superior socioeconomic status as from outstanding ability. There were very few exceptions to this rule. Furthermore, save for high intelligence, the personalities of these individuals appear to have had as little in common as would any random sample of similarly gifted seeing persons. Indeed, for the blind as for the seeing, the most important classes of personality determinants would appear to be hereditary attributes and predispositions (i.e., constitution, intellectual level, and certain traits of temperament), within the framework of the interpersonal dynamics of the immediate family. For any given individual, these are proximal forces, while extrafamilial society within any particular cultural milieu is, by contrast, a distal influence. In short, unrealistic cultural attitudes regarding blindness manifest no simple or direct effects on the behavior or personality composition of blind persons.

In Chapter 6, we reviewed the findings of contemporary research on the adjustment of the visually handicapped and found that blindness, as such, produces direct effects only in the areas of mobility and information processing. With respect to personal and social adjustment, blindness does not exert any unequivocal long term effects. No particular pattern of personality traits characterizes the blind as a group, setting them apart from the sighted or, for that matter, from any other group of physically deviant individuals. Nor can any such distinctions be made between the congenitally or early blind and persons blinded in later life. Regarding the partially sighted in contrast to the totally blind, many studies show greater maladjustment in the former group, yet the tendency is not marked and, in any case, does not stem from specific psychological weaknesses inherent in the condition of partial vision. Any sight at all should be objectively desirable, for even if it is not practically useful, it can, at least, still be enjoyed. The adjustment problems of the partially seeing appear to consist chiefly of the tendency to experience conflicting identities, viz., that of a sighted person versus that of a blind person. Such individuals may take longer to make a good adjustment than the totally blind, but once this identity conflict is resolved, they will experience no more stress or internal frustration than the totally blind and probably even less, to the extent that they possess functional vision. Although blindness by itself is not associated with fundamental changes in personality—i.e., effects of a major and enduring nature—traumatic loss of vision after age five is connected with certain typical short term emotional reactions: an immediate state of shock, which is soon followed by a longer period of profound depression. Such responses, however, constitute a normal reaction to physical trauma involving the loss of an important body part or function and are not exclusively linked to blindness. Persons whose pretraumatic personality was essentially healthy will usually recover from the depressive phase within a few weeks to a few months, with the emerging personality pattern being generally the same as that which existed prior to trauma. Contrariwise, psychologically unhealthy individuals or those with latent psychopathological traits will tend to show more severe symptoms after trauma, with the form of the symptoms following the pattern of the pretraumatic pathology. Given reasonable conditions of heredity and environment, blindness is, at worst, a relatively circumscribed handicap, not a generalized or massive disability. However, the handicapping effects of blindness become increasingly serious in proportion as the condition occurs together with other disabilities, e.g., mental illness, brain damage, mental retardation, cerebral palsy, deafness, orthopedic conditions, the various infirmities associated with old age, and so on.

In Chapters 7 and 8, we discussed research dealing with the dream life of the blind, being especially interested in dreams as a vehicle to the understanding of personality. In terms of imaginal content, we found that the dream reports of persons blinded after age seven are scarcely distinguishable from those of the seeing.

Likewise, the congenitally or early blind differ from the sighted only with respect to the absence of dream vision. In regard to thematic or narrative content, as well as personality factors affecting dreaming, individual differences in our blind subjects clearly predominated over group trends. In this connection, the method of quantitative content analysis has proved to be just as revealing in studies of the dreams of the blind as it has in those dealing with the dreams of the seeing. However, such investigations, like the adjustment research referred to above, disclose no consistent pattern of personality traits unique to the blind or to any particular subclass of visually handicapped individuals.

In closing, it may be concluded that blindness does virtually nothing to the personality. This is also apparently true with respect to other physical disabilities.

Index

About the author—

An associate professor of psychology at California State University, Fresno, Dr. Kirtley is also in practice as a marriage and family counselor. Previously he was affiliated with a Veterans Administration hospital.

Since 1973, Dr. Kirtley has been vice-president of the Central Valley Chapter, National Federation of the Blind of California.

The author has published many articles relating to his research work. These have appeared in the *Journal of Psychology, Journal of Consulting and Clinical Psychology, Psychological Reports,* and *Psychiatric Spectator.*